M000111325

Investment
Leadership and
Portfolio Management

Founded in 1807, John Wiley & Sons is the oldest independent publishing company in the United States. With offices in North America, Europe, Australia and Asia, Wiley is globally committed to developing and marketing print and electronic products and services for our customers' professional and personal knowledge and understanding.

The Wiley Finance series contains books written specifically for finance and investment professionals as well as sophisticated individual investors and their financial advisors. Book topics range from portfolio management to e-commerce, risk management, financial engineering, valuation and financial instrument analysis, as well as much more.

For a list of available titles, visit our Web site at www.WileyFinance.com.

Investment Leadership and Portfolio Management

The Path to Successful Stewardship for Investment Firms

BRIAN SINGER
GREG FEDORINCHIK

WILEY

John Wiley & Sons, Inc.

Published by John Wiley & Sons, Inc., Hoboken, New Jersey.
Published simultaneously in Canada.

For general information on our other products and services or for technical support, please
contact our Customer Care Department within the United States at (800) 762-2974, outside
the United States at (317) 572-3993 or fax (317) 572-4002.

Wiley also publishes its books in a variety of electronic formats. Some content that appears in
print may not be available in electronic books. For more information about Wiley products,
visit our web site at www.wiley.com.

Library of Congress Cataloging-in-Publication Data:

Singer, Brian, 1960–
    Investment leadership and portfolio management : the path to successful
stewardship for investment firms / Brian Singer, Greg Fedorinchik, Barry
Mandinach.
        p.   cm. – (Wiley finance series)
    Includes bibliographical references and index.
    ISBN 978-0-470-43540-3 (cloth)
    1. Portfolio management.   2. Investments.   I. Fedorinchik, Greg, 1970-
II. Mandinach, Barry, 1956-   III. Title.
    HG4529.5.S556 2009
    332.6–dc22

                                                                        2009020140

Printed in the United States of America

10   9   8   7   6   5   4   3   2   1

Contents

Preface

In Murfreesboro, TN, childhood home of one of the co-authors, a weathered farmer walks out to get the morning newspaper in her usual morning back pain. Mary had forgotten to take her nightly painkiller to treat arthritis in her back and the impact of her weekly immune system inhibitor injection was beginning to wane. Regardless, she hobbles back into the old wood farmhouse and settles in to an easy chair, molded to her body after years of this morning ritual. She reads the local newspaper, building up the energy to mount the tractor for another day's labor.

Mary spots an article in the newspaper about a terrorist attack in Southeast Asia. She has never heard of the terrorist group, but she is certain that "some Muslim group" is behind the devastation. Mary hates Muslims and is sure that they hate her for her fundamentalist Christian beliefs. No bother, though, as they are on the other side of the world and Muslims are unlikely to have any influence on her narrow existence in this rural little corner of the world.

She couldn't be more wrong. What Mary doesn't realize is that both of the drugs she uses to control her daily pain would not have been possible without the generous financial support of those individuals whom she unjustly loathes. Conversely, the people who produce her pills may equally dislike Mary for her bigotry and hatred; yet they enable her to get up on most days to live a pain-free existence. Moreover, their investments created two successful drugs—interestingly developed by an Israeli company—that garnered generous returns supporting unprecedented infrastructure building around the world.

It is not from the benevolence of the butcher, the brewer, or the baker, that we expect our dinner, but from their regard to their own interest. We address ourselves, not to their humanity but from their regard to their own interest. We address ourselves, not to their humanity but to their self-love, and never talk to them of our own necessities but of their advantages . . . He generally, indeed, neither intends to promote the public interest, nor knows how much he is promoting it . . . He intends only his own gain, and he is in this, as

in many other cases, led by an invisible hand *to promote an end
which was no part of his intention.*

—Adam Smith

These parties don't know and perhaps can't stand each other, yet they
depend on, benefit from, and support each other on a daily basis. How can
this happen?

ARE WE SETTING A GOOD EXAMPLE FOR OUR CHILDREN?

To understand how this happens every second of every day, consider a
common misperception that was so eloquently portrayed in Tom Wolfe's
The Bonfire of the Vanities (Random House, 2001). Sherman McCoy, a
self-styled "Master of the Universe" bond trader on Wall Street, is asked by
his daughter, Campbell, what he does for a living. The question is prompted
by the fact that seven-year-old Campbell's friend's dad produces tangible
things at his printing business and Campbell wants to tell her friend what
her daddy does.

After several failed attempts to explain what he does, Sherman's wife
Judy explains that, "Daddy doesn't build roads or hospitals, and that he
doesn't help build them." Rather, Judy explains, "Just imagine that a bond
is a slice of cake, and you didn't bake the cake, but every time you hand
somebody a slice of the cake a tiny little bit comes off, like a little crumb,
and you keep that. . . . Imagine little crumbs, but lots of little crumbs. If you
pass around enough slices of cake, pretty soon you have enough crumbs
to make a *gigantic* cake." (p. 239) Having equated the gains from bond
trading to gathering millions of "golden crumbs," Judy has implied, in
quite memorable manner, that Sherman doesn't produce anything tangible.
Sherman is portrayed as a parasite on the efforts of others.

While Tom Wolfe provided a wonderful story (and a *New York Times*
bestseller), he has shredded the contribution of investing. The critical role of
an investor is to locate the best and cheapest cakes in the world and make
them available to the individuals who want cakes the most. For providing
this service, they get a very small piece of the cakes—the crumbs. Most likely,
the consumer and baker don't know and will never know each other. In fact,
the consumer may hate the baker and the baker may, likewise, despise the
consumer, yet they merrily come to each other's service.

Mary, our rural farmer, benefits from the continuous efforts of investors
around the world. Investors evaluate every investment opportunity, every

request for money to build a business, research a drug, develop a new manufacturing process, and so on. When good opportunities are identified, they place capital in these opportunities. These same investors beseech entities that have capital to entrust it with them to make good decisions regarding which opportunities to support. Investors serve as stewards of society's wealth. That said, investors are not doing not-for-profit social work. Finding opportunities that may be profitable is incredibly difficult, and successful investors get and should get paid a lot of money. However, they should be successful to be paid handsomely, and it is difficult to distinguish success from randomly positive outcomes.

Another important consideration for investment managers is the fact that actually delivering successful performance outcomes to clients requires more than just improving the efficiency of the global allocation of capital, and generating value-added investment performance. It requires successful communication with clients that helps them overcome the natural human biases that often lead to poor investment outcomes. Succeeding in this endeavor is one of the greatest challenges in this business, and one that requires additional attention and great execution.

It is for these reasons that we have decided to write this book. After collectively accumulating nearly 70 years of experience, we feel a need to document the characteristics of firms that are and are likely to be successful stewards of client capital and the behaviors of these firms' leaders and their investment teams.

OVERVIEW OF THE BOOK

The book is a top-down analysis of successful strategies, structures, and actions that create an environment for generating strong investment performance and, most important, for delivering rewarding investor outcomes. Additionally, we discuss various aspects of the framework that we have found useful in this regard so that readers can examine real applications of the ideas. Each chapter can stand on its own and can be read in isolation; however, the chapters are best read in sequence.

The book begins with a discussion of the differences between investment firms and product firms. Both types of firms have their place in the industry, but they are motivated by different means and to different ends. The bulk of Chapter 1 focuses on the characteristics that are found in successful firms of both types, and includes discussion on the importance of culture, leadership, integrity, and the governance that must be in place to sustain investment success and superior investor outcomes.

Chapter 2 discusses "Building a Cathedral," with a focus on organizational mission, cultures, and values. It addresses some of the practical considerations required for living organizational values, setting mission and goals and measuring organizational success. We draw upon our own experiences and discuss what we have found to be successful and unsuccessful. The successful aspects of our experience will be delineated in detail for the useful application of senior managers in other investment firms.

Chapter 3 deals with some of the most important practical considerations in developing a meritocratic investment process that rewards individual contributions appropriately. We argue that far too much attention is paid to last year's performance results in determining the compensation of investment professionals. We outline and discuss our views on the two primary components of employee compensation, namely, performance and criticality. We lay out an approach that we have successfully employed for managing the compensation process and for encouraging individual development with a key focus on transparency.

Together, Chapters 4 and 5 discuss the importance of investment philosophy and process. The alignment of the two empowers individuals while setting clear boundaries to help govern the actions of investment professionals. These chapters explore a variety of issues related to fundamentally driven investment philosophies and processes. They also describe a number of the most important behavioral biases that serve to confound good investment decision making. Market behavior analysis can contribute significantly to successful execution of investment decision-making processes. In Chapter 5 we also cover theories of evolution and recently popularized notions of "black swan" tail events and their application to investing.

Chapter 6 demonstrates the importance of communication for superior investor outcomes, realizing that a successful investment process is equal parts investing and communication. Our experience has taught us that generating superior investment performance is extremely difficult but achievable for the highest quality firms. However, actually delivering superior investor outcomes raises additional challenges that most of the investment industry cannot achieve. Sound, consistent, and transparent communication with investors is the highest success strategy for achieving superior outcomes and helping investors avoid the pitfalls of performance chasing and other value-destroying behaviors.

Chapter 7 discusses incentive structures and fee models for asset management firms, challenging some of the pervasive models in the industry today. Some of the great wealth destruction of our time can be traced back to the basic culprit of flawed incentive structures. While the authors may disagree on the intent of various fee and incentive structures, we all agree that better alternatives exist than the status quo.

Chapter 8, the final chapter of the book, represents a distillation and summary of many of the most important concepts that we believe are presented here. If you have a limited time, and tend to prefer Cliff Notes over full texts, you may want to start with Chapter 8.

Interviews and surveys of numbers of individuals covering hundreds of different investment firms form the basis for much of the conclusions reached. Further, we have all had the opportunity to work for a number of both successful and ultimately unsuccessful ventures, spanning large firms and small firms, public firms and private firms, as well as our own entrepreneurial ventures.

Throughout the book, the importance of culture and integrity cannot be overstated. The greatest vulnerability to successful investment firms, teams, and processes is weakening or undermined culture and integrity. This is a point that will be raised again and again.

BRIAN SINGER

Acknowledgments

A number of individuals have contributed directly and indirectly to this work. The authors would like to give thanks to Alex McCarthy, April Powell, Edouard Senechal, and Brad Shade, all of whom provided editorial input as well as sweat labor at various stages in this process. Their hard work helped push this work to its completion.

We also need to thank our families for putting up with us through this past year. This is especially true of Linda, Margo, and Andy Singer, who put up with more than the usual number of rants from Brian. And of course Hilary, Tom, and Ted Fedorinchik—who will have been thankfully either too sleep deprived themselves or too young to remember this period of fatherhood in absentia.

We also would like to thank the hundreds of individuals who took part in conversations, interviews, and the other life experiences that shaped our views on a number of these topics.

CHAPTER 1

Characteristics of Successful Asset Management Firms

Generally speaking, employees and clients of asset management firms are looking for rewarding, long-term relationships with superior organizations. While newspapers and other media outlets provide frequent, often daily, scorecards of asset manager investment performance, determining superiority is difficult, requiring a long period of analysis. What does it mean to be superior? Identifying, understanding and implementing the characteristics of superior investment management firms is the key objective of this book.

Throughout this book we will relate a number of observations, some general and some very specific about various investment management firms. We will point to qualities of these firms that we, or those we interviewed, identified as positive or generally negative or disadvantageous. We are not however making recommendations for or against investing with these firms. The due diligence required to make such recommendations is beyond the scope of this book. We will simply use these firms as examples to identify and discuss the qualities that our research has identified as important for success.

Every investment firm performs two basic functions: the business function (marketing and client relations) and the investment function. We refer to firms that focus most energy on the business function generally as "product-driven" and those that focus most energy on the investment function generally as "investment-driven." These two functions often operate at cross purposes. Superior investment performance tends to attract assets from clients seeking attractive returns. This in turn may encourage product proliferation that feeds the business beast but undermines the sustainability of investment performance. A very small number of firms are built on a foundation that harmonizes the two functions. Vanguard is a product-driven firm with a low-cost business model. It delivers superior investment performance by distributing "passive" investment vehicles and avoiding the high

1

fees of actively managed vehicles. We say "passive" in quotations, because the overwhelming majority of passive vehicles are benchmarked against active indexes. It might be more appropriate to call this activity "index fund" investing. Deciding which index fund to invest in is an active decision. However, once invested in an index fund, the fund itself employs a rule-based active strategy. The rules may include capitalization, credit rating or style tilt, among others. Unless the index comprises the entire capital market, it is active. Regardless, following market nomenclature, we use "passive" and "active" in the more pedestrian sense. Passive strategies are those with close adherence to any benchmark or index. Active strategies, by most definitions, are those that take positions different from such an index with the goal of producing an attractive risk/return profile relative to the index.

Superior investment performance through active management is, on average, not compensated. After fees, active management, in general, is negatively compensated. Further, the skill required to add value through active investing is very hard to identify. Finally, finding the skilled managers who do exist is a daunting task. Vanguard is a safer alternative for those without the knowledge, experience, or resources—the vast majority of investors—to identify investment skill. This is not to say that index funds come without risk. Understanding the basic risk characteristics of various asset classes and index funds, or relying on an experienced advisor, remains a prerequisite to investing in any investment vehicle, active or passive. Despite the fact that we characterize Vanguard as a product-driven firm, John (Jack) Bogle, Vanguard's founder, speaks to the importance of client outcomes by admonishing the industry to prioritize stewardship over salesmanship. He deserves credit for undertaking this important endeavor and executing with excellence.

Capital Group is an active, investment-driven firm whose business model revolves around the delivery of superior long-term client outcomes. As Charles Ellis points out in *Capital: The Story of Long Term Investment Excellence*, "Capital Group, especially the American Funds mutual fund subsidiary, puts sound investing well ahead of sales or marketing in every business decision."[1] Charley goes so far as to say that Capital is paternalistic in its relationship with clients and potential clients. If an investment product is very salable, but not in the best interest of potential investors, then Capital will not sell the product. Capital has earned a reputation of operating in the best interest of current and prospective clients.

Why do some investment-driven and product-driven firms provide successful long-term employee and client relationships while others do not? It is impossible to provide a recipe for success, but it is possible to identify certain characteristics of successful firms. We identify five critical aspects of asset management firms that we believe significantly influence superiority and success:

1. Strong culture
2. Limited size and complexity
3. Clear governance of the business and investment functions
4. First-rate (non-hierarchical) investment leadership
5. Integrity

We surveyed investors, spoke with industry leaders, and drew upon our collective experiences with multiple product- and investment-driven firms to assess the importance of each characteristic in determining superiority and success. Each is covered in detail below.

This chapter, and much of the book, argues that unifying culture among a team of individuals from diverse backgrounds and educations is indispensable to the long-term, sustainable success of asset management organizations. Due to its importance, we begin with a discussion of culture and follow with a major challenge to its survivability—the allure of size—and to critical contributors to its sustenance: strong governance, capable leadership, and integrity.

YOU CAN TAKE THE BOY OUT OF THE CULTURE, BUT YOU CAN'T TAKE THE CULTURE OUT OF THE BOY

The culture of a firm is defined by the total set of shared and socially transmitted attitudes, values, aspirations, behaviors and practices of its employees. Superior asset management firms, whether product-driven or investment-driven, exude strong and positive cultures.

Consider two very different firms, both with strong and long-standing cultures. Vanguard's culture is one that includes cost-consciousness and client outcomes. Its Internet home page states, "Investment costs count: Keep more of what you earn. The average mutual fund charges six times as much as Vanguard does." Vanguard's desire to deliver strong client outcomes is enshrined in its structure; mutual fund clients are owners of the firm.

Jack Bogle espouses the interests of Vanguard's clients through the delivery of a range of low-cost investment vehicles. Jack is noted for his frugality. When an individual joins Vanguard, there is no question of the firm's strong culture. Prospective employees know that if they are hired, they are unlikely to be jetting around the world in private jets or vacationing on yachts any time in the near future.

Some shrug off the importance of a strong and positive culture as having no place in the hardened, individualist world of investment professionals.

This sentiment is unwise. While culture involves much more than just legal behavior, the U.S. legal system does not support the bravado of these investment professionals. The U.S. Department of Justice says, "A corporation is directed by its management and *management is responsible for a corporate culture* in which criminal conduct is either discouraged or tacitly encouraged."[2] The guidelines for determining culpability direct judges to evaluate whether the culture encourages ethical conduct. The upper echelon of asset management firms should not be cavalier about the cultures that they promote.

> *Cowardice asks the question – is it safe? Expediency asks the question – is it politic? Vanity asks the question – is it popular? And there comes a time when one must take a position that is neither, safe, or politic, nor popular; but one must take it because it is right.*
>
> —Dr. Martin Luther King, Jr.

A strong culture does not arise from just the encouragement of legal behavior; it comprises positive values, attitudes, and performance. However, the backbone of a strong culture in any organization is its values. In 1963, Thomas J. Watson Jr., the former CEO of IBM, wrote of the firm's core values (beliefs) in the booklet *A Business and Its Beliefs:*

> *I believe the real difference between success and failure in a corporation can very often be traced to the question of how well the organization brings out the great energies and talents of its people. What does it do to help these people find common cause with each other? ... And how can it sustain this common cause and send of direction through the many changes which take place from one generation to another? ... [I think the answer lies] in the power of what we call* beliefs *and the appeal these beliefs have for its people.... I firmly believe that any organization, in order to survive and achieve success, must have a sound set of beliefs on which it premises all its policies and actions. Next, I believe that the most important single factor in corporate success is faithful adherence to those beliefs.*[3]

If values are so important, why do they seem to be the same, or at least very similar, for most firms? Moreover, firms of limited integrity often espouse positive values while ostensibly functioning free from their influence. This is no more clearly demonstrated than by reviewing the values of the now defunct firm, Enron Corporation. Enron collapsed after a long-term pattern of unethical and illegal behavior was uncovered. Figure 1.1 displays Enron's values.

Communication

We have an obligation to communicate. Here, we take the time to talk with one another...and to listen. We believe that information is meant to move and that information moves people.

Respect

We treat others as we would like to be treated ourselves. We do not tolerate abusive or disrespectful treatment.

Integrity

We work with customers and prospects openly, honestly and sincerely. When we say we will do something, we will do it; when we say we cannot or will not do something, then we will not do it.

Excellence

We are satisfied with nothing less that the very best in everything we do.
We will continue to raise the bar for everyone. The great fun here will be for all of us to discover just how good we can really be.

FIGURE 1.1 Enron Corporation's Statement of Corporate Values
Source: www.enron.com (circa 1999)

Including the word "integrity" in Enron's values would be comical had its behaviors not destroyed the lives of so many employees and investors. The firm collapsed under the weight of executive fraud and conspiracy. Integrity is a value that Enron stated, but not one that it lived. While illegal behaviors are rare, values are more often stated than lived. We observe that many asset management firms create and display a set of values because it is a good marketing tool rather than any true set of guiding principles. One difference between firms with strong and positive cultures and other firms is the fact that their employees live the values that the firms display.

Case Study: Culture, a House Built on the Values Foundation

If a homebuilder starts from scratch, virtually any materials can be acquired and used. Eskimos in frigid environments use ice and snow. Native Americans used natural caves and cliffs or wood and animal skins. Similarly, the culture of a new firm can be determined at the outset and established by its initial and founding employees. Bill Hewlett and David Packard started Hewlett Packard with a clear set of values, the HP Way. The HP Way emerged from "deep convictions about the way business *should* be built.... [These convictions are] held *independent* of the current management fashions of the day."[4]

If a construction project is a renovation, then the builder is constrained by the existing structure, characteristics, and materials. Similarly, the materials for growing a firm, its people, must be consistent with what is already in place. Once a firm is established, the cumulative discussions and actions of every employee constitute a shared set of values and a culture that dictates recruitment, hiring, evaluation, and termination decisions.

A firm's values are not the firm's culture; they are a small aspect of the culture but arguably the most critical. Values comprise a small set of guiding principles of the organization. Capital Group, noted for its strong culture and superior mutual fund performance for example, has a culture that arises from its values. The Internet home page for Capital Group states that it offers "challenging opportunities in a highly collaborative, respectful, state-of-the-art environment."[5] Job candidates are told that Capital Group seeks individuals with specific characteristics common to all its employees: integrity, collaboration, respect, curiosity, accountability, detail-orientation, and humility.

And the Survey Says...

To test our hypothesis that firms with strong and positive cultures provide superior client outcomes, we segmented all firms into either the investment-driven or the product-driven category and queried investment professionals from around the world through surveys and interviews regarding superiority of the firms within their respective categories. Investment-driven firms are those with realized generally strong investment performance and a high potential for sustainable, superior investment performance. Product-driven firms have high client satisfaction based on offering features other than but not excluding investment performance. The non-investment features behind product-driven firms are low fees, client service, advice, diversification, and breadth.

We were not surprised to find that our queries confirmed the hypothesis. Superior firms, whether investment- or product-driven, generally possess strong and positive cultures that support their missions. In fact, of the firms covered in our research, culture was the most consistent and important differentiator of the quality of a firm. Of course some firms with strong cultures fail and others with weak cultures thrive for a period of time. However, it appears that a strong positive culture is a necessary, if not sufficient, characteristic of long-term superiority of asset management firms. The anecdotal evidence from our interviews suggests that these firms' leadership teams were able to develop shared values and culture while also maintaining and encouraging the individuality of the team's members.

Our findings are not unique and should not surprise readers familiar with extant literature. In *High Performing Investment Teams*, Jim Ware identifies key factors that help the best firms attract, retain, and motivate top talent. Among these factors are 1) leadership credibility and trust and 2) organizational culture and purpose. Further down the list is total compensation.[6] Jim observes that *values* motivate *behaviors* that in turn drive *results*. These values and behaviors are manifestations of culture.

Blake Grossman, CEO of Barclays Global Investors, observed in a presentation at the 2008 CFA Institute Annual Conference that innovation success factors at asset management firms include culture and evangelism. Readers are well advised to regard Blake's observations. He has built an organization that attracts and retains talent and continues to innovate products that target client needs. Barclays Global Investors has been a success story under Blake's leadership.

The American Funds subsidiary of Capital Group has a long history of strong investment performance and superior client service. Its culture has remained consistent since the beginning:

> We are protective of the way we do business. For more than 75 years, we have remained single-minded in our desire to do right by our investors without compromising our desire to do right by our associates. We invest in our associates using the same thoughtful, deliberate approach we use to invest in companies.[7]

The legacy and heritage of American Funds is clear, but perhaps investors should begin to be concerned. The Capital Group home page explicitly states that American Funds is "one of the three largest mutual fund families in the U.S."[8] Neither size nor growth is a foundational value of the American Funds unit that generated a long history of superior investment performance and client outcomes. Size is often an irresistible siren's song that draws many asset management firms away from their founding and successful cultures. Has this allure become too strong for American Funds?

The Capital Guardian and Capital International institutional subsidiaries of Capital Group define their missions as superior investment performance. Unlike the American Funds subsidiary, however, they curiously do not mention client results. Perhaps this is one reason why the success of Capital Guardian and Capital International have been limited and varied, especially relative to the mutual fund unit.

SIZE MATTERS, BUT NOT IN THE WAY MOST PEOPLE BELIEVE

While it is not difficult to identify the incentives that drive asset management firms to grow beyond their optimal size for superior performance, it is difficult to discern whether an asset management firm has grown beyond its optimal size. Consider two $25 billion asset management firms, one with a single capability that is $25 billion and one with 250 different capabilities each with about $100 million in assets. Both firms manage the same amount of money, but the former can manage a simple, liquid strategy without much distraction as there is only one set of investment characteristics and all clients receive identical performance and very close to identical service and communication. The latter suffers from myriad distractions that include multiple investment objectives, varied client communications, untold hours of contract negotiations and back office chaos. Size is determined not only by the assets under management, but also the number of different capabilities the firm manages.

Returning to the American Funds example, they have grown to have quite a large asset base, but have done so with relatively few capabilities. Similarly, Dodge & Cox delivered superior investment performance as it grew to be large on a limited set of capabilities. During the credit crisis of 2007 and 2008, however, Dodge and Cox stumbled. Perhaps it grew too large in assets under management (AuM) despite a limited set of capabilities. Perhaps this is nothing more than the inevitable stumble incurred by all but the luckiest of truly superior active investment managers and firms. American Funds and Dodge & Cox are examples of investment-driven firms that may have expanded beyond the viable size for maintaining investment superiority. By limiting the number of capabilities that they manage, both firms have been able to sustain tremendous AuM growth. But, all good things must come to an end, and their growth rates have potentially given them too much of a good thing.

Vanguard, on the other hand, seems to be able to grow far beyond the size of other asset management firms in both AuM and number of capabilities. Unlike American Funds and Dodge & Cox, Vanguard is a product-driven firm. It uses size to maintain or lower costs, as a benefit to its clients. Perhaps there exists a viable limit to Vanguard's growth, but for now it seems to know no bounds in the growth of its low-cost, passive business.

As in Technology, Small is Good

Size matters for investment-driven firms, but it does so via the confluence of AuM and the number of capabilities. Product-driven firms, especially those of the passive variety, can grow to be very large in both AuM and capabilities without compromising client outcomes. Our research confirms the hypothesis that asset management firms with a large number of capabilities and high AuM are either product-driven firms or investment-driven firms that have evolved, despite the inevitable protestations, into product-driven firms. Unlike those that start as superior product-driven firms, large investment-driven firms struggle to generate superior client outcomes. As investment-driven firms grow, they become product-driven and ultimately provide poor investment performance and substandard client service.

Charley Ellis confirms this to be "the major problem that confronts, and often confounds, most investment management organizations: Investment success leads to asset growth that eventually overloads the organization's capacity to produce superior investment results."[9] However, total assets under management seems less of an investment performance inhibitor than the number of capabilities. Currently, most diversified investment-driven firms in excess of $25 to $30 billion find it difficult to maintain their investment edge. Over time, with capital market growth, trading platform improvement, and trading simplification by more sophisticated derivatives, the size limit for superior investment performance will grow. For a multi-asset investment firm, these factors should lead to growth of the size limit by about 7 percent to 9 percent per annum. In 2009, the cap seems to be around $25 billion. If capital markets grow at a normal rate, then in 2015 this cap will grow to something on the order of $40 billion. Of course, this is a generalization. The size limit that begins to erode performance of a firm is dependent on the firm's structure and approach, its investment process, complexity and the liquidity of its positions and strategies.

Complexity is the true Achilles heel of size. A firm's AuM can grow, but, by limiting the number of capabilities, an investment-driven firm can often retain focus and expand beyond the limits of firms that allow product proliferation. The same can be said of pension plans, endowment, foundations, sovereign wealth funds, individuals, and other multimanager investment structures. As the number of managers increase, complexity grows and investment focus often diminishes.

Perversely, when manager research teams identify a superior investment firm with a strong culture, they often direct such a flow of funds to that firm that they sow the seeds of their own demise—the firm grows beyond its optimal size. Perhaps that is why investment awards, consultant buy lists, and 5-star Morningstar ratings, are often seen as kisses of death for investment-driven firms.

Figure 1.2 provides confirmation from the perspective of the multimanager environment of manager research teams. As the number of investment managers increases, distraction as measured by additional man-hours spent *per manager* increases. The result is less focus on each investment manager.[10]

The constraint is not the number of people employed by the multimanager investment firm. Complexity diminishes the fiduciary time spent on manager research and selection as the number of managers grows. Increasing investment staff and indefinitely expanding back-office capacity is not an

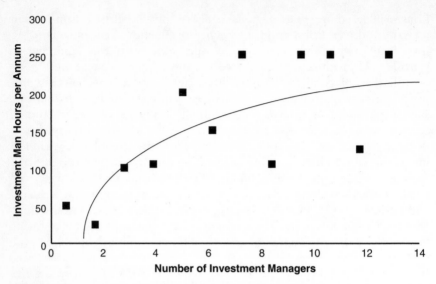

FIGURE 1.2 Application to Investment Management Structures
Source: Watson Wyatt Global Asset Study Survey, 1999.

option. As a rough guide, our research and experience suggests that about 15 to 25 capabilities is the maximum for a typical multimanager investment-driven organization. To be effective on a larger scale is possible, but it requires resources dedicated and specialized by discipline. However, for most multimanager firms 25 capabilities is the point the organization begins to migrate into a high-cost, product-driven operation. Again, this number is a generalization. With multimanager firms the capability limit is dependent on the skill, experience, history, process, and strategies employed by the firm. A few institutionally focused, investment-driven firms have demonstrated the ability to consistently deliver successful client outcomes by covering more than 25 capabilities, but they are the exception, not the rule.

The dividing line of size between investment and product-driven firms is fuzzy. Firms within a relatively wide size and capability range can be either investment or product oriented. We find that firms with few capabilities and less AuM will generally be investment-driven firms with the potential to deliver superior investment performance. Our research led to a matrix that can help guide clients in distinguishing between investment-driven and product-driven organizations.

Figure 1.3 portrays the size and capability characteristics of investment-driven and product-driven firms. The demarcation lines are not precise and firms between the dashed lines can be either investment- or product-driven. Generally speaking, superior product-driven firms can be about any size,

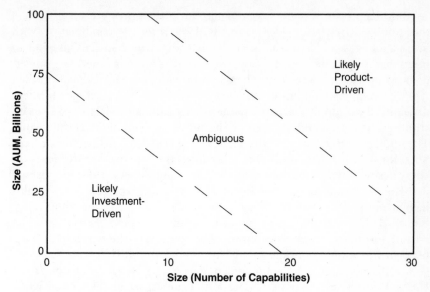

FIGURE 1.3 Investment-driven vs. Product-driven firms

from small start-up to Vanguard-like behemoth. Thus Figure 1.3 applies to investment-driven firms that evolve into product-driven firms as they grow. Notice that the capability constraint is much more restrictive than that of AuM.

Case Study: The Trojan Horse of Client-Centricity

In the mid-1990s, Gary Brinson sold Brinson Partners to Swiss Bank Corporation (SBC). At the time, the firm had less than $50 billion in assets and a limited number of capabilities. Gary was the guardian of a strong and positive investment culture and an undeniable culture built to deliver superior client outcomes. Several years after the acquisition, in the summer of 1999, Gary asked Peter Wuffli, SBC's CFO, to take over as CEO of the asset management division. Much to his credit, Peter allowed the culture that was Brinson Partners to remain intact. A further combination with Union Bank of Switzerland and the existence of "The Three Tribes"—Brinson Partners, Phillips & Drew and the Switzerland-based employees of the combined firm—created stresses that could not be contained. Capabilities began to proliferate as the temptation of revenue growth overwhelmed the investment focus. Shareholders' demands for short-term AuM and revenue growth obliged the shift to a product-driven organization.

But the pressures on the asset management division were stronger than those obliged by shareholder demands. UBS, after the combination with Swiss Bank, adopted a one-bank model that was client centric. This came to mean that the private bank division, because of its revenue generating power, dictated the culture of the entire bank, and a wide range investment product was created and sold in the name of client-centricity. The asset management division, which supplied product to the private banking division as well as institutional clients, could not contain the cultural spread of the private bank. The soldiers were loose inside the walls. Client-centricity no longer meant the quest for superior client outcomes; it became a thin veil for the satisfaction of client desire rather than client need. Salesmanship superseded stewardship.

The asset management division of UBS grew from 3 percent of the bank's income in the late 1990s to about 10 percent at the time of the credit crisis, but much like the investment bank, it became a "client-centric" product creator for private bank distribution. The cultures of the two largest independent investment boutiques that had existed within UBS were fused together. Brinson Partners, the fundamental value-oriented, investment-driven U.S. subsidiary and Phillips & Drew its counterpart in the United Kingdom, became a significant supplier of product to UBS's private bank. As the asset management division grew to more than $800 billion the previously strong investment cultures collapsed. Through no fault of anybody in asset management, it was simply impossible to sustain the independent investment cultures that had previously bred success. It was simply asking too much to limit AuM growth against the pressures of product-driven client-centricity and ever more shareholder value—or more precisely perhaps, *quarterly* shareholder value.

The long-term superior investment performance of Brinson Partners and Phillips & Drew were threatened on two fronts: weakening culture and rapid growth. No leadership team could hold back the private bank's cultural deluge. Superior client outcomes were trumped by shareholder demands for more value (in the form of a rising stock price) and the private bank's cultural influence. Only a governance structure and leadership team that prevented the merger in the first place could have prevented the decline. In the case of Brinson Partners, Gary was the governance structure and the leadership team. He saw the flood waters coming and decided it was time to head for higher ground.

GOVERNANCE: THE GUARDIAN OF AN INVESTMENT-DRIVEN FIRM

There is no way to prevent an investment-driven firm from becoming a product-driven firm, but there are ways to limit the possibility. This section begins with an examination of a firm's mission statement before moving on to consideration of CEO and CIO authorities and responsibilities, as well as board of directors composition, and incentives. We provide practical recommendations for a governance model that sustains a growing firm's investment focus from one generation of leadership to the next.

Mission Statement

The articulated mission of a firm is important to both culture and governance. Top-performing firms use it to inspire a sense of possibility and to create organizational alignment. The best firms use it as the foundation of organizational planning, by asking how each individual and each team in the organization specifically contribute to the acheivement of the mission. For investment-driven firms, the mission plays an even more critical role in maintaing the integrity of the firm's approach.

The mission statement is the first line of defense against the deterioration of an investment-driven organization. The mission statement is a clear articulation of why a firm exists. For an investment-driven asset management firm, the mission statement clearly states that the firm's focus is superior investment performance. It will include phrases like "superior investment performance" and "the premier investment firm." The mission statements of firms that our research identified as the highest quality from the standpoint of culture share striking similarities in their focus on striving for excellence. While not all mission statements are clearly identified as such, the firm's mission is clearly understood by its employees and supported by the firm's employee and client communications.

GREAT FIRMS SEEK EXCELLENCE IN DELIVERING THEIR VALUE PROPOSITION TO CLIENTS

A number of firms in our survey were identifed as best in class with respect to their percieved focus on performance excellence. Some excerpts of their mission priorities are shown below:

- "Our investment teams are singularly focused on providing top tier investment performance." - Adams Street Partners

(Continued)

GREAT FIRMS SEEK EXCELLENCE IN DELIVERING
THEIR VALUE PROPOSITION TO CLIENTS (*Continued*)

- "My overriding objective is excellence... I'll do whatever it takes to make the company great." - Bridgewater Investments
- "We see the firm's mission as the following, in order of importance: 1.) To deliver superior investment performance and advice to our clients." - GMO LLC

While these are just a few examples, what we see is a primary focus on generating superior investment performance. The best firms get their employees aligned behind the mission of performance excellence. They use the mission statement to inspire a sense of possibility and pride.

We will talk in greater depth about mission statements in Chapter 2. At this juncture it is worth following a short tangent to contemplate the precise wording of the mission and, more importantly, monitoring the mission statement for changes that signal cultural shifts.

The mission statement should be offered as the first and foremost marketing statement of an investment-driven firm. Mission statement prominence affirms the supreme investment focus of the manager and the employees. Clients should seek and confirm their mission alignment to a manager's before pursuing any other manager information. Consistency of manager and client mission statements forestalls future problems.

Hodgson, Breban, Ford, Streatfield and Urwin similarly recommend that the client or its proxy, investment consultants in their article, comprehend the asset manager's mission and governance structure.[11] The insight is important, but often the execution falls far short of the mark. Frequently, asset manager alignment is considered after the manager passes various consultant or client determined screens, primarily the three-year investment performance screen. Alignment of missions should be determined before screens of performance are considered.

More important, a prominent mission statement is more difficult to dodge or modify than an inconspicuous or nonexistent mission statement. As investment professionals, we have spent many days wrangling over mission statement wording with business management colleagues. We find that such wrangling is often the beginning of the end—especially when it contemplates dilution of the focus on investment excellence. In investment-driven firms, morphing of the mission statement is often motivated by a strengthening business function as AuM grows. The mission statement becomes modified in a manner that allows the investment professionals and business function to claim congruence. Often the changes are subtle. The phrase "*the* premier investment firm" may be substituted with "*a* premier investment firm." Investment excellence may be diluted through adding emphasis to popular phrases like "client-centric" to the mission statement. There is nothing wrong with being client-centric, but such a change in the mission statement is a potential signal of more nefarious forces working in the background.

Board Composition

If the mission statement is a first line of defense of an investment advisory firm, board composition is the next barricade preventing an investment firm from becoming a product firm across leadership tenures. Best practices for board composition suggest assembling mostly independent directors in order to protect shareholder interests; but while an independent board is good for owner protection, it may not be appropriate for an investment firm.

Among the stakeholders of an investment firm are not only the owners, who are often the investment and business professionals themselves, but also the clients. Investment firm boards should be designed to protect the critical interests of owners and clients, both of whom want to retain an investment-driven culture.

In an investment organization, unlike a publicly listed company, management has a fiduciary responsibility to act in the best interest of its primary stakeholder, the client. Management is not and should not be prioritizing the interests of shareholders. Practically speaking, the supremacy of client interests means that investment-driven asset management firms should not be listed firms or divisions of listed firms. Otherwise, the primacy of client outcomes would be threatened and ultimately diminished.

In the case of many publicly registered mutual funds and even privately structured investment funds or offshore corporations, there are in fact boards of directors whose stated objective is ensuring that investors are treated appropriately and that the investment manager is acting in a way that maximizes results for all investors. In fact, these boards have the ability to terminate the investment management firm (or advisor) to the fund. However, in practice, we see very few instances in which this actually happens. In the world of hedge funds, we even see a number of professional firms who specialize in carrying out these directorial duties. These are firms that exist and are organized primarily to supply directors to the boards of hedge funds. These firms exemplify a common principal-agent conflict. These directors are hired by the principals of the advising firms. Further, some individuals are known to be directors representing 100 different boards or more.

2008–2009 CASE STUDY: INVESTORS UNITE TO DRIVE DIRECTOR ACCOUNTABILITY

In the hedge fund fallout of 2008 and 2009, we expect to see the issue of board independence gain increasing attention in the hedge fund industry. The independence of and incentives of board members will and should be highly scrutinized. Institutional investors and capital allocators are in a position to help push needed change in this area and to hold directors more accountable. One instance we are aware of demonstrates a case of positive change, and how institutional investors can help drive this positive change.

The advisor to a certain investment fund, organized as an offshore limited liability corporation, claimed that they were commited to working with their investors, and ultimately doing whatever their investors wanted for the fund. Through a period of very challenging performance, the advisor continued to cling to a losing investment strategy and suspended the ability of its investors to redeem from the fund, while continually destroying investment value. The advisor continued to take its management fee during this period of suspended redemptions. A group of the fund's investors united and brought a plan to the advisor to try to realign incentives and push for change. This included an orderly timeline for a winding down of the fund and a fee that was based on a percentage of capital that was returned to investors (as opposed to a regular management fee charged on assets under management each quarter). The advisor balked at the suggestions of the investor group.

The investor group comprised about one-third of the fund's investor base. They asked the advisor to call a shareholder meeting to discuss the plan with other investors. This call for a shareholder meeting was also stalled and ultimately rejected by the advisor. So, while the firm had an independent board of directors, the advisor itself would not take the investor group's recommendation for a shareholder meeting to the board. Ultimately, the group contacted the board members directly and at first had a similar result. The directors, despite having confirmation of the desire of at least a third of the fund to do so, were unresponsive to the request. Eventually the investor group was able to get the shareholder meeting called, but only by using their collective clout and applying pressure to the firm that supplied the advisor's board of directors.

We would not be suprised to see a more organized approach to these types of situations as a result of recent experiences. There is an opportunity for industry associations or perhaps organizations like proxy voting services to formalize processes such as these for identifying and coordinating activities among collective shareholder groups. Given the inherent principle-agent conflicts of existing board structures, this may present the best viable solution to protecting investor interests.

Corporations and Limited Liability Companies (LLCs) can have boards with governance authority. In theory, client representation on these boards would protect their interests. In practice, clients would spurn the legal liability of board membership. Limited Partnerships (LPs) do not have boards with governance authority. The general partner(s) manage the partnership along the lines of a corporate board. Thus, direct client involvement on governing boards is difficult and unlikely.

A common occurrence today is for investment firms to create an Advisory Board. These typically include insiders and clients, along with big-name academics and investors. This structure gives the appearance of enhanced client protection, but it generally does not protect client interests. Unfortunately, the Advisory Board concept is more often than not about appearances and motivated by marketing—clever and comforting, but ultimately ineffectual. Advisory Boards are good, but care should be taken to discern its role as a governing versus promotional entity.

We conclude these thoughts about boards by saying that undoubtedly, appropriately structured boards with true independence can help to protect investor interests. However, we must also note that experience has taught us that aligning client and manager interests is not necessarily best accomplished through board composition, but rather through significant manager co-investment. When managers have significant personal capital invested alongside clients, it can be a powerful driver of incentive alignment. We will reflect throughout this book on the importance of incentive alignment.

CEO and CIO Authorities

We found a strong preference among those we interviewed on the topic of CEO and CIO authorities. Simply stated: Firms that are successful, especially across multiple leadership generations, delegate CEO and CIO titles and authorities to a single individual. In many cases there is no CEO title, with the CIO taking on both sets of authorities. A critical separation is that of

CIO and Chief Operating Officer (COO). The COO has authority over and responsibility for managing the affairs of the investment business. The CIO focus on investment process and strategy, as well as policy matters that could threaten the firm's investment focus.

Investment-driven firms tend to have a single officer with authority over executive and investment activities. Since successful firms are typically small and simple, there is no need for separation. Product-driven firms, on the other hand, tend to be larger and more complex, requiring the separation of the CEO and CIO titles and authorities. Separation of these authorities provides yet another sign of a product-driven firm. Even if the firm is small and has strong investment performance, it is susceptible to shifting away from its investment kernel.

If for some reason the CEO and CIO responsibilities are separated, legal documentation ensuring the de facto alignment of CEO and CIO authorities with the investment-driven mission is appropriate. Unfortunately, these incentives are very difficult to craft without overly constraining governance documents. Firms with separate CEO and CIO titles can be extremely successful over a single generation of leadership. Firms like Arrowstreet Capital have alignment of objectives, desires and values, but Arrowstreet Capital's powerful and well articulated mission reflect the guiding principles of the CEO and CIO.

Incentives

The confluence of mission statement and values, board composition, and CEO/CIO authorities are the governance backbone of investment-driven organizations. Given a clear mission statement and unambiguously articulated CEO/CIO authorities, the board must act to incentivize congruent management behaviors. The CEO/CIO is responsible and must be remunerated for superior long-term investment performance, superior client outcomes, and guarding the mission and values. If the CEO/CIO begins to act in a manner that is incongruous, then the board should reduce remuneration and, if actions are not realigned, begin the process of finding a replacement.

Later chapters elaborate on how to define superior investment performance and client outcomes, and discuss reinforcement of and barriers to desired outcomes. Briefly, though, investment performance can be achieved by an investment-driven organization that objectively evaluates and rewards its employees. Chapters 2 and 3 provide a straightforward set of tools for creating appropriate incentives for all management and staff. The board incentivizes the CEO/CIO, and the Management Committee, using these tools, incentivizes all other employees, including themselves.

FOSTERING COLLABORATIVE FREEDOM: EVERYBODY IS A PEER

In the asset management community, as with many industries, professionals are promoted to management positions based on their investment or asset gathering success. As a result, the highest levels of these organizations are rife with individuals devoid of leadership or management skills. We have personally witnessed countless examples of this. The best investment professionals are often promoted into supervisory or leadership roles despite no experience or aptitude for leadership. Similarly, we have seen individuals with strong sales and client service skills promoted to lead business functions, devoid of the required leadership skills. Promoting the wrong individuals into these leadership positions is one of the most common and potentially negative drivers of firm performance. These decisions once made are difficult to undue and deserve much attention and planning. Our experience suggests that the fallout, more often than not, is that either arrogant coercion masquerades as leadership or anarchic complaisance precludes decision making.

The leadership spectrum ranges from hubristic control to detached anarchy, with control being more common. According to Gary Hamel, "Command-and-control systems reflect a deep mistrust of employees' commitment and competence."[12] We believe that Hamel is too strong in making this conclusion. The control leadership style results in compliance, but does so at the expense of creativity and peer engagement and contribution.

Military leadership, where individuals must act in concert or they threaten each other and the broad campaign, requires a firm leadership hierarchy and unquestioned compliance with leadership requests. Such a hierarchy does not preclude flexibility, but constrains it to occur within precise parameters. Additionally, processes or teams where individuals fill precise roles—with flexibility, innovation, and creativity of limited value—are amendable to command-and-control leadership styles.

Consider the leadership of Ross Perot, the founder of Electronic Data Systems (EDS), who started the firm in the 1960s and eventually left the organization in 1986. EDS provided technological and data management outsourcing for firms that needed to organize out-of-control systems. Control-based leadership was effective for EDS's assignments. The control environment is anecdotally supported by the strict dress code, including no facial hair. The Associated Press (AP) reported in 1997 on the loosening of a last vestige of Perot's leadership style. EDS relaxed its dress code to allow pantsuits for women. This aspect of the firm's strong culture survived for 10 years after Perot's departure.

Many of EDS's early employees, consistent with the firm's culture and Perot's command-and-control leadership style, came from the military, specifically the battlefields of Vietnam. These employees, and subsequent employees, function in a military-like environment. So much so that in the late 1970s EDS undertook a military campaign. In 1978, two EDS employees were taken hostage in Tehran, Iran. The U.S. and Iran governments failed to act on behalf of the hostages, so Perot and his leadership team launched operation HOTFOOT (Help Our Two Friends Out Of Tehran).

Perot recruited retired U.S. Army Green Beret Arthur D. "Bull" Simons to command a rescue mission. Perot slipped into Iran, posing as a news courier, and informed the hostages of an impending rescue mission. EDS employees were recruited for the mission, and the two hostages were successfully liberated.

According to Glenn Johnson, a member of the rescue team, the team executed the mission because it was something that needed to be done. Clearly, command-and-control leadership can be successful for teams with a precise mission and clear roles.

Leadership disengagement, at the other end of the spectrum, is spawned from either fear or complacency and nurtured in a power vacuum. The result is anarchy and an organization incapable of making decisions at all levels. Anarchy is not intentional. A former colleague of ours epitomizes leadership disengagement and demonstrated how anarchy evolves. This colleague espoused and supported whatever idea had most recently come across his desk. He was firmly behind the proposal and plan until the next distraction waltzed in front of him. As a result, none of his peers or reports could discern direction; he was a complete power void.

The "product" of an investment-driven firm is superior investment performance. The product is made differently every single day. The manufacturing environment changes every day. An investment firm is not a factory, and the CIO never knows which employee, from most senior to most junior, will offer a great investment idea or insight. In this regard, all employees are peers.

Whereas control is viable for precise missions and roles, and with a clear hierarchy, and anarchy involves the chaotic collection of individuals' independent endeavors, collaborative freedom is an important middle ground. But what does collaborative freedom mean to a leader?

Collaborative freedom is a leadership framework comprising mission, values, and objectives within which productive and creative activity occurs. The future, Hamel contends, will rely on more collaborative, peer-based leadership structures.[13] In the asset management industry, the real-time need for diverse perspectives and constructive disagreement suggests that leadership through collaborative freedom is of immediate importance.

This leadership style leaves tremendous authority to individuals. Individuals clearly see the desires of the leader and use this knowledge to plan and make decisions. The role of the leader is to establish evolving ends and allow management and staff a multitude of unspecified means with which to execute.

It may seem odd, but in 1944, near the end or World War II, a British economist published one of the best commentaries on leadership. Friedrick A. Hayek feared that the ideals of socialism and fascism, particularly in National Socialist Germany, the Soviet Union, and Italy, were too easily embraced by intellectuals around the world. He explored the manner in which these ideas adversely hijack the leaders and members of economic systems. Hayek's *The Road to Serfdom* is considered primarily a commentary on political systems, but the leadership ideas apply ubiquitously.[14]

Hayek could see the power of freedom and the greatness of leaders who afford freedom. He observed, "Whenever the barriers to the free exercise of human ingenuity were removed, man became rapidly able to satisfy ever widening ranges of desire."[15]

People ask the difference between a leader and a boss. The leader works in the open, and the boss in covert. The leader leads, and the boss drives.

—Theodore Roosevelt

In 1962, Alfred Chandler published *Strategy and Structure* about the organization of corporations, arguing that structure follows strategy. While the examples in Chandler's book argued that that strategy would lead to an organizational structure that facilitated successful implementation of the strategy, it identified a risk that such structure would subsequently dictate future strategies. Chandler reasoned that structure needed to be redesigned in order to support evolving strategy.[16]

Hamel also observed that

Management processes often contain subtle biases that favor continuity over change. Planning processes reinforce out-of-date views of customers and competitor, for instance; ... incentive systems provide larger rewards for caretaker managers than for internal entrepreneurs; [and] measurement systems understate the value of creating new strategic options.... Redistribute power to those who have most of their emotional equity invested in the future and have the least to lose from change.[17]

While Hamel's use of the word "power" is somewhat amorphous, his thesis clearly points to the limits of command-and-control leadership and the strengths of a collaborative freedom leadership system for fostering the continual change of structure to support evolving strategy. As Hayek observed decades earlier, "The fundamental principle that in the ordering of our affairs we should make as much use as possible of the spontaneous forces of society, and resort as little as possible to coercion, is capable of an infinite variety of applications."[18]

Bringing this theory back to reality today, our research is incredibly consistent. Top asset management firms embrace this type of transformational leadership. The culture of these firms emphasizes ideas over hierarchy and execution over intention.

Investment leadership depends on the voluntary cooperation of individuals, exploiting and leveraging each other's diverse skills and knowledge. A firm's culture, mission, objectives, and values define the framework within which this voluntary cooperation achieves desired outcomes for all employees and all clients. The leader identifies the ends while collaborative freedom determines the means and shapes strategy that in turn shapes the firm's

IDEAS OVER HIERARCHY

A number of firms in our survey were identified as best in class in hiring and cultivating talent. These firms are perceived to live the values they espouse as it relates to encouraging a peer-driven mangement style. The focus of these firms is on idea generation, collaboration, empowerment, and encouraging employees to openly debate and challenge one another in a constructive way. Creating this kind of culture is difficult, but the rewards for successful execution are evident.

- "Conflict in the pursuit of excellence is a terrific thing and is strongly encouraged, in fact demanded. There should be no (or as little as possible) hierarchy." - Ray Dalio, Bridgewater Investments
- "New hires often enjoy surprising amounts of responsibility, and we encourage collaboration, personal mentorships with senior team members, and the open exploration of ideas." - D.E. Shaw Group
- "Our primary goal is to recruit top-tier candidates, challenge their thinking, cultivate their talent, and ultimately help them succeed." - The Blackstone Group

structure. While there will always be leadership levels, each and every individual is a peer in the future of the organization. Chapters 2 and 3 elaborate on the implication of these concepts for the leadership and management of an investment organization.

> *Let a hundred flowers bloom and a hundred schools of thought contend.*
>
> —Chinese Proverb

Chandler's thesis is that execution is fostered by a structure that derives its form from the specified strategy. Culture, mission, values, and objectives lead to key performance indicators (KPIs) that provide continual guidance to all divisions, teams, and individuals to execute and make decisions consistent with strategy. Charley Ellis states that, "the long-term destinies of most investment management organizations are disproportionately determined by compromising decisions made during the very early years of the organizations history."[19] Ellis seems to be observing the fact that the initial strategy dictates a structure that later becomes compromising to the organizations.

In fact, he further observes that "success with a specific strategy all too often leads to the buildup of a corporate structure that gets more and more consistent and efficient—and eventually rigid. This appears to enhance efficiency, as reported results get better and better for a while. But over time, "the way we do things here gets celebrated and codified.... . The organizational structure, with its familiar practices and comfortable practitioners, they reinforce rising rigidity."[20] The leadership team establishes the ends and, ultimately, execution becomes a form of organizational and individual commitment and integrity.

INTEGRITY: AN UNQUESTIONABLE CHARACTERISTIC OF SUCCESS

Among its definitions, "integrity" is typically understood to mean strict adherence to a moral code. To us this is only part of it. Integrity has a mechanical as well as a moral meaning that is important for high-quality asset management firms, regardless of their focus.

Consider a complex machine, such as a voting card reader. If the voting machine is to have integrity, it must meet certain minimum standards without error or failure. Similarly, a gun that functions time-after-time without error is a complex instrument that is said to have integrity.

The shortest and surest way to live with honor in the world is to be in reality what we would appear to be.

—Socrates

As a leader or employee, integrity is about doing what you say you will do. Your actions match your words, without error or failure. Your actions are consistent and predictable.

2008–2009 CASE STUDY: 50 BILLION LESSONS LEARNED FROM BERNIE MADOFF

There are hundreds of lessons in recent history that demonstrate just how difficult it can be to assess integrity. There is one from the recent period that deserves special attention. Bernard Madoff, a well-known industry professional, was exposed as a conman after committing a fraud of epic proportions. While the tallying is not yet complete as of this writing, it appears that he swindled private and institutional investors out of somewhere between $30 billion and $50 billion by convincing them that he had a strategy that could make money no matter what and that he had been doing so for many years. In reality, he was falsifying documents and perpetrating perhaps the greatest investment scam of all time. That is a staggering amount of money, and it is larger than the gross national product of more than 100 recognized countries.

Do you think that the hundreds of individuals and institutions that "invested" capital with Bernard Madoff believed that he was not only an individual lacking integrity, but also a sociopath capable of deceitful wealth destruction of the scale that appears to be the case? Of course not. For whatever reason, he had their complete trust. Sometimes the smartest, most charismatic, and persuasive individuals end up demonstrating a remarkable lack of integrity. And this is a lesson for us all. Integrity is something that must be demonstrated by actions across time. Investors cannot be afraid to ask for transparency and verifiable evidence in support of claims. And most important, investors cannot shortcut their own processes, as it appears many did. Despite the clear lack of integrity in the case of Bernard Madoff, an investor with any kind of investment process and integrity of that process would have been hard pressed to ever allocate money to him in the first place.

Real integrity evidences itself in times of organizational stress. Integrity is doing the right thing in the face of adversity, exactly when it would be easiest not to. It is holding fast to your beliefs and principles with the knowledge that doing so will certainly cause greater pain in the short-run. Throughout this book, we will come back to the issues and importance of integrity.

CONCLUSION

A strong and positive culture, limited size, strong governance for the protection of client interests, collaborative leadership, and integrity are all components of an organization that does right by its clients. For investment-driven asset management organizations, "hoovering" assets is not in the clients' best interests. Limiting growth and size requires an additional overlay of integrity, the integrity to say "no" to capability variations, to assets under management growth that becomes a drag on investment performance, to taking more risk than a client is comfortable taking, to anything that has the potential to impede investment performance in any non-negligible manner.

According to our surveys and interviews, some of the most consistent examples of investment-driven firms include Brandes Investment Partners; Bridgewater Associates; Grantham, Mayo, Van Otterloo (GMO); and Marsico Capital Management.

In the late 1990s, GMO held firm to its value-based fundamental discipline and refused to buy the high-flying TMT stocks. Many of its clients terminated their relationship, perhaps inevitable but a failure of communication nonetheless, and GMO's AuM was halved. After the TMT bubble burst, clients understood GMO's high level of investment integrity, enabling a doubling of the initial asset base.

The American Funds subsidiary of the Capital Group is a unique investment-driven organization in that it has an extremely large AuM, but it has a strong culture and has limited the number of capabilities that it manages. The strength of culture and limited capabilities, despite high AuM, have enabled American Funds to sustain an investment-driven existence for decades.

Among product-driven firms and former investment-driven firms that have shifted into the product-driven category are Fidelity Investments (Mutual Funds), Nicholas-Applegate Capital Management, Northern Trust, Nuveen Investments, Schroeder Investment Management Limited, and The Vanguard Group.

The powerful incentive of 2 percent management fees and 20 percent performance fees to grow assets and weak governance structures compelled many hedge fund firms that were otherwise investment focused and possessed strong cultures to become extremely high priced, product-driven firms. Our survey identified a number of firms about which investors have growing concerns. Among these fallen angels, and avoiding the fraudulent, are Bear Stearns Asset Management, Goldman Sachs Asset Management, Highbridge Capital Management, and MAN Investments. Their actions, focus, and integrity in the days ahead will have a great impact on their ultimate success or failure.

Transparency makes ethics and integrity easier. The bright light of transparency prevents the shadowy presence of misaligned incentives to drive investment-driven asset management firms from their initial core purpose— investment performance and client outcomes. Absent transparency, the culture can change, size can become a priority, governance can falter, and leadership can wane. Justice Louis Brandeis coined a phrase that should garner our attention when he said, "Sunlight is the best disinfectant." He was referring to transparency and honesty in public policy. But whether talking about the relations of a firm with its employees or with its clients, we would all do well to take heed.

In this chapter we have identified a number of characteristics of high-quality asset management firms. We focused on the importance of a strong culture and what that means for successful asset management firms. We also discussed the hazards posed by growth of assets and proliferation of products. Lastly we reiterated the importance of effective governance, leadership, and integrity. In Chapters 2 and 3 we will outline a more prescriptive framework for building a successful asset management firm. This starts with another detailed look at mission statements and values. However, we quickly move into a discussion of the practical considerations for setting up management and governance structures and identify best practices for execution of the mission.

CHAPTER 2

Building a Cathedral

A Framework for Turning the Mission into Collective Action

This and the following chapter will outline our unique model for effective leadership and management. As leaders it is critically important to embrace the organizational values, mission, and goals to provide a framework to make the necessary and sometimes difficult decisions about your strategy, your organization, and your employees. It is equally important to align individual and team objective setting and performance measurement in ways that help to achieve the mission.

To reveal the important role that mission statements play in guiding employee behavior and eventually the long-term success of your investment firm, we first need to tell you a story. This story focuses not only on the importance of what, as CIOs, our employees are doing but also how they perceive what they are doing as part of the larger purpose of the organization.

One day, a lady walks down the street and passes a man working by the side of the road. The lady asks, "What are you doing?" He says, "I'm cutting stone." She walks a little further down the road and sees another man doing exactly the same thing and asks of him, "What are you doing?" This man responds, "Cutting cornerstones for a building." She continues walking down the road and not too far down she passes another man, again cutting stone, and asks, "What are you doing?" This man says, "Building a cathedral."

This anecdote demonstrates the important purpose of a mission statement for all employees, as well as the importance for investment professionals to have an investment philosophy statement. Employees must see the big picture and how they contribute to it, and not just the narrow function that they are fulfilling on a day-to-day basis. If your employees respond to the question, "What are you doing?" with something analogous to "Building a cathedral," then the leadership is doing its job.

A FRAMEWORK FOR EFFECTIVE LEADERSHIP AND MANAGEMENT

Table 2.1 outlines a basic framework for effecting leadership and management that can be adapted to most organizations. In the sections that follow, we will not address every aspect of the process for execution of this framework, but we touch on the most critical parts as well as the lessons that experience has taught, in the hopes that some of our mistakes can be sidestepped. It is okay to make mistakes, but it is best to learn from the mistakes of others when we can.

> *Good judgment comes from experience, and a lot of that comes from bad judgment.*
>
> —Will Rogers

While we are not aiming to write a management self-help book, we acknowledge that a prescriptive approach may be interpreted as such. We are also cognizant that a prescriptive approach such as this has limitations

TABLE 2.1   A Framework for Effective Leadership and Management

Component of the Framework	Who Is Responsible?
Determine & Live Organizational Values (Enduring)	All employees
Create a Mission Statement and/or Investment Philosophy Statement (Enduring)	CEO, CIO, Board of Directors, Management Committee
Set Strategic Goals for the Organization (1 to 5 Year View)	Management Committee
Establish Team Goals & KPIs (1 to 5 Year)	Team Heads & Management Committee
Establish Individual Goals & KPIs (1 Year and 3 Year)	Individual & Manager
Evaluate Individual, Team, and Organizational Performance along criticality and performance dimensions (Annual)	All (with differing responsibilities for various aspects)
Communicate criticality and performance at all levels (At least Annual)	All (with differing responsibilities for various aspects)
Align Remuneration with Merit Zones (Annual)	Management Committee

and is dependent on the structure and governance of each organization. For this we apologize in advance.

One thing that is critical to this process at *all* levels is a focus on personal accountability and collaborative assessment. It is incumbent on the individual to take an active role in the process of setting and evaluating their own objectives. Fostering a culture and organizational processes that make this happen is the job of the leadership team.

ESTABLISHING AND LIVING ORGANIZATIONAL VALUES

We discussed the importance of organizational values in Chapter 1. Values are individual to each organization, and we will not try to be prescriptive here with an approach for setting those values; however we will share an experience that may serve as a guide for others. Values flow up, down, and across an organization. That is to say that individuals influence the organization's values and vice versa. As a result the values need to be always present in the minds of those evaluating candidates for potential roles within the organization. Furthermore, in the highest quality organizations, the values can be found to impact the client experience or client outcome.

Taken together, an objective analysis of these two groups (clients and employees) may be the ultimate test of whether the stated values are in fact a credible reflection of the firm. Ultimately this process starts with the leader, and for an investment-driven organization, this starts with the CIO. Later in the chapter we will discuss in greater detail, the process for evaluating whether or not the organization is living its values. In any event, the values represent the ground that your cathedral will be built on, and as such deserve significant attention from the management team.

Setting Organizational Values: A Case in Point

When Brian Singer became the head of a global investment team responsible for managing nearly $200 billion of multi-asset portfolios, he needed to develop a strong and positive culture. The team was a relatively unmotivated and disparate collection of investment professionals from Brinson Partners (acquired by Swiss Bank Corporation), Phillips & Drew (acquired by Union Bank of Switzerland), a contingent of Swiss-based colleagues from these banks, and later a group from Mitchell Hutchins Asset Management (the "in-house" asset management group of the former Paine Webber). Each country and city of origin brought a unique culture. Complicating things further, the cultures of the predecessor organizations were completely different. Capturing the cultural divergence, the management team referred to the three original contingents as "The Three Tribes."

Brian turned to Jim Ware, the founder of Focus Consulting Group, to assist his effort to create a unified team. He did not know Jim at the time or his fledgling consulting operation, but Jim understood the problem and was excited to work with the team to identify common values and foster a unified focus. The ultimate outcome was more than originally envisioned possible.

The combined team and its management began a multiyear cathedral renovation project. Starting with a set of diverse cultures and attitudes, the group first embarked on a journey to discern common values and behaviors upon which to build a focused team.

We invited the management team to the Union League Club in Chicago for a meeting. Each person indicated what they expected and anticipated from their employment. We discussed our investment and business philosophies. The management team searched for common threads that would allow us to work together. Sometimes we agreed, and many times we disagreed. Luckily, "The Three Tribes" were comfortable with a fundamental investment philosophy that could enhance performance through the qualitative use of quantitative portfolio construction tools.

We plastered the walls with Post-It Notes of each individual's values in order to discern similarities and differences. After two days we identified shared values and a mutually agreed mission. We further refined our mission by specifying a set of strategic objectives that we would jointly pursue from our disparate locations and through the lenses of separate national cultures.

Most of the initial staff accepted the guiding principles and mission that we identified. To the benefit of all parties, the individuals who did not accept the organization's values and mission did not stay. Few were terminated. For most, the obvious lack of alignment was transparent, enabling each individual to decide for themselves to seek alternative employment. Employee commitment sorted itself with dignity. In almost all instances the motivation was clear and the outcome advantageous. Over the subsequent years, the team thrived. We delivered superior investment and business performance. We created new investment products that specifically targeted client needs. More than anything, we had pride in our work and enjoyed each other's company (for the most part anyway).

We took from this experience the observation that values and culture are grassroots in nature. They are not externally imposed. They emanate from individuals on the team and are espoused by those brought into the team. If starting from scratch, the culture and values can be prespecified and individuals can be hired with full knowledge of the values. If starting with a preexisting team, the values must be derived from and agreed by the individuals in place.

CREATING MISSION AND/OR INVESTMENT PHILOSOPHY STATEMENTS

Seeing the big picture provides context for the delegation of authority to subordinates. Individuals become involved in the organization, which leads to interest in and commitment to the cause of the organization (its mission and investment philosophy). It also leads to loyalty, as well as personal investment, in the organization.

> *The task of the leader is to get his people from where they are to where they have not been.*
> —Henry Kissinger

For investment-driven firms, as opposed to product-driven firms, the investment philosophy statement and the mission statement can potentially be rolled into one. The combined statement should indicate both *what* an organization seeks to accomplish and *how* it seeks to do it. Two prime case studies of how investment-driven firms have been able to fuse their investment philosophies and mission statements are Brinson Partners in the early and mid-1990s and Dodge & Cox today.

Mission Statement Case Study 1: Brinson Partners

In the years the authors spent with Brinson Partners, we witnessed the evolution of its investment philosophy and mission statements. In the beginning, Gary Brinson was the chief executive officer (CEO) and chief investment officer (CIO), and Brinson Partners had a very clear mission statement that wove together the mission and the investment philosophy of the organization:

> *Build the premier global institutional asset management firm by operating in asset classes and geographic areas where we can achieve excellence in the delivery of performance and client service.*

Gary used this mission and philosophy statement, his gravitas, and a strong team to drive the industry toward greater globalization and more effective use of asset allocation for portfolio risk management and return enhancement purposes. In fact, his sermons on asset allocation helped to create a new mainstream segment in the asset management industry—one that was focused principally on the allocation of assets across asset classes and geographies as a means of seeking return and reducing risk.

> *The best way to predict the future is to invent it.*
> —Alan Kay, originator of the Windows operating system

As a result, there was no confusion on the part of any employee that his or her priority was portfolio performance and client service. The attention to detail in all client interaction was extraordinary. Gary would let everybody know if a phone went unanswered or a presentation page had even a minor error. Everybody at the firm dreaded an "after-hours" call from Gary before he met with a client and the late-night fire drills correcting minor errors in his effort to uphold a standard that few could even hope to achieve. Periods of weak investment performance resulted in late night and weekend vigils to question our research, test our valuations, or pose alternative hypotheses. A lack of attention to detail and the slightest indication of investment indolence reflected poorly on the firm and would not be even marginally tolerated.

Over time, there was a shift from a combined mission and investment philosophy statement to separate statements that signaled a shift within the organization. In the Brinson Partners organization, every individual embraced the primacy of investment performance and client service. By 2001, the role of CEO and CIO had been separated, the mission statement indicated a broader direction for asset management, and the investment philosophy statement targeted only the investment professionals and signaled a shift in focus from evenly balanced top-down and bottom-up investing to a more diffused bottom-up, alpha boutique orientation. Alpha boutiques are typically small, independent organizations narrowly focused on the generation of superior investment performance in a particular asset class or with a specific investment style. Perceptive investors detected this fundamental shift in the organization.

Mission Statement Case Study 2: Dodge & Cox

The Dodge & Cox fund family also wove together the firm's mission and investment philosophy statements. It still puts this statement front and center in its messaging, "Our disciplined investment approach is guided by a long-term investment horizon, independent research, and portfolio diversification."[1] Moreover, there is a very focused statement that, *"Research is our common language ... We have found no quantitative model or research service that can replace the benefits of holding an onsite meeting with a company's management, conferring directly with its competitors, customers, and suppliers, or taking the time to analyze its financial record from top to bottom.*"[2] This serves clients as well as a disciplined, long-term, research-driven approach.

While not necessarily delivering superior investment performance all the time, Dodge & Cox has adhered to its investment philosophy to deliver superior investment performance over time.

STRATEGIC GOALS AND KEY PERFORMANCE INDICATORS

A process for setting strategic goals in an organization is critical for aligning the activities of employees with the mission statement. By strategic goals, we refer to desired accomplishments required for the firm to be moving tangibly in the direction of mission fulfillment. While a mission statement tends to live on without expiry, strategic goals are time bound. Strategic goals may be desired accomplishments for this year or for the next five years, or a combination of the two. The goal-setting process can involve input and data collection from all employees, but ultimately it is the responsibility of the management committee.

For investment firms, this goal setting tends to revolve around the achievement of realistic performance objectives, but can and should include goals related to client results and client satisfaction. This goal-setting process requires that the management committee evaluate the external environment as well as organizational resources. Goals can be stretch goals but must be perceived by employees as potentially attainable.

One of the most effective methods the authors have found for goal setting involves having all members of the senior management team, the firm's leaders, submit an imaginative futuristic description of the firm. This description is one that the management team member writes as if he or she is a journalist writing a feature article about the firm at some designated point in time in the future. This not only helps provide a document that highlights different views about strategic priorities, but it also helps the team execute specific initiatives that will help drive goal achievement. In our experience, it can also provide a creative release. Some of the artwork that has been submitted with such articles has left lasting impressions in our minds to say the least.

> *A leader does not necessarily need to be the most intelligent member of his group...rather he is the one with the clearest and most far-reaching vision.*
> —Sheikh Mohammed bin Rashid Al Maktoum

The establishment of the firm's strategic goals provides the roadmap for planning, budgeting, and resource allocations, and also importantly for team and individual objective setting. Measuring the attainment of these objectives at each level is the role of the Key Performance Indicator (KPI). If the mission and investment philosophy statement, like blueprints, communicate the architect's vision of the cathedral, these KPIs provide specific statements of each employee's objectives for building our cathedral. We recommend a set of KPIs for the firm and consistent sets of KPIs for each team. If an investment firm is to remain investment-driven, then the KPIs must predominantly reflect investment performance, and each employee, to varying degrees, must be held accountable for that investment performance.

Weighting Investment Performance versus Successful Client Outcomes

An appropriate set of KPIs for an investment-driven firm would dictate that something on the order of 60 percent of overall performance be based on investment performance, with the remaining 40 percent being based on building a platform for successful long-term client outcomes (see Figure 2.1). The use of the phrase "client outcomes" is a very important aspect of KPIs. While it is difficult at best to generate superior investment performance, it is much more difficult to provide superior investment outcomes for clients.

The investment performance KPIs are for naught if clients and ultimate beneficiaries do not experience the competence of the investment manager. Often this derives from inappropriate constraints that are agreed to increase

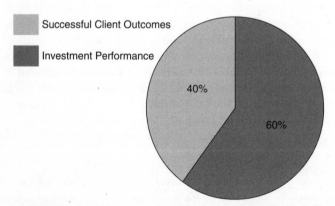

FIGURE 2.1   Suggested KPI weightings for an Investment-Focused Firm

the probability of winning an investment mandate or inappropriate risk calibration that results in early mandate termination.

Given this litany of caveats, how can the performance of investment and business professionals be effectively evaluated and incentivized? On the one hand, the management committee wants to create incentives that reward investment and business professionals for strong performance during their careers with the firm; competitors have a way of tempting away employees who are perceived (even if random) to be superior performers. On the other hand, the management committee must incentivize long-horizon thinking and investment performance that is consistent with the professionals' fiduciary responsibilities to the firm's clients.

While investment performance is the critical product of an investment organization, it would be inappropriate to consider it as the only criterion by which to evaluate employees. Investment performance reflects the confluence of all factors currently at play in the organization. However, it is only a single outcome from an infinite sequence of feasible return outcomes. Other pieces of information can provide valuable direction in assessing skill and competence.

Moreover, in building a platform for tomorrow's success, it is necessary to consider not only factors important to current realized investment performance, but also to incentivize a platform for future success. The collection of competencies that provide a skillful edge today may not provide an edge in the future. The organization and each individual must not be incentivized to trade future success for current success because of compensation structure. Instead, an ongoing process of research, development, experimentation, and innovation must be established and rewarded. Given the clients' relatively long investment horizon, achieving superior client outcomes directs the management committee to place something on the order of a 40 percent weight on KPIs associated with superior client outcomes over time via building and maintaining a platform for future success.

The assessment of each employee's success in building and maintaining a platform for future success is more qualitative than the process of assessing investment performance. The factors that are involved in this aspect of each employee's job are varied and can include:

- Innovation
- Independence
- Teamwork
- Research
- Transparency
- Client outcomes
- Values

ORGANIZATIONAL KEY PERFORMANCE INDICATORS: HYPOTHETICAL EXAMPLE

A simple example of a firm with a five-year investment horizon might construct KPIs that look something like that shown in the box below. The focus should always be return per unit of risk, with risk defined in a way that is relevant for the particular strategy or approach.

60% Risk-Adjusted Investment Performance

	1-Year Information Ratio*	3-Year Information Ratio	5-Year Information Ratio	1-Year Peer Ranking	3-Year Peer Ranking	5-Year Peer Ranking
Weighting>	10%	15%	25%	10%	15%	25%
Investment Strategy ABC	Goal: Greater than .5	Goal: Greater than .5	Goal: Greater than .5	Goal: Top third	Goal: Top third	Goal: Top third

* Information ratio measures excess return or alpha divided by the tracking error or relative risk of a portfolio compared with its benchmark. We will discuss this further in Chapter 3.

40% Successful Client Outcomes

- 10 percent improvement in client service quality ratings from client feedback survey.
- Successful development, rollout, and 50 percent client usage of new online reporting tool.
- Successful development and rollout of new risk reporting program and inclusion of statistics in client reporting and client presentations.
- Assets Under Management
  - Priority 1: Asset retention.
  - Priority 2: Development of new relationships with long-term investors.

Of course, KPIs will be different for every organization and may focus on different metrics. The important thing is that they are thoughtfully developed and communicated to all whose function contributes to accomplishing them. The weightings given to different performance periods for evaluation purposes will also vary. In the next chapter, however, we will make the case for significantly higher weightings applied to longer term performance numbers.

The intent of this system is to target and substantially meet the KPIs, although the organization should not be expected to meet the target for each KPI every year. Our experience suggests that all employees should, to varying degrees, be held accountable for investment and business performance KPIs. If all employees are accountable,[3] they have an incentive to understand how their jobs influence investment performance. Under an incentive structure of broad accountability for investment KPI achievement, employees take an interest in investment decisions and begin to modify their behaviors to improve investment analysis, decision making, and implementation. Similarly, broad employee accountability for business performance, even if not directly within the realm of authority of the individual, leads to behaviors that indirectly influence business outcomes.

We do not want to suggest that people be held accountable for outcomes beyond their authorities. Rather, we want people to realize that their authorities extend beyond narrow job descriptions. Realization of these authorities increases the potential for a virtuous circle of superior investment and business performance, higher revenue, and higher compensation for all employees in the firm.

CONCLUSION

Developing and living organizational values is the foundation of leadership success. A shared mission is a second critical step and is derived from and supported by the organizational values. The word "shared," is critical here, and it is truly no easy task. It requires constant communication from the team at the top. Reviewing the mission and the organizational goals and KPIs as it relates to the mission is, well, mission critical. This overarching mission must be translated into actionable and measurable goals, which are measured by the organizational KPIs. We have put this framework in place and tested it over a number of years and with different organizations. In our view, it is requisite to the success of an investment organization—or any organization for that matter. In Chapter 3, we will dig deeper into some of the pragmatic considerations of this approach with a focus on measuring individual performance and appropriately setting individual compensation. Ultimately, truly successful organizations have a culture and approach that ensures the firm is a true meritocracy.

CHAPTER 3

Building a Meritocracy

Understanding, Evaluating, and Rewarding Employee Contributions

A chievement of individual and team KPIs is the basis for measuring performance. However, even in a well-structured meritocracy, it is not the sole determinant of an employee's absolute or relative compensation and promotion potential. Compensation and promotion should be driven by the objective assessment of employees across two dimensions, namely performance and criticality. Criticality is a measure of how important and integral the individual is in driving attainment of the organization's goals. Performance is a measure of the degree to which KPIs have been met over the measurement period. We will discuss our approach more specifically later in this chapter.

PERFORMANCE: A DEEPER DIVE

It is important to outline this basic compensation methodology up front to help frame thinking about evaluation processes. Figure 3.1 provides important context for thinking about criticality and performance. Utilizing this evaluation framework and communicating to employees along these dimensions serves many purposes. Chiefly, it helps to set employee expectations and facilitates faster decision making with respect to employee hiring, firing, and compensation decisions. We will expand on this framework and discuss more practical implementation ideas and consideration later in the chapter. But first, we focus on the more general questions of determining the appropriate weightings of KPIs in assessing performance and the horizon over which performance should be evaluated.

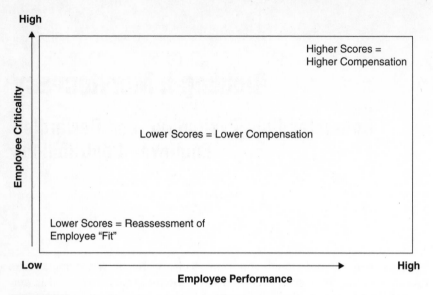

FIGURE 3.1 The Two Dimensions of Meritocracy: Criticality & Performance

HORIZON: THE FALLACY OF THE THREE-YEAR TRACK RECORD

We have always found the three-year period typically used to evaluate investment performance and to make manager hiring and firing decisions to be laughably short. It could even be characterized as a violation of the fiduciary responsibilities of most trustees and agents. The three-year investment track record that is at the foundation of most manager or fund hiring and firing decisions makes almost no statistical sense.[1] Yet, it is precisely this brief time period that makes it so difficult for clients to experience investment performance of successful managers and for managers to create opportunities for long-term investors.

> *There is a danger of expecting the results of the future to be predicted from the past.*
>
> —John Maynard Keynes

There is a big problem that dogs everyone involved in performance analysis—no one can be certain that investment skill exists for a manager. A very simple exercise demonstrates how difficult it is to ascertain the skill level

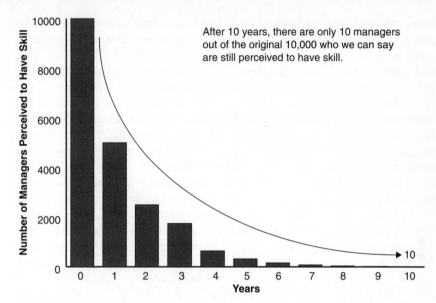

After 10 years, there are only 10 managers out of the original 10,000 who we can say are still perceived to have skill.

FIGURE 3.2   Randomness and the Appearance of Skill

of an investment manager. Assume that there are 10,000 investors. Imagine, for example that these are the investment managers behind the mutual funds listed in the performance section of the *Wall Street Journal*. Further, assume that no manager has skill, either positive or negative. Each year, we would expect half of the managers to outperform their benchmarks. After one year, 5,000 managers would have outperformed their benchmarks. After two years, the number would be 2,500, and so it goes. Figure 3.2 demonstrates the number of managers who would have outperformed their respective benchmarks after the number of years indicated on the horizontal axis.

In this "real world" situation, despite the absence of any skill on the part of any manager, after 10 years about 10 managers would have been expected to beat their benchmarks in each and every year. Could this mean that the Bill Millers and Peter Lynches lauded by the investing public that presumes observed performance to be the ultimate indicator of investment competence are merely random outcomes?

Investors, historically, have shown a tendency to chase after these 10 managers, while dumping managers in lower deciles. If there really were skill in the investment community and this randomness were the extent of factors that confound performance analysis, investors would have the opportunity to achieve superior outcomes by applying statistical tools to

long-term performance track records to identify and select superior managers. However, investors and agents do not consider 10-year performance
track records; they typically consider three-year track records. After three
years, more than 1,000 of our unskilled managers would be deemed superior to the crowd and, as historical data shows, money would flow from
the randomly poor managers to the 1,000 randomly successful managers.
Let's face it; if you can get a job making a fee on transactions that move
money from one manager to another and you lack integrity, then your career
should make you a wealthy individual. If you have integrity, then you would
attempt to move your clients out of this fee treadmill.

The CFA Institute reports that there were about 54,000 mutual funds at
year-end 2003.[2] Of these, only 15 percent were U.S. based, or about 8,500
funds. Not too dissimilar from the 10,000 assumed in the example above.
If there are 54,000 mutual funds and performance was purely random (e.g.,
no manager is skilled), then roughly 50 of them would outperform their
benchmarks every year for 10 years. There is no doubt that fund analysts
worldwide would pontificate the myriad skills, insights, and prescience of
these 50 fund managers. Worst of all is that they would likely recommend
portfolios combining subsets of these 50 funds to demonstrate their "back
tested" prowess in designing multimanager investments. (An aside that is
developed in Chapter 4, it is prudent to ask the fund analysts what they were
recommending 10 (or three) years ago, not what they are recommending now
based on prior performance.)

Performance Analysis When No Skill Exists

Assume that a manager has skill, with the ability to add 100 bps of added
value per year at a standard deviation of excess returns over the benchmark
of 4 percent. The manager's skill can be measured by the ratio of the actual
added value to the standard deviation of annual added values. This ratio is
referred to as the information ratio (IR):

$$IR = \frac{\text{added value}}{\text{standard deviation of added values}}$$

It is important to state that the added value of *annual* returns is used.
Any stated IR has an implicit time horizon built into the calculation. For
example, assume that an investor adds 50 bps per quarter in excess of the
benchmark and does so with a 2 percent nonannualized standard deviation
of quarterly returns. The IR can be a multitude of numbers, but the two
obvious ones would be the quarterly IR and the annual IR:

	Return	Standard Deviation	Information Ratio (IR)
Quarterly[a]	0.50%	2.00%	0.25
Annually[b]	1.93%	4.00%	0.48

[a] The quarterly added value and volatility are not annualized and the IR is simply the return divided by the volatility.

[b] The annualized added value assumes quarterly returns that are independent and identically distributed (iid) and typically can be approximated as $\{1 + \text{quarterly return} - \text{variance}/2\}^4 - 1$, or $\{1 + 0.50\% - [(2.00\%^2)/2]\}^4 - 1$. The annualized volatility is calculated as quarterly volatility$^* \sqrt{4}$. The IR is the return divided by the volatility.

Since the return increases about linearly with time (linearly if the volatility is zero) and the standard deviation increases with the square root of time, the IR increases with the lengthening of the measurement horizon.[3]

If returns are unrelated from one period to the next and have the same return characteristics in each period, then we can make some statements about the probability that the manager's skill is observable. Given that realized investment performance is a proxy of the manager's true skill, what is the probability that this skilled manager appears unskilled? The IR is the tool we use to undertake this analysis. Figure 3.3 shows the probability

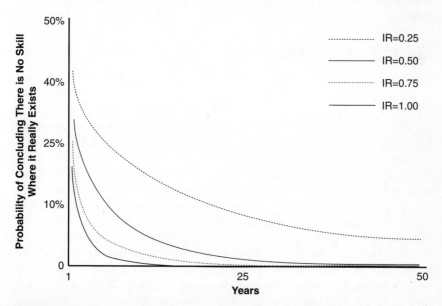

FIGURE 3.3 Certainty of Investment Performance over Time

of concluding that a skilled manager, with skill measured by the IR, is unskilled.

If the manager has an annualized IR of 0.25, then after three years there is nearly a 35 percent chance that historical performance, being only a sample of the true performance, indicates that the manager has no skill. It would take nearly 50 years to reduce the probability of inappropriately assessing the manager's skill to about 5 percent. Since most managers, regardless of competence, declare an IR of 0.50, the probability of inaccurately concluding the manager has no skill remains above 20 percent.

In measuring investment performance, these subtleties dictate not only an accurate accounting, but also a clear understanding of that accounting. We think that it is best to use annualized returns, volatilities, and information ratios. The occurrence of serially correlated returns and the analysis of illiquid assets require additional analysis for better understanding and performance analysis.[4]

All managers want to be skilled, and all agents and clients want to hire managers with skill. Regardless, integrity compels us to distinguish between what we want to be true and what we can objectively conclude is true. Yes, we want to identify skill after three years. Despite our desires, we must accept tremendous investment performance uncertainty, even when we know that the manager we are evaluating has skill. When we do not know, the task of selecting and compensating is even more of a fool's errand than most in the industry are willing to admit.

Case Study: Defined Benefit Plans

Consider the investment horizon of defined benefit (DB) plan beneficiaries. Generally speaking, DB plans are pay-as-you-go schemes that place the burden on the sponsoring companies to pay specified benefits to employees upon retirement. Most DB plans provide incentives for pensioners to wait until Social Security retirement age to start receiving benefits, which is 65 years old in the United States. Currently, the life expectancy for a 65-year-old male is nearly another 20 years. For someone who wishes to maintain principal until death and then pass the principal down to his or her heirs, 20 years would be the time horizon. Twenty years would be the mean of the life expectancy distribution, and there is variation around it, with a positive skew. Some pensioners would not seek to maintain principal, but draw down the principal over time. These people have a shorter time horizon. In essence, the life expectancy could be equal to or less than the 20-year investment horizon. Regardless, the duration—the expected time to retiree cash flow from the date of retirement—is about eight to nine years. Depending on the DB plan's ratio of active to retired employees, the investment horizon is in all likelihood at least nine years.

Personal savings may reflect a shorter-term desire for future cash flow than conventional DB plans, but, since current state and private systems are unlikely to meet the cash flow desires (as opposed to needs) of most individuals, the personal saving investment horizon is likely to be longer than three years. Despite the tendency for many individuals to invest with very short time horizons, investor appreciation of the wealth that they will require to support acceptable future living standards (as opposed to desire) is probably too low.

Other pools of wealth, such as sovereign wealth funds, endowments, and foundations, generally are perceived to have long investment horizons, much longer than three years.

PERFORMANCE ANALYSIS: PRACTICALLY SPEAKING

The main point here is that it is often very difficult to differentiate good (or poor) performance from good (or poor) outcomes. Performance data alone will almost never provide a clear picture. Two things that can help are

1. Objective performance attribution methodologies and processes that are designed to reflect the investment process, and
2. Setting expectations ex-ante regarding environments in which the strategy should outperform or underperform (and then evaluating realized performance against those expectations).

Like the evaluation of investment managers, employee of investment firms should be measured on what they have accomplished. Employees should also be mentored for what they are capable of accomplishing. While difficult, measurement and analysis of past performance is the easier of the two. Support and guidance when the team comes under fire for justifiable and unavoidable poor performance is orders of magnitude more difficult.

Performance Attribution: Ex-Post Analysis

We are known for our research on the separation of asset and currency investment decisions and performance analysis.[5] Our intent was to develop an attribution methodology that paralleled our investment process. Tangentially, we specified a general framework that applies to all asset and currency analysis. Other separations of investment decisions can and should be built into this framework to measure performance along the same dimensions that investment professionals have authorities and are held accountable.

Performance Perversion: Ex-Ante Expectations

Any skillful fundamentally based investment process will tend to generate superior performance when prices move toward fundamental values (as defined by the investment process). The process should generally perform poorly when prices move away from fundamental values. However, as prices move away from fundamental values, the opportunity for future superior performance increases. When we worked at UBS Global Asset Management, our team developed an opportunity set measure that rose as prices moved away from values and declined as prices converged on values. The key is to design portfolios that limit poor performance as the opportunity set grows and capitalize on a shrinking opportunity set. Figure 3.4 provides a hypothetical example of this process over time.

From 1997 to 2000 (period II) and from 2005 to 2007 (period V), the arrows indicate the opportunity measure in the dotted line rose dramatically. Currency performance was "poor," indicated by the downward-sloping arrows (periods II and V). However, given the magnitude of investment opportunity increases as prices moved away from values, the "poor" performance was actually commendable. Subsequent to each of these "poor" performance periods, periods III and VI, as the opportunities drop, superior performance is captured in even greater measure. Based on these observations, titular "poor" performance should have been rewarded. Conversely, of course, positive performance concurrent with a widening opportunity set may not be rewarded, and may even be considered a red flag of inadvertent risk exposure.

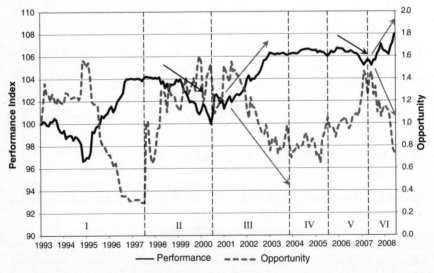

FIGURE 3.4   Opportunity versus Performance

There is no doubt that the incentive structure of superior investment firms must exceed the typical three-year horizon that permeates the investment industry. So why does the industry seem transfixed with the three-year investment horizon? We credit two primary factors:

1. Behavioral factors that result in subrational investment decisions on the part of investment principals—beneficiaries and money managers.
2. The chain of agents between the investment firms and beneficiaries must justify their fees and, in so doing, actively make decisions even when the basis for those decisions does not exist.

Chapters 4 and 5 delve into these issues in greater detail, but consider the array of agents that interject themselves into the saving and investment processes:

- Morningstar, Lipper, and other fund-ranking and analysis entities
- Consultants
- Investment staff
- Human resources staff
- Trustees
- Boards of directors
- Financial advisors
- Government agencies

These agents can make a powerful contribution, and regulation often requires their intercession into the saving and investment processes. However, the intention of these agents, despite any higher purpose, falls unconscionably short of their execution. Like investors, agents often are dismal failures and do little to improve the lot of the principals that they purport to benefit and protect.

Taking these considerations in conjunction, it appears that many fiduciaries may in fact be detrimental to the process of providing for future consumption, whether they are investment firms or agents. These players are simply responding to their incentives, and all the carping in the world won't change the situation. Rather, the incentives need to change, and the first place to look for the incentives is in the fees. The second is in job stability. Both involve issues of integrity, ethics, and money. The importance of unquestionable integrity and ethics permeates this book. The importance of money is addressed specifically in Chapter 5.

> *Most of economics can be summarized in four words: 'People respond to incentives.' The rest is commentary.*
> —Steven E. Landsburg

Finally, in the process of evaluating three-year performance track records, many principals and agents place an inordinate importance on the most recent year's performance. In considering a manager, an individual or firm will typically look at a table of one-, two- and three-year performances, considering each of equal importance. If so, the one-year performance will inadvertently receive a weight of over 60 percent—the full 33 1/3 percent weight on the one-year performance plus half of the 33 1/3 percent weight on the two-year number plus one-third of the 33 1/3 percent weight on the three-year number. The second-year performance outcome will receive about a 30 percent weight and the third-year outcome will receive about a 10 percent weight. See Table 3.1.

Even if only the three- and five-year performance numbers are considered equally, each of the first three years receive about a 25 percent weight and years four and five only about a 10 percent weight. Even equal consideration of the five- and ten-year performance histories results in 75 percent of the weight on the first five years and 25 percent on the second five years.

To get beyond the endemic short-termism that prevails, the CIO should establish a performance weighting criterion that places weights on the order of 50 percent on the 10-year return, 30 percent on the five-year return, 15 percent on the three-year return, and 5 percent on the one-year return *and* have the integrity to say "no" to clients who want the skills of the manager but are uncomfortable with the long investment horizon. Integrity requires the CIO to recognize the long investment horizons (based on future consumption needs) of the clients and the reality of uncertainty in measuring skill. Furthermore, the CIO is similarly compelled to reject clients who do not live up to the same level of integrity and fiduciary accountability.

Even with the weighting 60/40 scheme proffered above, there is a significant chance that an investment manager or employee with skill will be deemed to have no skill. However, anything shorter is likely to create instability in the employment of key investment staff. For this reason, and despite the rigorous approach described in this chapter, performance evaluation must be a human process. Individuals who adhere to the investment philosophy and follow the investment process should be *expected* to underperform in many periods.

TOP-DOWN AND BOTTOM-UP APPROACH TO DETERMINING PERFORMANCE

The process of evaluating each employee's performance is top-down, beginning with an evaluation of the firm, proceeding to evaluations of each

TABLE 3.1 Appropriately Weighting Investment Performance Periods

Year	Weighting the historical returns according to this column…	…implies weighting the individual annual return as in this column.	Weighting the historical returns according to this column…	…implies weighting the individual annual return as in this column.	Weighting the historical returns according to this column…	…implies weighting the individual annual return as in this column.	Weighting the historical returns according to this column…	…implies weighting the individual annual return as in this column.
1	33%	61%		27%		15%	5%	21%
2	33%	26%		27%		15%		16%
3	33%	11%	50%	27%		15%	15%	16%
4		0%		10%		15%		11%
5		0%	50%	10%	50%	15%	30%	11%
6		0%		0%		5%		5%
7		0%		0%		5%		5%
8		0%		0%		5%		5%
9		0%		0%		5%		5%
10		0%		0%	50%	5%	50%	5%
Total	100%	100%	100%	100%	100%	100%	100%	100%

team, and ending with the evaluation of each individual. The CEO, CIO, and the executive management team evaluate the firm's performance, focusing primarily on investment performance and building a platform for future investment success. Secondary consideration is given to assets under management (AuM) growth. This reflects a bit of a "build it and they will come" mentality. However, for a firm holding out investment performance as its raison d'etre (as opposed to socially responsible or passive investing), a core competence of superior investment performance is the only ethical way to raise assets.

Second, as noted in Chapter 1, successful asset management firms limit the number of capabilities managed, limit the assets under management, and in good conscience turn clients and assets away.

> *Just say no.*
> —Nancy Reagan

Thus, each and every employee is responsible for investment performance, and the KPIs of the firm subsume the KPIs of the investment team and the KPIs of each employee. This provides an incentive for every employee to act in a manner that directly or indirectly improves investment analysis, decision, implementation, and client communication.

After evaluating the performance of the organization, executive management evaluates team performance. The primary reason that the executive management team discusses performance together is that each team's execution depends on the other teams' performance. Thus, it is inappropriate to fault one team for its failure to execute if that failure is a function of the team's dependence on another team's performance. If there is a failure to execute, the root cause must bear the brunt of the poor performance score.

> *Execution supersedes intention.*
> —Brinson Partners, Inc. "Guiding Principles"

Each team is evaluated relative to that team's KPIs, the aggregation of which is consistent with the firm's overall KPIs. Once the team has received a KPI performance rating, the individuals in the team can be evaluated according to their KPIs. Again, this is accomplished by the joint evaluation of the executive management team. The evaluation of each individual by the entire management team has a couple of important and positive externalities:

Uniformity – some managers are harder graders than others.

Understanding – each manager learns about the functions of other teams and accountabilities, strengths, and weaknesses of each employee.

Leverage – increased ability to leverage the talents of each employee across the organization.

Consistency – prevents favoritism and discrimination.

Since the aggregation of the individuals' KPIs must combine to the KPI performance score of the team, and that of the teams' KPIs to the firm's KPIs, each employee is evaluated in an objective and consistent manner with full appreciation of the firm's mission and KPIs. Everybody in the organization knows about and works to improve investment competence and performance.

DESIGNING YOUR RATING SYSTEM TO HELP MAKE THE DIFFICULT DECISIONS

In our experience, we have seen that it is beneficial to ask all performance scores to range between 1 and 4, only 1, 2, 3, and 4 are allowed. A score of 1 is bad and a score of 4 is good. The use of an even number of performance scores forces each manager to avoid the tendency to select the midpoint. Each employee must be scored with good or bad performance.

If the firm performs as expected, then a distribution of all employees' performance scores would follow a bell curve shape. If the firm does poorly and gives itself an overall performance score of 1.5, then the distribution for all employees would be negatively skewed. See Figure 3.5.

If the firm does well, with a performance score of 3.5, then the distribution would be positively skewed.

Since performance scores range from 1 to 4, and only scores of 1, 2, 3, or 4 are allowed, managers are prevented from taking the easy out of selecting a middling performance score. As a coin must fall on either heads or tails, each employee must be deemed to have performed poorly or well. In the end, after much discussion among the management team, employees can be moved on an exceptional basis to a 2.5 score. Employees who have worked less than a year automatically receive a 2.5 score as the performance evaluation period is typically too short to be meaningful. Since the performance score is ordinal, it is the rank that matters and not the distance from 2 to 5 or from 1 to 3 that matters. Thus, the ordering of 1, 2, 2.5, 3, and 4 can be recategorized as scores between 1 and 5. The small number of 2.5 scores becomes 3 and the previous 3 and 4 scores are increased to 4 and 5.

If roughly 10 percent of the employees are new or are determined to have simply and exactly met their expectations, then the distributions would appear as shown in Figure 3.6.

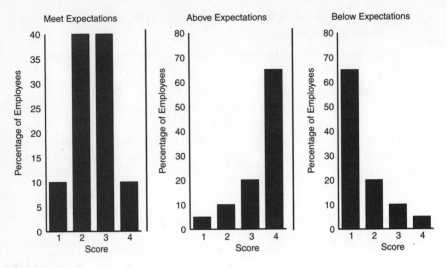

FIGURE 3.5 Employee Performance Distributions and Skew

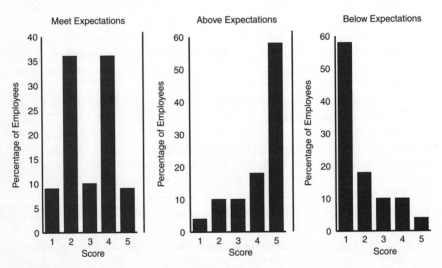

FIGURE 3.6 Distribution of Performance Ratings

WHAT DOES THE PERFORMANCE SCORE REALLY MEAN?

The performance score is not an absolute measure of how well a team or an employee performs. Rather, it is a measure of performance relative to KPIs. An investment professional may have identified good investment opportunities, but if that is the employee's job and the opportunities are in line with what would generally be expected, then a middling performance score is warranted. Let's face it, investment professionals are generally not an underpaid lot. Further, outsized reward is not warranted if KPIs are merely met. If the analyst has not generated many investment opportunities, then performance would be below KPI expectations and the performance score would be low. Thus, an investment team that focuses on generating superior investment performance must have more than normal investment skill and outcomes to achieve higher than normal, or median, compensation. Ideally, any additional income that accrues to or disappears from the organization becomes an equity or partnership interest.

Now that we have come up with a real measure for employee performance that avoids many of the pitfalls of a traditional method, we need to define the next criteria of employee effectiveness, and that is criticality.

CRITICALITY: A DEEPER DIVE

As discussed earlier, it is not sufficient simply to evaluate the performance of each employee relative to that employee's KPIs. If a junior analyst with limited authority and responsibility and a senior portfolio manager with much

LARGE VERSUS SMALL ORGANIZATIONS AND THE EFFECTIVENESS OF THE MODEL

Obviously, this structure benefits small, stand-alone firms over asset management organizations within large or publicly held financial firms. Large financial firms have an incentive to respond to shorter-term parent or shareholder interests over longer-term beneficiary interests of the asset management division. While this tension exists for all investment operations, the separation between the owner and the clients of an asset management division in a large organization is so great that fiduciary interests are questionably upheld. It is difficult to build durable governance and compensation structures that successfully reward owners consistent with clients. It is an even more monumental task in large financial firms.

more authority and responsibility both demonstrate superior performance relative to their KPIs, it would be inappropriate to compensate them equally. Why? Not because one is "senior" or has more tenure within the organization. Rather, they should be paid based on their criticality and importance to the organization. Thus, while each employee can have a performance score of 1 through 4 (or 1 through 5 on an adjusted basis), each employee should be ranked in terms of criticality using the same scale

Criticality is hierarchical, with one person at the top and another person at the bottom. Each employee, regardless of function, can be sorted according to his criticality to the organization. In an investment organization, the investment professionals will tend to be the most critical, but by no means the only individuals of high criticality.

It is crucial to appreciate the fact that it is both the individual and the role the individual fills that determine criticality. This realization demonstrates that criticality is the responsibility of the employee and the employee's manager. Superior execution by an employee in a certain function creates criticality in and of that function that did not previously exist.

Case Study: Letting Your Employees Increase Their Own Criticality

A young man working for me in an administrative capacity, monitoring derivative positions in our portfolios, cognizant of the investment professionals' intent, discovered a means of eliminating an undesirable mismatch in some portfolio hedges. After fully researching his alternative, he proposed and the investment team adopted his recommendation. Over the course of the subsequent investment cycle, this change added significantly to portfolio performance.

> *Laws control the lesser man. Right conduct controls the greater one.*
> —Chinese Proverb

This individual migrated from more mundane performance monitoring activities to more critical portfolio construction activities. This high performance individual garnered greater authority and responsibility in his existing job and positioned himself for potential promotion to a function of even greater criticality. Responsibility shifted to the manager to identify functions that could further leverage this person's knowledge and competence, affording greater opportunities for him to advance his criticality.

Case Study: Criticality Incentivizes Innovation

Criticality is not a one-way street that sees people increasing in criticality. High performing teams and organizations tend to continuously improve and sometimes leave members behind. The way this tends to manifest itself is in a criticality ranking that does not move up or, in fact, slips backward. The investment team that I most recently worked with provided several examples of this. Over a period of three years utilizing this process, we saw that we were building a higher and higher quality team, raising the bar for everyone. Members that had been ranked at the average level of criticality either moved up or moved down, often without any significant change to their overall roles in the organization. In other words, doing the same job you did last year tended to push people's criticality down. In this way, a focus on criticality improves the organization by incentivizing people to innovate.

Why Is Criticality So . . . Critical?

Criticality is a measure of authority and responsibility accrued after years of demonstrably superior decision making in situations of uncertainty. Decision-making responsibilities span a spectrum from no risk to high and systemic risk. Risk is determined by the degree of difficulty, time available, and habituation.

> *Experience is not what happens to you, it is what you do with what happens to you.*
>
> —Aldous Huxley

The Hierarchy of Choice in Figure 3.7 segments criticality according to the riskiness of decisions and the title of the individual likely to make the decisions. At the right of the figure, the angled text provides descriptive support for the types of decisions typically made at each level of criticality. We realize that not all asset management firms are structured with this title hierarchy, but the framework is generally applicable to all organizations.

Many organizations sacrifice the opportunity to incur higher criticality and risk-taking in favor of safer and more reliable management procedures. While these arrangements attempt to improve efficiency, they tend to impede the extraordinary. It is no accident that daring and innovation wane as organizations grow large and successful. Maintaining high levels of efficiency requires that leadership shun hindrances to and explicitly reward criticality; otherwise, management procedures yield nothing more than a higher level of mediocrity.

> *The man at the top of the intellectual pyramid contributes the most to all those below him, but gets nothing except his material payment, receiving no intellectual bonus from others . . . The man at the bottom who, left to himself, would starve . . . contributes nothing (intellectually) to those above him but receives the bonus of all their brains.*
>
> —Ayn Rand

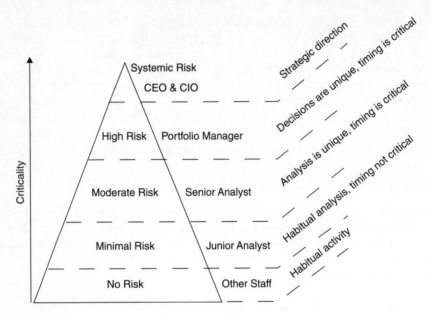

FIGURE 3.7 A Look at the Hierarchy of Choice

The ranking and rewarding of individuals according to criticality is an important leadership function, and a simple procedure each year can accomplish this task. Each manager ranks his team in order of criticality and then picks the most critical and important employee in his staff. These top employees are then compared across teams and ranked. The process moves down one level of employee criticality and comparisons are made between employees being currently considered and those already ranked. The process concludes when the least critical employee is identified and a list of ranked employees is completed.

For example, an investment team may begin with consideration of several portfolio managers at the top of the criticality ranking. Each portfolio manager is discussed and ranked relative to the others. Moving down the criticality spectrum, analysts can be considered.[6] Some of these analysts may have extended their activities beyond analysis, becoming actively involved in developing successful strategies for implementing their research and designing portfolio risk exposures. These individuals are making themselves more critical to the organization and should be ranked above other senior analysts. This process should proceed down to less critical positions, from analysts and junior analysts to quantitative support functions and so on.

The Benefits of Communicating Criticality

As with the performance discussions, ranking discussions lead to greater appreciation of the criticality and importance of each team and each individual, despite the very different function they may perform. All managers learn that the outcome of the organization depends on more than just his team; it depends on how his team relies on the execution of the other teams. Second, each manager gains a better understanding of the function and contribution of each employee in the organization. Third, there is a degree of personal connection that is built between managers and what would otherwise be nameless employees. Finally, and probably most important, there is the role this process plays in advancing the careers, creating opportunities, and enhancing the aspirations of employees. When the management team understands and knows the roles and performance of each employee, then managers are better able to fill positions and promote from the internal pool of talent.

MERIT ZONES: PUTTING IT ALL TOGETHER

Consistently and objectively ranking each employee according to criticality and scoring each employee's performance enables compensation and promotion decisions that lead to appropriate incentives for employee performance. In Figure 3.8, a scatterplot is used to separate each individual into distinct *Merit Zones*. Each employee is represented by a square icon on the Merit Zone chart. The scatterplot is divided into six merit zones by five dashed iso-merit lines. Two employees on a single dashed curve would have same merit. Performance and criticality are not considered equivalent. In this example, criticality is considered about 2.5 times as important as performance in determining merit. Such a trade-off is determined by and different for each firm, but personal experience suggests that the 2.5:1 ratio is generally an appropriate starting point

There are three employees in Merit Zone 1. These employees may be in different functions and have different criticality grades and performance scores. Regardless, they are considered to have high and very similar worth to the organization. Similarly, there are four individuals in Merit Zone 2. These four employees are of similar worth to the organization, but less than that of the individuals in Merit Zone 1. Figure 3.9 shows a hypothetical distribution of all employees across the merit zones.

There are relatively few employees in the highest or lowest merit zones. Those in the highest merit zone should be the ones that executive management nurtures, retains, and compensates. Those in the lowest merit zone should be addressed remedially or terminated. The individual in Merit Zone

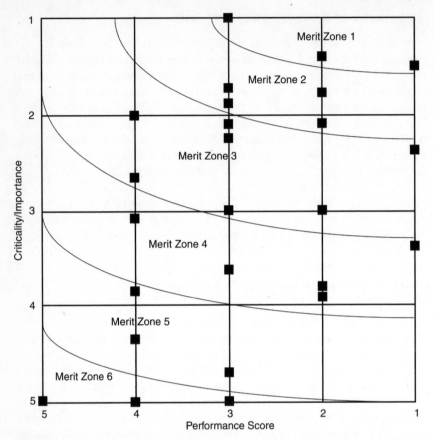

FIGURE 3.8 Employees Fall Into Different Merit Zones

6 and a performance score of 3 should be coached for better performance and potentially for more authority and responsibility of a higher merit zone. The other two individuals in Merit Zone 6, and perhaps the low-performing individual in Merit Zone 5, should be considered for termination (see Figure 3.9).

> *The iron rule of nature is: you get what you reward for. If you want ants to come, you put sugar on the floor.*
>
> —Charles Munger

It is worth reiterating that each employee has been considered in a consistent and objective manner and that the opportunity for favoritism or discrimination has been significantly reduced or eliminated. Moreover,

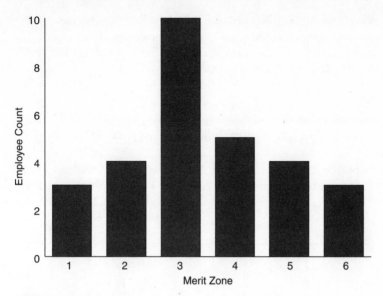

FIGURE 3.9 Distribution of Employees Across Merit Zones

knowledge of each employee has permeated the executive management team. In larger organizations—our experience suggests something over about 100 people—the process can filter down to lower levels of management. The management team involved in the highest-level discussions can extend the process to their management teams, ensuring consistency and limiting senior management distraction. Decisions regarding promotion, training, and termination can be made with less uncertainty and more confidence.

COMMUNICATION OF PERFORMANCE AND CRITICALITY

While some information is confidential, the vast majority of information is withheld because it creates uncomfortable situations for leadership. It is easier to withhold information and not address issues head-on than it is to allow them to slowly fester without much notice. However, transparency and integrity create the basis for trust among management and staff.

Perhaps the greatest benefit of the Merit Zone diagram is the ability to communicate with each employee in an honest and transparent manner. In traditional settings, each employee is typically informed of performance in isolation, with limited ability to grasp both the absolute and relative nature of performance. Moreover, managers have a tendency to practice avoidance behavior when communicating performance, resulting in the conveyance of inaccurate and, even worse, misleading performance information. The Merit Zone diagram facilitates clear communication and reduces the ability of managers to practice avoidance behavior.

> *The ultimate result of shielding men from the effects of folly is to fill the world with fools.*
> —Herbert Spencer, English Philosopher (1820–1903)

Each employee is shown the Merit Zone chart and told which square represents him or her. For example, an employee may be told that he is the square with the green circle in Merit Zone 3 (see Figure 3.10). The dialog

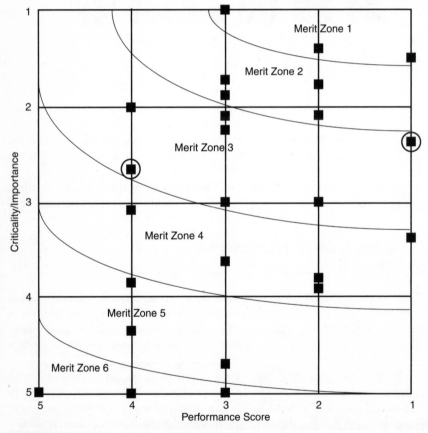

FIGURE 3.10   A Closer Look at Merit Zone 3

can and should include discussions of criticality—why there are roughly 10 employees of greater and 20 of lesser criticality. More important, given the strong performance score, he can and should be told of likely promotion and opportunities for career advancement in the coming year. The evaluation discussion easily segues into the aspirations of the employee and the desires and needs of the organization. The outcome is an agreement that in the coming year a promotion will involve more authority and accountability and the potential for greater compensation. Commensurately, his KPIs will reflect the higher level of authority and accountability that comes with the promotion.

The more difficult and necessary discussion occurs with the individual in Merit Zone 3 and circled in red. This individual is as critical as the employee circled in green, but has failed to deliver at the performance level expected of an employee with KPIs of a Merit Zone 3 employee. The opportunity exists for his manager to discuss the performance shortfall and measures that should be taken to improve performance in the future. This may lead to a discussion of training or a shift in functional responsibilities. It may be the case that this individual is valuable, but the function fails to enable the value—merit—to be realized.

> *When people are made to feel secure and important and appreciated, it will no longer be necessary for them to whittle down others in order to seem bigger by comparison.*
>
> —Virginia Arcastle

We have found that individuals on both ends of the performance spectrum and in high or low criticality appreciate the clarity that the Merit Zone diagram provides. In many instances these individuals were unaware that they were not performing at the desired level, thinking that their performance was better than was really the case. Similarly, these individuals perceive their criticality to be unrealistically high. When these instances arise, discussions of means for advancing criticality or improving performance are openly sought and actively acted upon.

It is clear that criticality is a function of the leader and the employee and, within the KPI guidelines, performance is a function of the individual. There are no surprises when it comes to compensation or promotion. Each individual is aware of where they stand in the organization and how they execute relative to their KPIs and relative to others' performance and their KPIs.

Merit Zones and Compensation

The split between salary and incentive compensation is determined by the organization, function, and culture. Certain countries, such as Switzerland

THE RISK/REWARD PROFILE OF SALARY VERSUS INCENTIVE-BASED COMPENSATION

Investment functions tend to place less emphasis on salary and more on incentive-based compensation. Back office functions tend to lean toward salary. A proclivity for salary should not result in a one-to-one trade-off with incentive compensation; rather, a shift to salary from incentive should result in lower total compensation. Compensation that prioritizes incentive uncertainty over salary stability should be higher than salary-oriented compensation structures, imparting a compensation risk premium on those who incur compensation risk.

and Japan, tend to place more importance on salary and compensation stability. Other countries, such as the United Kingdom and the United States, tend to prefer a riskier compensation structure that places more importance on the incentive component of total compensation. Regardless, the Merit Zone approach enables consideration of total compensation and simplified accommodation of these cultural differences.

Obviously, higher merit zones should be paid more than lower merit zones. Given both the criticality and the high performance of Merit Zone 1 individuals, their total compensation should be significantly higher than other merit zone individuals. A good beginning rule of thumb provides for a doubling of total compensation for each increment in merit zone. Figure 3.11 demonstrates an appropriate pay scale.

While each organization and management team must determine the exact shape of this curve, the doubling of total compensation for each merit zone is appropriate for highly competitive organizations with large incentive components of total compensation. Organizations with a lower incentive component would find a lower compensation differential to be appropriate.

Experience is a hard teacher. She gives the test first and the lessons afterwards.

—Anonymous

Distribution of Compensation

The final stage of compensation is to distribute the compensation pool across all employees in all merit zones. This brings together the Merit Zone

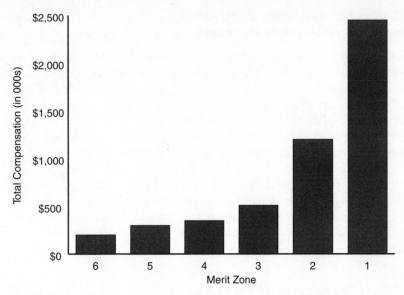

FIGURE 3.11   Total Compensation per Employee (by Merit Zone)

Distribution and the Total Compensation per Employee diagrams. Each individual in a merit zone should be compensated similarly and consistent with the above curve. This can be determined by a simple goal seek function in any spreadsheet. The goal seek would establish the compensation of the top merit zone (each lower merit zone would drop by one half) and multiply the number of individuals in each merit zone by that merit zone's total compensation in order to sum to the total compensation pool.

The total compensation that is indicated for each individual is absolutely consistent with every other employee. Each employee is evaluated objectively and consistently, and compensation is similarly anchored. However, it would be inappropriate to presume that this numeric process would result in the correct total compensation for each employee. While the calculated total compensation is objective and consistent, it does not reflect a multitude of other factors that should be taken into consideration in determining the compensation of each employee. For this reason, it is critical that each manager act as a human intermediary between the quantitative recommendation and the actual compensation each employee receives. The quantitative approach provides a rigorous foundation for the final total compensation number determined by each manager with specific knowledge of unique considerations for each employee.

Case Study: Communicating Merit Zones and Improving Employee Performance

One colleague, whom I found to be nearly as hardheaded and recalcitrant as me, proved to be a particular challenge. He was set on his team's direction; however, his desires were only partially consistent with the KPIs of the group. We had many discussions over the year, but he didn't seem to absorb the inconsistency of direction. Merit zone discussions at the end of the year revealed an unexpected decline in performance and the criticality of his position. The change in merit zone and an open discussion of its motivation lead to alignment of direction, consistent with group KPIs. Over time, we worked together very well and both came to respect each other highly for our strengths, diversity, and open questioning of each other's views. While I do not believe that I was able to fully bring out the potential of this individual, he became a valuable team member and there was never any consideration by me of replacing him.

Case Study: The Dangers of Not Effectively Communicating Performance

The last case illustrates how effective communication can lead directly to improved performance. On the other hand, we would like to illustrate the dangers of what can happen when this is not done with another anecdote. While researching and writing this chapter we had the opportunity to meet a junior employee of a local financial services company. He told us the story of how he had come to work at his current employer and that his current position was actually the third position he had held for the third employer in as many years. He told us that he essentially held the same responsibilities in all three positions.

Why did he make these moves? The answer to him was simple: In all of his previous positions his former employers were not able to clearly demonstrate to him in his annual evaluations his performance and criticality. They were not transparent, and as a result, he perceived his compensation to be the luck of the draw as opposed to the conclusion of a model.

VALUES AND COMPENSATION

A firm's values have yet to be considered as part of employment decisions and ongoing evaluation and compensation processes. During the hiring process, candidates should be introduced to the values of the organization, and a portion of an interview should include a values discussion. The employer should clearly communicate the importance of values in promotion and compensation considerations, and the candidate should understand that the values are more than words on a piece of paper.

Values should be considered in two ways during the evaluation process. First, manager intermediation in the compensation process provides the ability to adjust compensation and, assuming the employee's actions are aligned with the values, communicate the degree to which each employee lives the values of the firm. Second, and more fundamental, is the assessment of future employment based on two dimensions: values and performance.

There is no such thing as a small breach of integrity.
—Tom Peters

An organization that maintains the highest level of integrity is objective, consistent, and transparent with employees. Further, high-integrity organizations place greater importance on employee alignment with values than on good performance. This does not imply that poor performance is

VALUES AND THE INTERVIEW PROCESS—NO BETTER TIME TO START THAN FROM THE BEGINNING!

Despite what appears to be an important part of the interview process, we have found that managers tend to avoid values discussions, perhaps because they threaten the swaggering and aloof image of an independent investment professional—the "Dirty Harry" of finance. Even worse, we witnessed interview processes that were distinctly indicative of low-integrity cultures. A colleague once proudly conveyed an interview technique he used to determine whether job candidates were really prepared for the global travel demands of the position. The technique, he proclaimed, was to ask each candidate her passport number. If the candidate gave a number, then it signaled comfort with international travel, or the intelligence to fabricate a number that the interviewer could not verify. If the interviewee did not give a number, then he or she was simply not smart enough for the position. Astonishing! This individual created an interview technique that was calibrated to identify individuals lacking integrity—they are clever enough to lie and, worse, to begin the process to realize ultimately that it is valued.

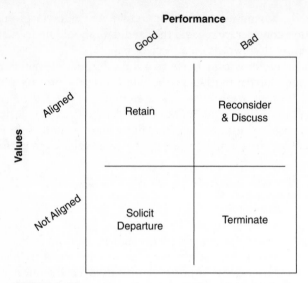

FIGURE 3.12   A Values-Based Framework for Hiring and Firing Decisions

acceptable. Rather, it indicates that a failure to live the values of the organization is unacceptable. A simple decision matrix is shown in Figure 3.12.

An employee whose actions are aligned with the values of the organization and whose performance is good should be retained. This is the easiest employment decision as it requires no decision at all. Without question, we can see that an employee whose values are not aligned and whose performance is a risk to the organization should be terminated. Again, this employment decision is easy. The termination decision is determined primarily by the failure to live values rather than poor performance. Substandard performance simply makes the decision effortless and unremarkable.

The two other potential outcomes are somewhat more difficult. An employee whose actions are not aligned with the values of the organization and whose performance is good is ultimately unacceptable. However, it is best to solicit the departure of the employee with a clear indication of the reasons. While performance is good, the individual is likely to be happier and more productive at another organization. Unless a failure to live the values involves unethical behavior, the departure should be solicited rather than abruptly performed.

Finally, an employee whose actions are aligned with the firm's values but whose performance is bad should be reconsidered with open and honest performance discussions. Such employees may be able to perform at a higher level if the function changes or if their understanding was misplaced.

Integrity considerations are critical to the success of an investment organization. The ultimate termination of employees who do not live the firm's values is the only thing that separates Enrons and WorldComs from other organizations. All firms espouse superior values. Only those whose culture revolves around the values and that require the employees to live the values thrive and survive to the benefit of all stakeholders, including clients.

CONCLUSION

The objectivity, consistency, and transparency of our model are frightening at first. We can warn you that you should not be surprised when management and employees push back in the early stages of implementation. However, as time passes, the benefits overwhelm preexisting fears and all parties find the process and outcomes to be superior to previously experienced evaluation processes. The Merit Zone process has integrity and helps to foster higher levels of integrity and transparency in the organization. Arrogance that is bred in isolation by groups that perceive their contributions to be the linchpin of the organization gives way to humility and appreciation of the contributions of others. This is a strong foundation for management and employee relations and for the career development that all parties desire.

CHAPTER **4**

Investment Philosophy and Process

A Lofty Cathedral Needs a Deep Foundation

The foundation upon which a successful investment management organization is built is its investment philosophy and investment process. In this chapter, we discuss the role both play in the path to successful stewardship for investment firms. The philosophy and process provide a basis for leadership and for team affairs and, as such, are critical markers for viable firm structure and compromising firm transformation.

This chapter lays the groundwork for a more detailed discussion of investment process implementation in Chapter 5.

THE IMPORTANCE OF INVESTMENT PHILOSOPHY AND PROCESS IN INVESTMENT ORGANIZATIONS

An investment philosophy is a set of principles that guides the investment activities of the organization. Philosophy statements often include words like "fundamental," "quantitative," "team-based," "value," "growth," "momentum," or "contrarian." The investment philosophy statement communicates *how* an investment organization accomplishes something, not *what* the investment organization seeks to accomplish.

In this book, we focus our efforts on active investing as opposed to passive investing. As such, the investment philosophy statements that we consider are those of active investment-driven organizations. This is not to say that passive investing is wrong. There is a lot of merit in the construction of a passive and well-diversified investment portfolio. The truth is that many individuals are not sophisticated investors, and even among those who are, we would argue that only a minority actually possess the skills necessary to identify active managers that will beat the market.

As Bill Sharpe discussed it back in 1991, investing can be thought of as a zero-sum game.[1] All investors can be classified as passive or active. The passive investors, by definition, get the market return, while active investors can be split into two categories: those who beat the market and those who underperform the market. The cumulative performance of all these investors generates "market" performance. The gains of investors who beat the market are offset by the losses of those who underperform the market. Thus, active investing is adversarial; to beat the market and be a winner you have to take advantage of those who underperform.

Even though active investing can be thought of as a zero-sum game, it provides a tremendous benefit for society. In particular, the active investment process determines the price of all assets and results in the efficient allocation of resources across society. It would be inappropriate to conclude that because active investing is a zero-sum game, everybody should just invest passively. If this were to occur, the price mechanism would fail and resources would be inefficiently allocated across society, which is known as the Grossman-Stiglitz paradox.[2]

INVESTMENT PHILOSOPHY: CORE BELIEFS

Following the approach that we recommend creates a valuable investment edge, beginning with the specification of an investment philosophy to guide investment behaviors. As noted, the investment philosophy communicates *how* something will be done, not what will be done. The basic premise, which is often overlooked by many individuals in investment organizations, is that behaviors consistent with the investment philosophy statement are more critical than those inconsistent with the philosophy. Guided by the investment philosophy, each employee knows how to prioritize issues and where to focus their time. An excellent example of this can be found in the way Brinson Partners conveyed its philosophy to both clients and employees.

> *A hidden connection is stronger than an obvious one.*
> —Heraclitus of Ephesus

Figure 4.1 expresses to both clients and employees alike exacly what the focus of the partnership was and precisely what was considered important. The content of this presentation page was not unique to Brinson Partners. Nearly every organization speaks either directly or vaguely to these

Guiding Principles: The Equations

Equation #1
People   +   Process   +   Philosophy   =   Performance

Equation #1
Performance   =   Investment Results   +   Client Service

Equation #1
Maximum Performance   =   Maximum Business Results

FIGURE 4.1   Brinson Partners Equations
Source: Brinson Partners 1996 Annual Meeting.

behaviors somewhere in their literature. With Brinson Partners, however, this concept was more than just a marketing tool. The firm communicated unrelentingly—to both employees and clients—what was important and what behaviors should be prioritized. The mission statement and investment philosophy were essentially one, and every person in the organization, whether an investment professional or not, knew that the focus of the organization was investment performance and client service. Every endeavor of every individual was prioritized with that mission in mind. Brinson Partners further clarified *how* superior investment performance would be achieved by augmenting the investment philosophy statement, referring to a fundamental and research-driven investment culture that focused on determining the fundamental value of assets and asset classes. The Brinson Partners' example highlights the correct implementation of an investment philosphy. Conversely, we can find the opposite in the eventual evolution of this very same firm.

In 2001, after Brinson Partners had been bought by UBS and renamed "UBS Asset Management," the mission and the investment philosophy statements were separated. The mission statement no longer embraced the investment philosophy of the organization. It became a more generic asset management organization's mission: "Our mission is to be the best investment institution that invests across the breadth of the global capital market." Gone were references to investment performance and client service.

The investment philosophy was referred to as a "fundamental investment philosophy," and was targeted at just the investment professionals, rather than to all staff at the organization. The "fundamental investment philosophy" was as follows: "Ultimately the value of any security is permanently linked to the fundamentals which determine the present value of the cash flows the security can generate for current and successor owners. What a security is worth must be governed by the cash flow generation ability of the enterprise, the ability to grow, [and] the uncertainty of the discount rate applied to the flows available to the owners." The asset class references of the Brinson Partners days were gone and the firm's focus seemed to shift from an equal consideration of top-down and bottom-up toward predominantly bottom-up prioritization. Ultimately, a clean break was made from the past, and the investment organization became a collection of "alpha boutiques." In other words, the top-down focus was eschewed for the bottom-up security analysis of alpha boutiques, and with this, the consistent mission that had once permeated throughout all areas of the firm was lost.

There was nothing necessarily wrong with this mission shift, it merely reflected a shift in business strategy that was perhaps necessitated by the firm's size. Regardless, the mission shift signalled changes within the organization that would have pleased or displeased various clients.

While Brinson Partners provides great examples that the authors are intimately familiar with, there are also other invesment firms that have clearly and succinctly articulated investment philosophy statements. One of these is The Capital Group, whose investment philosophy statement, while lengthy, could not be more clear:

The companies that comprise The Capital Group share an investment philosophy that is distinguished by four key beliefs:
- We believe that solid research is fundamental to sound investment decisions. Our companies employ teams of experienced analysts who regularly gather in-depth, first-hand information on markets and companies around the globe.
- We believe that an investment decision should not be made lightly. In addition to providing extensive research, our investment professionals go to great lengths to determine the difference between the fundamental value of a company and its price in the marketplace.
- We believe in a long-term approach. It's part of the big-picture view our investment professionals take of the companies in which we invest. This is reflected by the typically low turnover of portfolio holdings. In addition, our investment professionals usually remain with us for many years and are compensated according to their investment results over time.
- We believe in the value of multiple perspectives. The assets of each fund or portfolio are divided among a number of portfolio managers. These managers make independent investment decisions and manage their portions as though they were separate funds. Over time, this method has contributed to consistency of results and continuity of management.[3]

While clear investment philosophy statements provide direction for employees, the impact on clients is more subtle and also more valuable. The investment philosophy statement provides a structure for all communication, assisting in accuracy and clarity. More importantly, it enables employees and clients to reach beyond simple statements about historical performance and to frame and contextualize various investment environments and issues across time.

For example, clients can leverage the investment philosophy statement in their analysis of an investment advisor. All investment activities and client communications can be evaluated against the philosophy statement, eliminating the ever-seductive "spin." Any deviation in communication or change in the mission and/or investment philosophy statement should be considered an immediate red flag, regardless of actual investment performance. Conversely, the client-facing professionals of the investment advisor can use the philosophy statement to put short-term performance in its correct context, and help clients refocus their attention to their long-term investment goals.

The investment organization's mission statement and its investment philosophy statement are enduring tenants specifying the organization's purpose and, as Collins and Porras state in *Built to Last*, "a perpetual guiding star on the horizon; not to be confused with the specific goals or business strategies." Based on the research of Collins and Porras, fiddling with the mission or investment philosophy statement should be a cause for concern for both employees and clients of the organization.[4]

INVESTMENT PROCESS: CONTROL AND ANARCHY

Investment process statements provide greater specificity than the investment philosophy statement, communicating the realm of activities employees can undertake on a day-to-day basis. It provides a framework for prioritization and for the successful integration of disparate individuals within the organization, divisions of the organization, and the entire organization as a whole. The language of an investment process statement, while often simple, is more precise than the language of an investment philosophy statement. Unfortunately, less than essential attention is often placed on the investment process, perhaps because it is so simple and seemingly redundant. In the following sections we will examine how we, and others, construct their investment process.

To begin, a well-constructed investment philosophy and process, with clearly defined boundaries, will create an environment where the CIO does not need to micromanage. Rather, behaviors that are within the boundaries should be considered acceptable and desirable, even if they are not behaviors that the CIO would undertake. Borrowing an often repeated management dictum, the CIO can hire the best people and step partially out of the way, allowing employees' investment contributions to succeed or fail. In this manner, success is likely to prevail and the CIO leverages the unique knowledge and skills of each and every individual on the investment team. It is our belief that the absence of investment process boundaries results in ad hoc micromanagement by the CIO and the collapse of the investment team into one individual: the CIO. Ultimately investment professionals become bit players in the CIO's "investment theater." We will discuss the role of the CIO and how he can best leverage the unique skills of the investment team, later in the chapter.

> *Few things help an individual more than to place responsibility upon him and to let him know that you trust him.*
> —Booker T. Washington

With this philosophical foundation properly defined, the investment process can be liberating, as opposed to constraining. As an aside, it is important that this liberty not be confused with anarchy. There is a continuum from absolute control to anarchy. Control-oriented people and anarchists tend to see control and anarchy as an either-or situation, with nothing in between. Control-oriented people see anything short of heavy-handed control as anarchy. Conversely, anarchists tend to view any measure of control as the only alternative to anarchy. However, within the spectrum from absolute control to anarchy there exists the freedom of self-governance. Herb Kelleher, executive chairman and former CEO of Southwest Airlines, characterizes the intermediate realm of freedom from the perspective of a successful leader:

> *I've never had control and I never wanted it. If you create an environment where the people truly participate, you don't need control. They know what needs to be done and they do it. And the more the people devote themselves to your cause on a voluntary basis, a willing basis, the fewer hierarchs and control mechanisms you need.... We're not looking for blind obedience. We're looking for people who on their own initiative want to be doing what they're doing because they consider it to be a worthy objective.... The fact that I cannot possibly know everything that goes on in our operation—and don't pretend to—is a source of competitive advantage. The freedom, informality, and interplay that people enjoy allows (sic) them to act in the best interests of the company.[5]*

In getting back to the investment process, Figure 4.2, taken from the CFA Institute curriculum, identifies three elements of the process: planning,

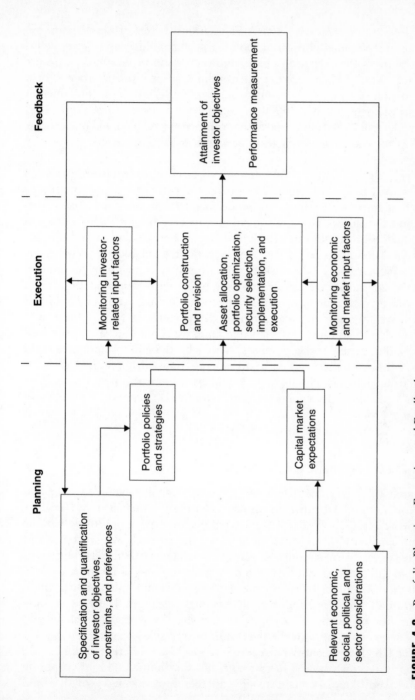

FIGURE 4.2 Portfolio Planning, Execution, and Feedback
Source: CFA Institute curriculum.

execution, and feedback (p. 495).[6] The leftmost boxes of the diagram expand on the planning portion of the process, the middle three boxes delineate aspects of the execution phase, and the rightmost box focuses on the feedback phase. Taken together, this outlines an investment process for a fundamental-oriented investment organization. This can imply fundamental analysis of the economy, fundamental analysis of factors affecting assets, and fundamental analysis of the actual value of assets. We build our process around the fundamental valuation of assets, though this is not necessarily the norm.

Typically, fundamental investment processes of macroinvestment firms are designed to build strategies based on forecasts of macroeconomic or other fundamental variables that are deemed to influence asset classes, sectors, and industries. There are a number of very bright, highly educated individuals who develop strategies in this way, but we tend to find this approach less desirable. To us, it is reminiscent of the old joke that economists are like pickup sticks, when asked a question they come down pointing in every direction. If, for example, we were to gather recommendations from macrostrategists around the world at any point in time, surely we could find 10 very well thought out and articulated arguments as to why the equity markets should go down. At the same time, we could find 10 equally well thought out, articulated arguments as to why the equity markets should go up. Mind you, these would be arguments coming from individuals with PhDs from the best schools, and would be accompanied by tremendous amounts of data, fancy equations, and novel charts to support their positive or negative views.

Let us examine a recent specific example.

Case Study: Pickup Stick Analysis

In March 2007, Dresdner Kleinwort offered a bearish view on the S&P 500 and, concurrently, UBS investment research offered a bullish view. Dresdner Kleinwort's bearish view was predicated on the expectation of vulnerable economic activity. The U.S. economy, Dresdner argued, was susceptible to weakness because the household sector was in financial deficit. This financial deficit meant that companies would have weak top-line, or revenue, growth. In addition, Dresdner felt that price-earnings (PE) multiple pressure would accelerate during the period of trend-earnings weakness. These views were well backed up in the research report, leaving Dresdner to conclude that "we remain equity bears while the rest of the sell side is sanguine."[7]

The UBS Investment Bank research report had a different outlook. UBS felt that the economy was in fact soft, but that household and corporate incomes were likely to remain strong, and, therefore, earnings growth would remain reasonable. Moreover, UBS felt that softness in the economy was already priced into the equity market. Contrary to Dresdner, UBS felt that PE multiples were likely to expand based on their view that the economy would be soft, but not weak. Finally, UBS offered that market risk aversion was high at that point in time and likely to come down subsequent to a recent volatility spike. This decline in market risk aversion would lead to lower discount rates and therefore higher equity prices. In their report, UBS concluded, "we believe that ongoing market turbulence has more to do with positioning, risk management and profit-taking than with any significant change in the underlying fundamentals. Thus, we recommend . . . to add to positions in global equities."[8]

Both the UBS Investment Bank report and the Dresdner Kleinwort reports seem reasonable. If inclined to choose one view or the other, most professional investors would likely find brilliant the report supporting their own view.

Forecasting: The Fools Gold of Investing

In the end, an investment process based on the forecasts of investment strategists is vulnerable to a communication bias. Based on some research that had come from Harvard, Jeff Diermeier, the head of US Equities at Brinson Partners, opined that a superior investment team could be constructed by hiring people with limited communication skills. Such individuals, he observed, rely on analytical strength rather than on persuasive proficiency to succeed. Moreover, the common discussion and forecasting of economic variables considers the wrong variables—economic, not the asset variables—and results in what could be considered a strategist's beauty contest. Investment decisions would come down not to the better analysis, but rather to the most articulate conveyor of that analysis. Macrostrategists, for this reason, are often skilled at public relations and quite capable of persuading market participants of the appropriateness and superiority of their views. They are not necessarily good at strategy formulation.

> *Those who have knowledge, don't predict. Those who predict don't have knowledge.*
>
> —Lao Tsu 6th century BC

The best way to avoid becoming prisoner to the best communicator is to put in place an investment process that is predicated on direct fundamental asset valuation, as opposed to indirect forecasting of economic or fundamental market variables. This and the next chapter will frequently return to the importance of fundamental asset valuation as a critical tool to avoid weak, though perhaps stimulating, analysis and instead be a tool for objectivity in highly emotional times. Ideally, analysts should focus on discounting future cash flows in order to determine the fundamental value that they would be willing to pay for an asset or asset class. The investment process begins with a focus on determining fundamental value by garnering cash flow and discount rate information.

Forecasting is inevitable, but consideration of objectively determined cash flows rather than subjectively driven asset prices is imperative. Once determined, fundamental value is a current observation that circumvents the behavioral whims of market participants and persuasive abilities of investment strategists.

AVOIDING THE PITFALLS OF BEHAVIORAL BIASES

Even with a specific fundamental valuation launching point for the investment process, there are several potential pitfalls that first need to be illuminated. The literature of behavioral economics and finance highlight a number of these human biases that can lead to suboptimal decision making. However, our experience has shown a tendency for four main culprits to throw sand in the gears of an otherwise sound investment approach:

1. Perceived reality
2. Too much information
3. The confirmation bias
4. Belief perseverance bias

After discussing these potential pitfuls, we will return to the implementation of the investment process.

Perceiving or Constructing Reality

The first pitfall has to do with the gathering of facts. An analyst's function often has been referred to as the assimilation of an information mosaic that allows the analyst and/or portfolio manager to infer a big picture and make investment decisions. It is seductive to think of the process as simply obtaining more and more facts, like tiles filling the mosaic; however, the truth is that it is impossible to simply gather a plethora of facts. The reason is that facts do not speak for themselves. Rather, they are interpreted from the perspective of the observer. The analyst provides context, and that context is a function of his or her ethnicity, education, experience, training, culture, and so on. According to Richard J. Heuer Jr.'s book, *Psychology of Intelligent Analysis*, "judgment is what analysts use to fill gaps in their knowledge. It entails going beyond the available information and is the principal means of coping with uncertainty. It always involves an analytical leap, from the known into the uncertain."[9]

> *Reality is merely an illusion, although a very persistent one.*
> —Albert Einstein

Heuer observes that the perception component of analysis is really an active, rather than a passive, process. This means that the analyst "constructs, rather than records 'reality'."[10] While Heuer refers to this in a negative manner, implying that prior experiences will taint each analyst's perception process in an adverse manner, we have the opposite view. We maintain that the alternative perceptions of each individual be considered positive. We noted in Chapter 1 that the cultural environments at many of the highest quality firms are constructed exactly with this notion in mind. Different interpretations that arise from diversity of experience, education, culture, and so on allow the facts to be perceived in ways that afford the construction of different realities—a different perspective from each analyst. This diversity of perception depends less on understanding and enables the construction of not just a primary mental model of a situation, but also a number of alternative mental models, or hypotheses. Each model depends on collective understandings that derive from diverse individual perceptions. A small but sufficiently diverse pool of *skilled* analysts can overcome missteps in the reality construction process. To the degree that a skilled investment team's diversity is better than the market's and the competition's, reality construction becomes a positive investment edge. But, this can only happen when an organizational culture supports this type of behavior.

What prevents an unending stream of irreconcilable mental models characterizing every single situation? How can the construction of all of these different mental models be done in a controlled manner? The investment philosophy statement is necessary in this regard, but it is not sufficient. An explicit investment process—one that provides a framework into which each analyst plugs his or her alternative mental model—needs to be put in place. The combination of a precise investment philosophy statement and a well-defined investment process is critical for the analysts and portfolio managers to function.

Too Much Information, or Analysis Paralysis

The second potential pitfall is the desire to gather more facts to clarify the investment landscape. It is fairly standard in the investment industry for strategists and pundits to comment that more information is needed before decisions can be made. Unfortunately, capital markets are sufficiently anticipatory and efficient that by the time these pundits get the information they desire it will be too late to act. Investment managers need to act *before* all of the information is in place. It is inappropriate to expect that more and better information will provide sufficient clarity for the analyst or portfolio manager to make decisions. In fact, a layperson would make great decisions if *all* the relevant information were gathered. The raison d'etre of the investment manager is the capability to make decisions with moderate, or even scant, information.

The key is not the acquiring of larger quantities of information, but rather that relevant information is efficiently used. Markets are sufficiently complex that the number of variables having an impact on asset prices is virtually infinite. If investment analysts manage to identify the requisite and accessible facts and construct alternative realities to vet, then perceived fundamental value will be close to an omniscient being's understanding of true value. Hence, the most critical aspect of the decision-making process is the ability to use available information to the greatest degree possible. There will often be an analyst who, like a neoclassical painter, wants to capture every detail of the investment scene with absolute precision. Unfortunately, decisions will rarely be forthcoming, except unsurprisingly when the painting of the preconceived picture has been completed. In these situations, the individual should be prodded to take more of an impressionist approach, capturing the primary perception of the scenery and mentally filling in the detail of the full landscape. This point cannot be reiterated enough: *It is not about more information; it is about using the right information effectively.* The specifics of the investment process that we develop in this and the subsequent chapter focus critically on enhancing information value and leveraging fundamental asset valuation to avoid investment pitfalls.

Confirmation and Belief Perseverance Biases

Nassim Taleb suggests further pitfalls to information gathering: the confirmation bias and the belief perseverance bias. The confirmation bias is the tendency for individuals to seek information that confirms an existing opinion they possess. The belief perseverance bias is an individual's natural resistance to changing previously held opinions.[11]

To help combat these pitfalls, we prefer to think of information as either "flow" information or "stock" information. Flow information addresses the change of a variable; for example, inflation as the change of prices, income as the increase or decrease of wealth, or any of the plethora of economic statistics that are reported to change on a month-by-month basis. Stock information addresses the concept of a measurable level. For example, one can think of net worth as the stock variable that gives rise to income, the flow variable. Recently, investors have been obsessed with the hundreds of billions of dollars of subprime and Alt-A mortgage defaults, without realizing that this is a relatively small portion of over $80 trillion of household assets and over $50 trillion of household net worth.[12] The perspective of the stock information seems to be lost in the downpour of flow information that inundates investors every single day. Unfortunately, the confirmation and belief perseverance biases are supported by almost all of the flow information that is transmitted regularly regarding economies and capital markets.

What is read in research reports and regularly heard in the media is information of the flow variety. The reasons are simple: Flow data is very easy to obtain relative to stock data and is much more interesting to report. For example, it is more enticing to refer to a $500 billion increase in household assets in any given year than it is to report that household assets increased by 0.67 percent from $83.5 trillion to $84 trillion. Without knowing that the base is on the order of $84 trillion, the $500 billion change seems much more significant. To highlight this point even further, let us consider an example from the field of science.

In 2003, scientists discovered that the Milky Way (the home galaxy of planet Earth) incurred a massive collision with the Canis Major dwarf galaxy. The Milky Way ripped the Canis Major dwarf galaxy apart and absorbed an estimated one billion stars. This sounds pretty massive—one billion stars. Yet the Milky Way has an estimated nearly 200 billion stars and the collision with another galaxy is actually a process that occurs continuously, feeding the growth of larger galaxies. The "flow" of one billion stars slamming into our galaxy sounds pretty impressive, until one considers the "stock" of 200 billion (some say as many as 400 billion) stars in the Milky Way. It just is not as exciting to say that the Milky Way is expected to grow from 200 billion to 201 billion stars over the coming millennia. And such is the nature of the frequently churned out research reports and commentary on the financial industry.

To produce a monthly research report, or to be a daily talking head on the news media, the focus has to be on flow information. These reports and information are always touted as being relevant or even critical, but in reality the information does more to increase, and occasionally decrease, confidence than it does to increase knowledge. This information flow supports both the confirmation and belief perseverance biases.

Figure 4.3 is from Richard Heuer's previously referenced book *Psychology of Intelligent Analysis* (page 68,[13] referencing footnote 53[14]). What this chart shows is that an increase in information gathered, while increasing confidence, does not necessarily increase accuracy. In the valuation of an asset, the endless stream of flow information serves primarily to increase confidence, but seldom does it increase accuracy beyond that attained by

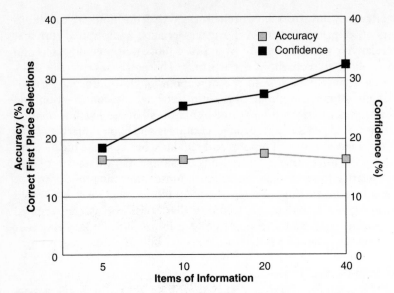

FIGURE 4.3   More Information Breeds Confidence, But Not Accuracy
Source: Richard Heuer, ed. *Psychology of Intelligence Analysis*. New York: Nova Novinka, 2005.

the first few items of information. The mosaic can look like an impressionist painting or the completely detailed renderings of the realist genre, but the picture is available from the less rich impressionist depiction. More detail does not change the picture.

In his book, *The Wisdom of Crowds*,[15] James Surowiecki refers to a study conducted by Paul Andreasen at MIT in the late 1980s. The study divided students into two groups. Each group was given a portfolio of stocks that they were allowed to trade in the open market. Each group was also provided with fundamental information about every stock in their portfolio that would give some indication of a fair price. One group was able to see the changes in the prices of their stocks. The other group was able to see the changes in the prices of their stocks and was given a stream of financial news that purported to explain the changes in stock prices. The study found that the students who did not have access to news performed far better than the group that had the news feed. Andreasen found that the group with access to news overreacted to that news, overplaying the importance of the information, while failing to question the usefulness of the information.

This evidence has important implications for how good analysts spend their time. The confirmation and belief perseverance behavioral pitfalls, and the uncertainty of any asset value estimate, suggest the need for a more robust investment process, not more information. The holy grail is a process that extends beyond just valuation, opening doors to factors that not only determine an asset's fundamental *value*, but also the market behaviors that determine its *price*.

CONCLUSION

The investment philosophy and process provide guidance for leadership decisions and employee behaviors. Based on our investment proclivities, we offered a fundamental philosophy as an example that can be used to steer leaders and investment staff clear of many behavioral biases that dog the overwhelming majority of investors. Ultimately, investment professionals make decisions based on limited information and, absent the foundation of a strong philosphy and process, can succumb to these pitfalls. Clearly, adopting a philosophy and process does not preclude the many mistakes that investors make, but it provides a first and foundational step in the right direction. The absence of a philosophy and process, on the other hand, opens the door to a multitude of inappropriate and investment performance hindering behaviors.

The investment philosophy is cast in stone, immutable. The investment environment evolves, however, and the process needs to evolve as well. To retain an investment edge, the investment process must remain at least one step ahead of capital market developments. The following chapter focuses on the investment process in response to evolving market conditions.

CHAPTER 5

Investment Process in an Evolving World

Adopting an investment philosophy and process is no investment panacea. They provide essential boundaries for leaders and investment professionals, but little else. In this chapter we discuss the investment process, paying particular attention to leadership, staff, and market behaviors, especially during extreme periods such as the deleveraging-driven market crash of 2008/early 2009. We examine the hurdles that market behavior creates for disciplined, fundamental investors and ways to combat and benefit from these challenges. This chapter provides some practical implications for the CIO, examining the role he must play in both the construction and management of an investment team. Finally, we conclude by providing some concepts on optimal portfolio design.

In the Introduction to *Investment Management,* Aswath Damodaran observes the inordinate focus of energy put into investment philosophies and strategies, and lack of focus on the investment process.[1] Given that creating an investment process is so simple, and that it is such a critical component of a successful investment organization, the lack of attention seems odd. There exists a belief that decisions made by the Warren Buffets and Bill Millers of the industry are based on a gut feeling or a sixth sense. This is decidedly not the case. The truth of the matter is that the only gut feel or sixth sense in successful investing is discipline and hard work. There is no magic bullet.

> *Opportunity is missed by most people because it is dressed in overalls and looks like work.*
>
> —Thomas Edison

Discipline and hard work cannot simply focus on gathering more information. Reading more analyst reports will not be helpful, and reading more newspapers really does not add anything of value to the situation. Rather, drawing upon the diversity of the investment team to dissect market behavior and turn each mental model sideways or upside down is what is required for successful investing.

> *Somebody who only reads newspapers and at best books of contemporary authors looks to me like an extremely nearsighted person who scorns eyeglasses. He is completely dependent on the prejudices and fashions of his times, since he never gets to see or hear anything else.*
>
> —Albert Einstein

IMPLEMENTATION OVERVIEW: THE "HOW" OF THE INVESTMENT PROCESS

The investment process combines with a firm's mission, values, and philosophy to define and prioritize a broad set of acceptable behaviors. Pension plans, endowments, foundations, individuals, and sovereign wealth funds develop investment guidelines that specify their investment objectives and constraints. From an investment manager's perspective, this client policy-setting process is outside the realm of the manager's investment process. In developing the investment process that we use in this chapter, the execution phase specified in the CFA Institute curriculum (as introduced in Chapter 4, Figure 4.2) is pertinent to the investment manager. Since we narrowly focus on execution, a simple structure for the investment process is sufficient. This chapter adopts a process of the three components, shown in Figure 5.1 that we believe is a valuable tool for investment leadership to deliver superior investment performance.

Beyond putting an investment process in place, leadership must foster its ongoing implementation. The CIO and other investment leadership must use the investment process to specify authorities and provide boundaries within which there is unfettered freedom. The investment process provides the most basic set of boundaries defining acceptable activities for investment professionals.

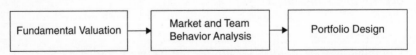

FIGURE 5.1 Three Components of the Investment Process

A leader whose power is manifest via control will find this structure uncomfortable. A less control-oriented leader, however, will leverage the philosophy and process to lead the investment team without micromanaging, providing each investment professional with more freedom than would otherwise be the case. Through experience working in both control-oriented and collaborative freedom-oriented investment environments, we find that the control-oriented environment can survive, but only in the short run. The collaborative freedom-oriented environment lays the foundation for long-run success—affording experience, opportunities to groom successors, and garnering long-term loyalty and commitment of all employees.

Allowing investment professionals to roam freely within the confines of the investment philosophy, process and values enables their analysis and research to be limited only by their imaginations. This is confirmed by Dov Seidman in his book *How*.[2] Seidman observes that truly innovative and successful investment teams work on the edge of chaos at all times. Chaos should not, and does not, imply a lack of discipline or structure. As shown in Figure 5.2, a well-established investment philosophy that is understood by all firm employees, coupled with an established investment process, provides the foundation and framework for innovative freedom—freedom to construct different realities and mold divergent perspectives—by everybody associated with the organization. A broad but bounded area of collaborative freedom is prescribed within which all behaviors are acceptable and desired, even if not agreed by all—especially the organization's leadership.

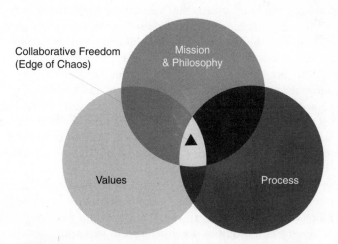

FIGURE 5.2 True Collaborative Freedom is the Intersection of Organizational Values, Mission, Philosophy, and Process Adapted from *How* by Dov Seidman.

FUNDAMENTAL VALUATION

Referring to our proposed investment process diagram, the first stage is the fundamental valuation of all assets and asset classes. Each asset has a fundamental value. Even though this is a simple statement, and "asset" is a simple concept, the financial community has confounded the concept immeasurably.

Since we assert that "asset" is a simple concept, let's begin by reviewing its basic definition: Assets are claims on future income that arise from saving. There are two ways to save:[3]

1. Lend or give up current income in exchange for future income, and
2. Buy and operate durable (capital) goods for future cash flow.

There are two fundamental instruments associated with these two forms of saving:[4]

1. Bonds for lending, and
2. Equities for owning durable (capital) goods.

Bonds are a transfer of current income from one person to another and, therefore, a transfer of current income for future income by the bond acquirer. Buying the bond means that you forfeit funds today (current consumption) in order to receive an income stream in the future (future consumption). Equity is the residual ownership claim on durable (capital) goods. Buying an equity means that you forfeit funds today for a piece (share) of a capital goods pool that can be sold in the future. The total asset pool is nothing more than the aggregation of all equities and bonds.

There are subsets of these basic assets, such as venture capital, and derivatives of these assets (like futures or swaps), but the basic elements are equities and bonds. Additionally, some assets, such as convertible bonds, mix the characteristics of equities and bonds, but again, the fundamental building blocks remain equities and bonds.

Many things can be traded, but that does not make them assets. Commodities and art are good examples. Commodities can be traded, and the active trading of commodities may add to one's wealth, but commodities are not assets. Buying commodities is neither a form of lending nor the creation of a claim on a durable (capital) good. If something is not an asset, then it does not have a fundamental value. It does have a price determined by demand and supply, and future prices may be predicted by knowledgeable traders, but that does not make commodities an asset any more than it would make an eggplant an asset.

The fundamental value of an asset is merely the discounted value of its future cash flows. There exist a plethora of texts on fundamental valuation. For a more in-depth analysis of this topic, we refer interested readers to the CFA Program and its curriculum,[5] Benjamin Graham's or David Dodd's *Security Analysis,* and Aswath Damodaran *Investment Valuation.*[6] While it is useful to defer to these texts for the mechanics of fundamental valuation, there are several critical aspects that we address.

First, if every asset is valued based on the present value of future cash flows, then investment strategies can be set on an apples-to-apples basis. All asset classes, whether equities or bonds, can be identically evaluated. It is common in the financial industry for equity investors to look at PE ratios, PEG ratios, and other fundamental variables, while bond investors evaluate yield spreads. The problem is that fundamental equity variables are not the same as fundamental bond variables, preventing equity markets and bond markets from being compared on an equal footing. Thus, in order to set macro strategies across asset classes, all asset classes are preferably valued in exactly the same manner—discounting future cash flows. This enables, for example, Japanese bonds to be compared equivalently with German equities as investment alternatives.

Second, valuation is, to the greatest degree feasible, a snapshot of the current situation from the perspective of the investor. By "snapshot of the current situation," we mean the concurrent calculation of the fundamental values of all asset classes. Within the valuation process there is an embedded forecast of cash flows and an estimate of future uncertainty underpinning discount rates, but fundamental value is a measure at a specific instant. These fundamental values can be compared to market prices at exactly the same moment in time. Thus, all discrepancies between market prices and fundamental values can be compared across all asset classes on a consistent basis. Moreover, they can be compared with price and value discrepancies at any other point in time on a consistent basis.

Third, the key role for the CIO employing this approach is maintaining a disciplined adherence to the fundamental valuation process, ensuring the integrity of fundamental valuation models, and fostering evolution in response to new analytical tools. Maintaining discipline is by no means an easy task. The greater the need for discipline, the stronger the test of the CIO's and each investment professional's will. Let us consider Benjamin Graham, the father of fundamental analysis. Jason Zweig wrote in "The Intelligent Investor" column of *The Wall Street Journal* during the 2008 financial crisis, "Even the greatest investors have felt the same kind of fear and pain you are probably feeling. For proof, look no further than *Security Analysis....*

Graham was one of the best money managers of the 20th century, a brilliant analyst and market historian, and Warren Buffett's most influential teacher and mentor. . . . Graham himself stuck largely with stocks in his investment fund. But at the conclusion of his book, he advised the institutional investors among his readers to shun the stock market entirely and invest in bonds. Graham doubted they could stomach 'the heavy responsibilities and recurring uncertainties' stirred up by stocks."[7]

Within the simple three-stage process adopted in this book, fundamental investors begin by valuing assets. Historically, knowing fundamental values for assets provided a significant edge, but several developments have altered that environment. For several decades, the CFA Institute and numerous university graduate programs have churned out hundreds of thousands of individuals who are well schooled in the art and science of valuation. Knowing how to determine the fundamental values of assets makes an analyst one of a large, similarly trained community. There are still valuation advantages that can be garnered through hard work and analytical innovation, but the opportunities are more limited than was previously the case.

MARKET BEHAVIOR AND HOW IT CHALLENGES THE FUNDAMENTAL INVESTOR

Today, the fundamental investment process must extend beyond asset valuation. In fact, future opportunities for the investment community are likely to reside more in superior understanding of market behavior and portfolio construction competence than in fundamental analysis. Behavioral and portfolio design advantages derive not only from the fact that prices can deviate from fundamental values for long periods of time and by destructive magnitudes, but also because portfolio solvency can be threatened by deviations between market prices and fundamental values for assets. Fundamental valuation is necessary, but it is no longer sufficient.

> *The market can stay irrational longer than you can remain solvent.*
> —John Maynard Keynes

Market Behavior and Large Events: The First Challenge to Fundamental Value Investing

The second component of the three-step investment process is market and team behavior analysis. This is a topic that has gained increasing popularity in the past couple of decades. Over this period, the industry has been peppered with an endless stream of anecdotes and stories about how individual investors make mistakes when presented with various games. While this is an often talked about subject, most investment professionals never seem to get past the anecdotes to theory development. Moreover, there was a lot written about individual behavior, but much less written about group behavior. Without question, there have been some seminal books on crowd behavior and manias, beginning with Charles Mackay's book originally titled *Memoirs of Extraordinary Popular Delusions*, published in 1841.[8] Somewhat more recently, in 1978, Charles Kindleberger penned *Manias, Panics and Crashes*, addressing the origins of such events. Finally, Edward Chancellor published *Devil Take the Hindmost: A History of Financial Speculation* in 1999. These books have laid the foundation for modern thinking on crowd behavior, and we consider them essential reading for any macro investor.

But it was not until three books were published in the first decade of this millennium that we felt significant progress could be made to incorporate crowd behavior into the investment decision-making processes. The first book to be published was *Ubiquity: Why Catastrophes Happen*, by Mark Buchanan in 2000.[9] This book is popular science writing that barely addresses capital markets. James Surowiecki published *The Wisdom of Crowds* in 2004.[10] Surowiecki's well-written book covers a broad number of topics, including financial markets and the impact of crowd behavior. Finally, Philip Ball published *Critical Mass: How One Thing Leads to Another* in 2004.[11] Ball, like Buchanan, is a popular science writer, and *Critical Mass* ranges far and wide. It moves through all manner of physics topics, addressing markets and the interaction of economic agents (the players in the economy) midway through the book. However, the book never addresses directly the issue of market behavior as it impacts investors. All three books go beyond chronicling crowd events and probe the origins, or perhaps more appropriately, the context of interactive agents[12] and crowd behavior.

We will leave it to the reader to read one or more of the many standard behavioral finance textbooks. The standard textbooks address mental accounting, confidence biases, prospect theory, and other standard theories of individual investor behavior.[13]

We focus on some new frontiers of physics, physiology, and psychology to argue that fundamental valuation provides necessary, but incomplete, information when asset returns are not normally distributed. As part of this discussion, we argue that the interactivity of reasoning individuals creates crowd behavior, which in turn results in the non-normal distributions that render fundamental valuation insufficient.

Before delving into market behavior, it is useful to draw a comparison between the analysis of market behavior and fundamental value—the first two components of the investment process that we have put in place. As noted, fundamental value is a snapshot at any point in time from the perspective of the investor. Market behavior analysis should be undertaken on the same basis, avoiding forecasts of future market prices and other fundamental variables. As such, market behavior analysis encompasses the understanding of market prices, as opposed to fundamental values, from the perspective of all other market participants at a specific point in time. In short, market behavior analysis is an attempt to understand why prices deviate from fundamental values.

Analysts and academics have observed for a long time that fat-tailed distributions are more descriptive of asset returns than the more commonly used symmetric normal distribution.[14] Beyond the fat-tail construct, Nassim Taleb extended the work of Benoit Mandelbrot to popularize the phrase "black swans" in his 2007 book titled *The Black Swan: The Impact of the Highly Improbable*.[15,16] In particular, a black swan is a low-probability, high-impact event that could be considered inconceivable. It is hard to make any statement about the distribution of returns when one considers the potential for a black swan.

Our industry owes a debt of gratitude to Nassim Taleb. The enjoyable insistence of his writing style, replete with Taleb's experiences and observations, makes Mandelbrot accessible. We only wish that more investors had learned the lessons that Taleb has so eloquently taught.

For someone who is such a promoter of the terrors of unknown unknowns, Taleb holds tremendous certitude about the perfection of his own ideas. He recommends that instead of putting your money in medium risk investments, you should put 85 percent to 90 percent in extremely safe instruments like Treasury bills. He qualifies the safe instruments, saying they should be "as safe a class of instruments as you can manage to find on this planet." The remaining 10 percent to 15 percent should be placed in extremely speculative bets, "as leveraged as possible (like options), preferably venture capital-style portfolios." This is a portfolio designed not to blow up from a black swan (the loss of 15 percent is sufferable), while at the same time producing a small return day-in and day-out from the low-risk investment.

This recommendation, however, is thin pabulum for investors and should be considered an ill-informed and ill-formed portfolio. This portfolio is the equivalent of a survivalist hiding out in the mountains in fear of a low-probability catastrophe that he is, in the end, ill-equipped to counter. This is not an existence that we would necessarily tout for others to pursue. If the survivalist's portfolio is inappropriate, how can an investor incorporate Taleb's analysis and invest for higher future consumption? The answer begins with the determination of *fundamental value*—drawing upon the distinction that was made earlier about stock and flow information. The existence of fundamental value is a stock number that renders the news flow nonrandom. While the news may appear random and push market prices both away from and toward fundamental values, fundamental value acts somewhat like gravity in that it is a continuous pull on market prices in a nonrandom direction. Black swans, as Taleb presents them, result from the random flow of news, ignoring the important stock concept of fundamental value that influences news and its interpretation.

The first step in avoiding black swans is to invest only in things that have fundamental values. The second requires an *evolutionary perspective* on capital markets, and an appreciation for the fact that, over time, the returns incurred by exposures to the occasional black swan may be better for investors and society, even if incredibly destructive black swans occur. Each individual must function in the current environment and realize that watching the horizon in anticipation of a black swan event is a waste of energy and resources. In short, you don't need to predict a black swan; you just need to appreciate the evolving vulnerability. Taleb appropriately advises against trying to predict black swans, suggesting that it only makes you more vulnerable to the ones that you did not predict. Moreover, Taleb suggests that black swans "can be caused and exacerbated *by their being unexpected*." Finally, leverage can be useful, but it exposes the investor to losses in excess of invested capital and can exacerbate liquidity difficulties during extreme events. Leverage is like candy, good when used in moderation.

Taleb's view of modern portfolio theory may be borne of anger at analysts who base their quantitative models on assumptions of normally distributed asset price returns. This anger is somewhat warranted, but we must remember that models based on normal distributions are simply tools. Let's again turn to science for a parallel analogy. In physics classes, we learn about Johannes Kepler's *Laws of Planetary Motion* explanation for the orbits of planets, even though it is wrong. The reason for this is that an understanding of Kepler provides a foundation for understanding Einstein. It would be inappropriate not to teach the foundations before moving to much more complex concepts. Kepler's models are tools that open the door to many observations and much knowledge that does not require the complexity of Einstein. Back in the realm of finance, the assumption of normally distributed returns opens students to a world of higher-level finance. With each increment of knowledge, these students can grasp much more knowledge. And, we all must humbly observe that we are always students.

The theory espoused in this chapter is based on new advances in physics, psychology, and neuroeconomics, and it provides a valuable advance beyond Taleb's survivalist dead end. Taleb characterized history as opaque: We observe a single series of price changes perhaps leading to a catastrophic black swan event. Similarly, tumbling grains of sand may lead to an avalanche, but we cannot observe the infinite number of series of falling grains of sand and sand piles that did not occur. The theory supported here views history as translucent rather than opaque. The evolution of a sequence of price changes rewards certain characteristics in the marketplace, just as evolution rewards certain characteristics of living creatures. The sequence leads inexorably to a systemic vulnerability that can be anticipated, even if the specific event cannot be predicted.

Normally distributed returns independent of, and identically distributed to, prior returns make fundamental valuation of assets or asset classes sufficient for long horizon fundamental investors. Even if we assume fat-tailed return distributions, the long horizon investor would probably still be in pretty good shape using only fundamental valuation. It is once we begin to consider the potential for black swans, and comprehend the evolving history, as opposed to opaque history, of some black swans, that the power of our recommended "vulnerability model" of market behavior comes into play. History becomes translucent to the trained and experienced investment team.

The proposed theory takes a step beyond the prior assumptions of normal returns, fat-tailed distributions, and inconceivable black swans. The theory embraces the fact that group behavior is significantly impacted by the interaction of *reasoning* group members. Figure 5.3 provides a road map for the discussion.

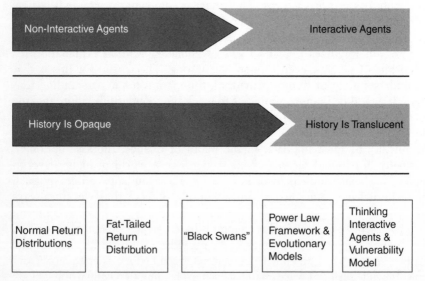

FIGURE 5.3   Roadmap for Building the Behavioral Research Framework

Market Behavior and Unknown Value: Is There Equilibrium?

This section develops a theory for accommodating crowd behavior in the macro investment decision-making process. The theory begins first with concepts developed in physics over the last 10 to 15 years. These concepts describe evolution, avalanches, earthquakes, and other black swan events. The theory is extended beyond simple interactive agents, such as grains of sand leading to an avalanche, to reasoning interactive agents, such as people, leading to manias, bubbles, crashes, and other significant market events.

Each asset has an intrinsic fundamental value reflecting its future cash flow potential. Unfortunately, uncertainty about future cash flows renders true fundamental value unknowable to market participants. One could ask who would have ever anticipated the rapid demise of Lehman Brothers? Clearly, the outcome was possible. In fact, it occurred. Analysts may or may not have anticipated that outcome, but that failure may simply reflect an inability to imagine the demise scenario or comprehend the evolving risk. While a higher being may know fundamental value, analysts endeavor every day to developing future cash flow projections that are discounted to determine their estimates of fundamental value.

Figure 5.4 demonstrates an asset's true fundamental value, and prices and perceived fundamental values over time. The market simultaneously aggregates evolving understanding of prior news and instantaneous comprehension of new information. The progressive understanding of prior information provides a continual, gentle force that pulls price toward fundamental value. This process is slow and modest relative to instantaneous reactions to new information and, therefore, has a largely undetectable influence on price. Regardless, the continual pull drives prices toward fundamental values.

Sophisticated analysts develop knowledgeable estimates of the true fundamental value of an asset. In aggregate, we might say that the market has a perception of fundamental value based on the analysis, communication, and persuasion of these sophisticated analysts. The perceived fundamental value varies around the true fundamental value that is ultimately unknowable. Since these analysts are not independent of each other, they often adopt similar views. In aggregate, across the sophisticated investor, the lack of independence frequently results in consistent biases and systematic deviation of their fundamental value estimates from true value. Moreover, the market at large, comprising both sophisticated and unsophisticated investors, effectuates prices that deviate from true fundamental value even further than perceived values generated by sophisticated analysts.

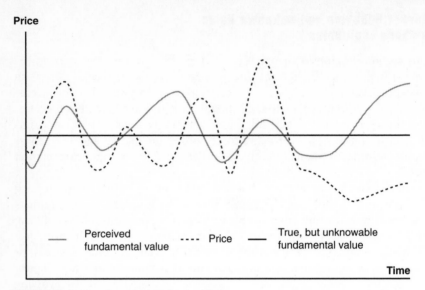

FIGURE 5.4   Fundamental Value and Price

*Have the courage of your knowledge and experience. If you have
formed a conclusion from the facts and if you know your judgment
is sound, act on it—even though others may hesitate or differ.
(You are neither right nor wrong because the crowd disagrees with
you. You are right because your data and reasoning are right.)*
                                                          —Benjamin Graham

Since true fundamental value is unknowable, and price noise is compounded by unsophisticated investors, can fundamental value really be an attractive force on market price? Alternatively, one could argue that everything is deterministic, and statistics, such as fundamental value expectations, are merely humans' means of parameterizing their ignorance. If values and behaviors are deterministic, which we do not believe is the case, despite the argument's viability, then analysts are simply ignorant of the fact and use statistical analysis to improve understanding of the unknown.

Obviously, this discussion can become quite philosophical, but as long as true fundamental values exist, known or not, exchanges of assets in a marketplace exist, and endeavors of market participants to understand fundamental values occurs, there exists a convergent force. This force may be small and frequently dominated by short-term noise, but it does exist and does pull prices toward values.

At any point in time, analysts' estimates of fundamental values are based on existing knowledge. Market participants should expect prices to gravitate toward the analysts' perceptions of fundamental values. There is advantage to buying assets when their prices are below the analysts' perceived fundamental values, and there is advantage to selling assets when the converse is true. Such buying and selling would reflect a behavioral edge, but not a knowledge edge. A knowledge edge would arise from determining an asset value estimate that is superior to that of sophisticated analysts.

Mandelbrot's interest in price behavior, and Taleb's subsequent interest in black swans, treats all price histories identically. Cotton prices, the original interest of Mandelbrot, reflect the economic equilibrium of supply and demand. Asset prices, however, reflect the economic equilibrium of supply and demand, but they also are grounded by the weak force of fundamental values. One can predict cotton and asset prices, but knowledge of an asset's fundamental value is distinct from the forecast of its future price.

> *I would say if Charlie Munger and I have any advantage it's not because we're so smart, it is because we're rational and we very seldom let extraneous factors interfere with our thoughts. We don't let other people's opinion interfere with it. . . . We try to get fearful when others are greedy. We try to get greedy when others are fearful. We try to avoid any kind of imitation of other people's behavior. And those are the factors that cause smart people to get bad results.*
>
> —Warren Buffett

To obtain a knowledge edge, the analyst must push the boundaries of knowledge beyond what is currently known to capture what is unknown but knowable. This is the endeavor of humankind. There will always be unknown unknowns that afford the opportunity for black swans. However, it has become convenient to declare every significant market price change a black swan when the unknown was, in fact, knowable. The more that market participants know, the less they need to parameterize, or characterize, their unknowns with statistics. However, in their quest for knowledge, analysts should never forget that there likely are unknowns that are not knowable in any relevant time frame. This awareness allows the analyst to avoid rejecting facts that do fit in the analysis when they start to appear. See Figure 5.5.

Evolution of price histories creates a knowable vulnerability in the marketplace. The fact that a vulnerability becomes known, however, does not mean that an outcome becomes predictable, but it does mean that we can understand heightened risk for large magnitude events. For example, we know California is vulnerable to earthquakes, yet we cannot predict

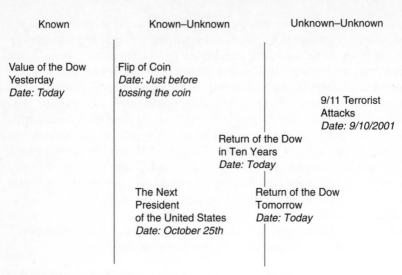

FIGURE 5.5 Body of Knowledge

exactly when they will occur. Until we fully understand this vulnerability, scientists must draw upon other means to further their understanding and manage risk. Similarly, markets are vulnerable to huge events, but our ability to identify true values is limited. Our ability to understand evolving market vulnerability by analyzing the behavioral responses of market participants to asset price deviations from fundamental values improves our investment edge.

Market Behavior and Evolution: A Step Beyond Black Swans

An enormous crater is hidden under the water of the Gulf of Mexico and the ground of the Yucatan Peninsula in Mexico. This crater, created by a comet that collided with the Earth 65 million years ago, is almost 200 km in diameter, but cannot be seen due to many millennia of dust and debris accumulation. Analysis of soil samples around the world indicate that the influence of this collision spanned the entire earth, extinguishing 95 percent of all species at that time. This extraordinary event eliminated all manner of dinosaurs, and it allowed many smaller animals, such as mammals and reptiles, to survive and begin to thrive.[17]

This scenario seems to make sense. A tremendous impact from the comet affected the atmosphere of the entire world and drove most species to extinction. However, this is not the only documented evidence of Earth suffering such a tremendous impact. There is evidence of a 100 km crater in Siberia and another slightly smaller crater at the mouth of the Chesapeake Bay in the United States. These were made about 35 million years ago, apparently by comets smashing into Earth. The conundrum is that fossil records show absolutely nothing unusual in terms of species extinction at that time.

Even more confusing, there is evidence of mass extinctions 210, 250, 365, and 440 million years ago. Yet there is no evidence of any significant event that was the catalyst for these extinctions. We may eventually find some causal event, but at this point in time we are unaware of anything similar to the comet that crashed into Earth 65 million years ago.

Why did the extinctions occur 65 million years ago, but not 35 million years ago? What caused them 210 or 440 million years ago? To understand, we will need to look at the process of evolution and the vulnerability it creates as it rewards certain characteristics that allow species to thrive and punishes others that cause species to disappear.

To help understand this evolutionary process, we created a hypothetical example of animal evolution. We accompanied this hypothetical scenario with diagrams to aid in visualizing the importance of evolution in creating environmental vulnerability. In this example we assume that the environment goes from a normal climate to a colder climate and sustains that colder climate for a long time. Figure 5.6 shows the initial normal climate

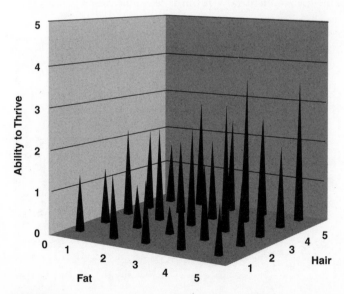

FIGURE 5.6   Evolution: Normal Climate Environment

environment. Animals have hair, some thick and some thin, as well as fat, again some thick and some thin. The distribution of each animal's exposure to these characterics is both random and normal.

Generally speaking, as the environment gets colder over an extended period of time, animals with more hair and more fat survive and thrive. Conversely, animals with very little hair and not much fat begin to disappear. Figure 5.7 portrays the late phase of the cold environment. As we can see, animals with more hair and fat flourish, and the population evolves to evidence a fitness peak for animals with these characteristics.

While this evolution toward more hair and more fat occurs, let's assume that global warming accelerates and temperatures rise rapidly, perhaps over a couple of decades. Additionally, assume that this warming creates a land bridge connecting the cold environment with a landmass where there exists a predator that has been rewarded by evolution for its speed, rather than for just thick hair and more fat.

It is not the strongest of the species that survives, nor the most intelligent, but the one most responsive to change.
—Charles Darwin

These fleet-footed predators find themselves in heaven, for around them they see nothing but fat, lumbering caloric packages upon which they can gorge. The environment now rewards less hair, less fat, and speed. So the

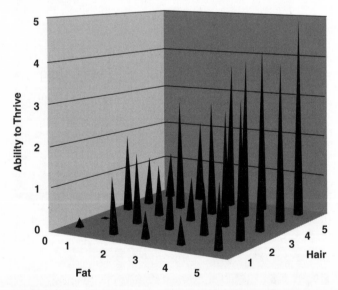

FIGURE 5.7   Evolution: Late Phase of Cold Environment

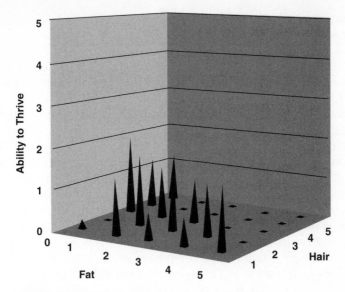

FIGURE 5.8 Evolution: Fast Predator or Hot Climate
Environment

slowest of the creatures, perhaps those with the most hair and fat, now
find themselves eliminated, as shown in Figure 5.8. If global warming had
occurred at an earlier time, before evolution had rewarded thick hair and
more fat, then the introduction of a new predator would not have been
catastrophic. But over time, the animals ironically become increasingly vulnerable for adopting the exact characteristics that enabled them to thrive in
the cold environment.

This is not too far-fetched. Dodo birds on the island of Mauritius were
eliminated by predators introduced to that environment by humans. The
dodo bird evolved to be flightless and fearless on an island that was isolated from its predators. When humans arrived, the birds were hunted to
extinction by humans and the predators they brought.

To realize the precariousness of the situation does not require predicting
the introduction of a fleet-footed predator or global warming. All that is
needed is to realize that animals well-suited to one environment may be
vulnerable in a different environment. The adaption process occurs slowly
and evolves characteristics that enhance systemic vulnerability.

Applying These Evolutionary Concepts

That was a long, and hopefully somewhat interesting, discussion of elementary evolutionary principles. But what does this hypothetical scenario have

to do with market behavior? The answer is an awful lot. In fact, we need only look back to the period of time between 2002 and 2009 to find an example of such evolution in the financial arena. Subsequent to 2002, capital markets were characterized by both low volatility and high liquidity. "Liquidity" can be a difficult term to define, but we use a broad interpretation that includes accommodative monetary conditions and credit availability. Over the period from 2002 to early 2007, investors initiated strategies that were rewarded in this environment. These positions included yield curve exposure, credit spread exposure, equity exposure (especially high-risk equities such as emerging market and small-cap equities), or currency carry trades.

In 2007 and 2008, liquidity dried up as financial institutions became concerned about providing credit to other financial institutions that may have been exposed to the precarious subprime mortgage market. By the summer of 2007, credit spreads began to widen. The characteristics that had been rewarded no longer were. In fact, the new environment of low liquidity and high volatility further punished investors as they tried to shed their positions. Instead of an environment of mutually reinforcing behavior, the environment shifted to one of mutually destructive behavior.

The years leading up to 2007 rewarded investors who incurred exposures that benefited from the unique low-volatility, high-liquidity environment. These investors were increasingly exposed to an emerging, and ultimately a fully developed, vulnerability. Investors who understood the vulnerability had the opportunity to take opposite positions and benefit from the collapse of an unsustainable environment. There were, however, two problems with being on the opposite side of the characteristics that were rewarded before 2007. First, contrarian positions were not, and would not, be rewarded until the environment changed. Predicting the timing of the change was difficult at best. Second, the steady flow of new participants in the strategies that were rewarded, and the exit of participants in strategies that were not rewarded, led to a reflexive response of market prices that further perpetuated the unsustainable environment and penalized any contrarian behavior.

Buchanan's *Ubiquity* and Ball's *Critical Mass* provide insight into the evolutionary behavior of market price and assist our behavioral analysis. Buchanan points out that, "Evolution accomplishes its ends through the triple action of variation, selection, and replication. In any population of rabbits, for example, some will see better, run faster, or think quicker than others. This is variation brought about by the process of mutation. These 'fitter' rabbits (i.e., those with the advantageous mutations) tend to live longer and produce more offspring than do weaker rabbits. This is selection. And because parents pass copies of their genes down to their offspring, the next generation almost certainly contains a greater proportion of fitter rabbits than did the last—a consequence of replication. The overall fitness of the population slowly increases."[18]

It appears that the population of market participants follows a similar triple-action process.[19] Rather than selection and replication working through offspring, the investment population respawns each performance period. Interestingly, and quite unexpectedly, Mark Buchanan published an article about the evolving environment during the drafting of this text. On October 1, 2008, as global equity markets perched at the edge of an abyss into which they would fall a couple of days later, Mark wrote "This Economy Does Not Compute" for *The New York Times*. Buchanan observed that economists were carting out traditional equilibrium theories to understand market developments, assuming markets have "no real internal dynamics of their own." Reflecting on the interactive agents in financial markets, Buchanan refers to markets as "self-propelling systems driven in large part by what investors believe other investors believe." Referring to an agent model of the economy by the Yale economist John Geanakoplos, along with two physicists, Doyne Farmer and Stephan Thurner, Buchanan states:

> *In the model, market participants, especially hedge funds, do what they do in real life—seeking profits by aiming for ever higher leverage, borrowing money to amplify the potential gains from their investments. More leverage tends to tie market actors into tight chains of financial interdependence, and the simulations show how this effect can push the market toward instability by making it more likely that trouble in one place—the failure of one investor to cover a position—will spread more easily elsewhere.*
>
> *That's not really surprising, of course. But the model also shows something that is not at all obvious. The instability doesn't grow in the market gradually, but arrives suddenly. Beyond a certain threshold the virtual market abruptly loses its stability in a "phase transition" akin to the way ice abruptly melts into liquid water. Beyond this point, collective financial meltdown becomes effectively certain. This is the kind of possibility that equilibrium thinking cannot even entertain.[20]*

Market participants acted rationally, responding to their incentives and bringing the financial system to a disequilibrium critical state that survived for years. Like an avalanche, the system came crashing down in a sudden phase transition to instability. The financial system became more vulnerable as agents adopted characteristics that were rewarded in the marketplace in a competition to thrive and survive. All the regulation in the world will not preclude future financial crises any more than they can prevent agents from responding to their incentives. As forest fires result in deadwood strewn across the forest floor and a forest that is increasing vulnerable to uncontainable fires, regulations tend to create deadwood market participants who do the same for the world financial system. Occasional crises are a health means for financial systems to weed the weak and fraudulent players.

The phase transition to instability of a financial system was documented and researched by Hyman Minsky, an economist at Washington University in St. Louis until his death in 1996. Minsky's "financial instability hypothesis" states that such instability is inherent in the financial system. Stability, he observed, is inherently destabilizing in exactly the way that Buchanan, Geanakoplos, Farmer, and Thurner hypothesize. For Minsky, stability creates vulnerability as debt begets more debt and more unstable debt structures. The financial system reaches a critical state that is vulnerable to collapse, the "Minsky Moment." While time is not the critical factor, the longer the financial system is stable, the more market participants adopt rewarded characteristics and the greater the vulnerability to a Minsky Moment.

Stop Dancing before the Music Stops

This evolutionary analogy plays itself out repeatedly in the investment world. How do you avoid disappearing if you have little fur and insufficient fat in cold times? Chuck Prince, the former CEO of Citigroup, was pressured to resign in 2007 shortly after the bank's subprime losses were exposed. If Prince had not "danced when the music played," would he have been fired by myopic shareholders long before the subprime debacle had run its course? Brinson Partners' experience in the late 1990s demonstrates the converse example. Rather than take part in the tech-buying frenzy and its rallying momentum, the firm eschewed the high-flying sector. As a result it lost roughly 40 percent of its assets to client withdrawals in 1998 and 1999 as it lagged the performance of a dot-com dominated S&P 500 index.

What can be done? Unfortunately, a foolproof solution does not exist. Rather, a broad array of responses must be used. First, in managing "other peoples' money," continual, transparent, and trustworthy lines of communication must be maintained with investors. Putting results in the best light, for example, should be avoided. Spin is a short-term palliative that often results in long-term distress for all parties.

Second, the worst-case scenario should always be portrayed, regardless of asset class, as complete loss. The only thing that changes is the probability of losing everything. Higher-risk assets have a higher probability of complete loss than lower-risk assets. Even cash under the mattress is a risky position.

The Germans witnessed the highest denomination of their currency go from a 50,000 Mark note in 1922 to a 100,000,000,000,000 Mark note in 1923. That old 50,000 Mark bill retrieved from under the mattress in 1923 would not have been very useful. Marks were more valuable as fire tender than they were for consumption. The inflation rate was 3,250,000 percent per month in 1923. Not to be outdone, the Greeks accomplished an inflation rate of 8,500,000,000 percent per month in 1944. Inflation-protected securities can experience default, even if the principal value cannot be inflated away. Investors must understand that there is the potential for extreme loss, and they must not hold any misguided perception that an investment is risk free. We will discuss how to properly educate clients on this reality in the next chapter.

Third, portfolios must be managed within acceptable risk parameters. Prices may be further away from fundamental values than they have ever been, but that does not mean that the discrepancy cannot become larger. Diversification must be across not only assets, but across behavioral assumptions, risk models, investment philosophies, and so on. Finally, fat and furry creatures may need to learn how to shave and to diet, very quickly. Lumbering, slow investors, like the large and complex firms mentioned in Chapter 1, are always vulnerable to rapid shifts in capital markets. Nimble investors and investors with the freedom to react and preact without bureaucratic approval processes may not catch the change in advance but they at least have the ability to respond. To shorten response times, we maintain what we call the "canary portfolio." Like a canary in a coal mine that succumbs to natural gas before the miners do, at the first instance of trouble the strategy can be instantaneously executed. The canary portfolio requires a simple decision to execute and not the additional complexity of strategy formulation.

Lessons from the Financial Crisis Now let's return to our example of low volatility and high liquidity from the years prior to 2007. As uncertainty grew regarding financial institutions and market participants increased exposures to securities that benefited in that particular environment, markets became more vulnerable and investors more skittish. Suddenly, in response to an event that would have passed with little notice a year or two earlier, all the investors who had taken on credit spread exposure, entered currency carry trades, and built high-risk equity exposure began to experience losses. It is difficult to precisely identify the catalyzing event. Many cite the February 2007 announcement by HSBC of higher loan-loss provisions on bad mortgages. Others point to the January 2007 Chapter 11 filing by Ownit Mortgage Solutions. The 3.3 percent nationwide median house price decline in the first quarter of 2006 may have been the straw that broke the backs of Ownit, Ameriquest, Mortgage Lenders Network USA, New Century Financial, and Countrywide Financial. Of course, we could identify the accommodative monetary policy of Alan Greenspan, who brought the Fed Funds rate down to one percent, the lowest in 45 years. Yet, the Community Reinvestment Act resulted in Fannie Mae's 2000 announcement that the Department of Housing and Urban Development will require it to dedicate 50% of its mortgage securitization business to low and moderate income families. Being extreme, we could go all the way back to the 1938 creation of the Federal National Mortgage Association, Fannie Mae, as part of Franklin Delano Roosevelt's New Deal.

Each of these developments was another grain of sand that led to the avalanche that is now referred to as the "Subprime Crisis" or "Credit Crisis." Why one grain of sand caused the avalanche and not the others is a mystery. Clearly, the financial situation had reached a critical state.

While not knowing what the catalyzing event would be, it was not too difficult to determine that there were large groups of investors vulnerable to a change in the capital market environment. Some investors that had realized the critical state of financial markets predicted the implosion of the subprime market. Some investors shorted subprime and Alt-A credit, various credit spreads, and currency carry trades. These investors who had shied away from the strategies that worked in the low-volatility, high-liquidity environment became the ultimate winners—the survivors. In late 2007 and 2008, financial markets were witness to the catastrophic extinction of market participants who focused on short-term returns and garnered comfort from hiding in the crowd. Such venerable institutions as Bear Stearns, Lehman Brothers, Merrill Lynch, and others disappeared. This period also witnessed the demise of a number of hedge funds, including Focus Capital, Peloton Partners, Sowood Capital Management, and Ospraie Fund.

In *The Wall Street Journal* on Tuesday, September 16, 2008, Jeremy Siegel was spot on in his understanding and characterization of this evolutionary process. "Few were willing to admit that subprime real estate loans could be as risky as equities. It was just too profitable to issue these mortgages. So eyes were closed and the money kept pouring in. Groupthink prevailed. To paraphrase John Maynard Keynes, it is much easier for a man to fail conventionally than to stand against the crowd and speak the truth."[21]

Being part of the herd and participating in groupthink might feel good in the short run, but absent a healthy dose of luck (which after the fact would be deemed skill), it is more than likely destined for failure. Standing against the crowd by adhering to the truth of fundamental value can be very painful and can even make the prudent investor appear to be stupid, but it is a foundation element of successful long-term investing.

The difficulty lies not in new ideas, but in escaping the old ones,
which ramify, or those brought up as most of us have been, into
every corner of our minds.

—John Maynard Keynes

Market Behavior: Noise and Time Horizons

In the short run investors are often motivated by the noise. Investors have
a tremendous incentive to capture short-run gains, even if they incur an
increasingly large exposure to an emerging market vulnerability. When everything blows up, the common refrains are "there was no historical prece-
dent," "the event was a six-sigma event that could not have been expected
by anybody," or even "this was an act of God." For a true fundamental
investor, these refrains ring hollow.

Do not wish for quick results, nor look for small advantages. If
you seek quick results, you will not reach the ultimate goal. If you
are led astray by small advantages, you will never accomplish great
things.

—Confucius

A Roman statesman writing under the pseudonym "Cato" observed that,
"there must certainly be a vast fund of stupidity in human nature, else
man would not be caught as they are, a thousand times over, by the same
snare, and while they yet remember their past misfortunes, go on to court
and encourage the causes to which they are owing, and which will again
produce them." It never ceases to amaze us that market participants seem
to fall into the same traps over and over again. We should not consider
these participants to be stupid or irrational; rather, we should think of their
behaviors as natural responses to incentives and, therefore, manageable by
a leader during the investment process.

Nothing is more terrible than ignorance in action.

—Johann Wolfgang von Goethe

Few clients seem enraged or emboldened enough to change these incentives so that the short-term horizon of managers is not pursued at the
expense of clients. It is difficult to fault market participants for simply responding to incentives that come from their clients. Markets reward certain
behaviors in the short run, and clients support managers in their pursuit of
short-run profits. We should expect managers to align on the characteristics that are rewarded in the market and become increasingly exposed to

a systemic vulnerability. When the evolutionary environment changes and these characteristics are no longer rewarded, or are severely punished, the systemic vulnerability will reveal itself in the results of clients, the rewards of long-term investment managers and the ravages of short-term managers.

To get a sense of how investment horizons have changed, consider the average holding period for stocks measured in years. Both Bain & Co. and Societe Generale provide corroborating evidence of declining investment horizons over the past five or six decades[22] as shown in Figure 5.9.

It is our opinion that the greatest opportunities for investment managers today originate in a long investment horizon. So many investment managers focus on short-term gains that many opportunities, requiring the commitment of capital for extended periods of time, remain under-exploited. It is not necessary for the long-horizon manager to identify the exact catalyst that will bring a vulnerability to an end. It is necessary only for the long-horizon manager to study the encroaching systemic vulnerability, identify the development of a critical state, and to position the portfolio to benefit from an ultimate transition to a new capital market environment. Inherent in any long-horizon investment strategy is the reality of short-term risk and occasionally extreme underperformance. The ability to weather that underperformance, and increase exposure to the risk factor that is causing the underperformance, is what confers opportunity to long-term investors.

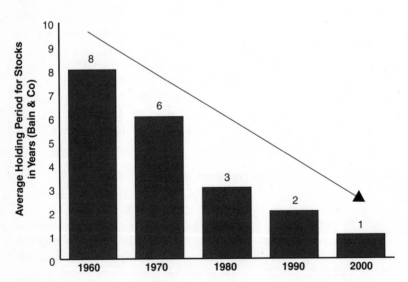

FIGURE 5.9   Average Stock Holding Periods Dramatically Decreasing
Source: Bain & Co.

Market Behavior and Critical States:
Empirical Evidence

Short-term price changes in financial markets that are in a critical state are strikingly similar to a number of phenomena in physics. They have a distinct feature whereby the magnitude, or size, of the outcome is inversely related to the probability of its occurrence. Specifically, it is similar to a power-law probability distribution. According to Philip Ball in *Critical Mass*, "the best way to show the power-law is to plot the logarithm of avalanche size against the logarithm of its probability: the graph then becomes a straight line." The slope of the line is equal to the exponent of the power-law. We view this concept in Figure 5.10.

This sand pile example portrays the relationship of probability and magnitude of a *disequilibrium* situation. As Ball observes, despite being nonequilibrium, the critical state is a stationary state from which the system predictably strays.[23] This disequilibrium but stationary state goes by the name, "critical state." Buchanan observes, "the lesson is this: when it comes to understanding something in a critical state, most of its details simply *do not matter*. Physicists refer to this considerable miracle as 'critical state universality,' and the principal has now been supported by thousands of experiments and computer simulations."[24] Buchanan refers to critical state

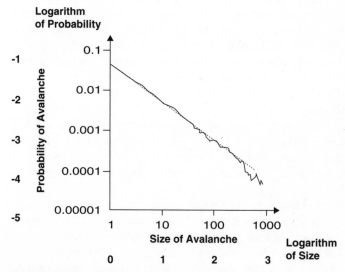

FIGURE 5.10 Anatomy of an Avalanche
Source: Philip Ball, *Critical Mass: How One Thing Leads to Another.*

universality as one of the most profound discoveries in theoretical physics in the last century.

Buchanan states, "To understand any real physical system in a critical state, you may as well forget all the real, messy details about that system." Recall our previous admonition to avoid the siren's appeal of more information and focus on using information more effectively. Despite ignoring the messy details of the real system, we still know that the system in a critical state—a non-equilibrium but nonetheless stationary state—will display predictable critical behavior. An important aspect of the critical state is that any system near its critical state is extremely responsive to disturbances.

To help simplify this concept, imagine dropping one grain of sand, followed by another grain of sand, and so on until a pile of sand arises. Each time a new grain of sand lands on the pile, the existing pile shifts a little bit and small groups of sand shift down the side of the pile. Occasionally, an avalanche of sand brings down a major portion of the pile. This sand pile is in a stationary but precariously critical state. The observed series of falling grains of sand is one of an infinite number of series that history could have provided. It is impossible to predict which grain of sand will result in an avalanche. More important, it is impossible to look at the historical sequence of grains of sand to determine which one would in fact cause the avalanche. We observe one outcome—the series of grains dropped on the pile—leading to an avalanche from an infinite number of other outcomes that may or may not have resulted in avalanches. The sand pile system reaches a critical state. In the critical state, each grain of sand may result in a range of disturbances from a mere jostling of an adjacent grain of sand to a full-fledged avalanche. The power-law function tells us that the log of the magnitude of these events is inversely proportional to the log of the probability of the event.

The cases of critical state universality have an important feature: Each of the individual agents—grains of sand in a sand pile, or as we will discuss in a moment, investors in financial markets—are interactive agents. They have both attractive and repulsive forces. Grains of sand have gravity attracting them toward each other and charge pushing them away from each other. Similarly, individual agents in financial markets influence others in the marketplace.

We can think of individuals in financial markets as analogous to grains of sand falling on a sand pile and the market system as being in a critical state. Contrary to equilibrium financial theory, the state would be non-equilibrium but stationary. Each investor's response to a new piece of information, like a grain of sand falling on a sand pile, could lead to a very small jostling of prices or a catastrophic avalanche of prices. Recalling Taleb, "history is opaque." With each new piece of information we have no idea whether the market response will be small or large. However, from critical state universality, we do know that the magnitude of market response will be inversely related to its frequency. *We find that the U.S. stock market prices demonstrate the power-law features of stationary critical states in the short run, using high frequency data, but not over long investment horizons. Over long horizons, the system gravitates to a normal distribution of returns that would be characteristic of an equilibrium state.*

A feature of systems that self-organize into critical states is that they are scale free. The magnitudes of scale-free variations are independent of the duration of the time intervals. Thus, if you graph Dow Jones Industrial Average (DJIA) log of daily price changes since 1885 against the log of the probability of those price changes, the chart would be a straight line and would look the same if it depicted monthly, quarterly, yearly, or other periodic data.

Figure 5.11 shows DJIA daily price change magnitudes (absolute values) in a graph designed to reveal whether the index level follows a power-law distribution. The vertical axis is the probability of a daily return event occurring depicted on a log scale. The horizontal axis is the daily returns, or price changes, also depicted on a log scale. Thus a 1 percent return occurred about every 10 days, about 10 percent of the time. The circular dots reflect

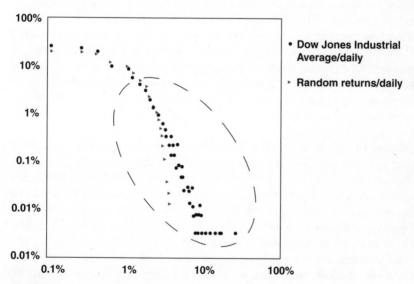

FIGURE 5.11 Stock Returns Do Not Appear Normally Distributed
Source: Samuel H. Williamson, "Daily Closing Values of the DJA in the United States, 1885 to Present," MeasuringWorth, 2008. URL: http://www.measuring worth.org/DJA/.

the actual data of the stock index since 1885, and triangular dots show simulated results for a normal distribution with non-annualized mean and standard deviation characteristics identical to that of the actual daily stock market return data.

Ball evaluated S&P data over one-minute time intervals and discovered that the data more closely resembles a power-law distribution than a normal distribution.[25] Shifting to daily data, we find that returns appear slightly more normal than the per minute data, but, excepting fat tails, roughly adhere to a power-law function. Higher frequency (daily), smaller magnitude returns that we studied also follow a trajectory that loosely resembles that of a normal distribution. The dots on the bottom-right of the chart are low-frequency (y-axis) and high-magnitude (x-axis) daily returns. The dotted oval identifies the range over which the data follow a trajectory more like power-law function than a normal distribution. This finding is consistent with that of Ball in *Critical Mass*.

The returns from about 1 percent to 10 percent follow a power-law function, deviating quite significantly from the simulated normal distribution. In this range, the market perches precariously in a non-equilibrium, but stationary, critical state. In this state, each piece of information can cause a small market response or large market response without our ability to forecast the outcome, and without our ability to point to history to understand that outcome. Humility does not come easily to industry professionals or associated media. As a result, the opacity of history is underappreciated and every market wiggle, large or small, is deemed to have been caused by some event or catalyst. We shun the catalyst identification game. It may be good for marketing, but it is basically a useless waste of investment time. Catalyst searching goes beyond analysis for more information, likely to improve confidence more than accuracy, to analysis of information that does not exist.

Over longer periods, unlike the interactive agents of physics, people in capital markets are thinking interactive agents. These thinking interactive agents have the ability to learn reflexively from their, and others, experiences. Over time, the thinking process causes the system to gravitate away from a rather precarious stationary critical state toward one that is more consistent with an equilibrium state of the Modern Portfolio Theory (MPT). In this state, price changes are normally distributed.

We can observe the system gravitating toward a normally distributed structure by looking at annual price change data in Figure 5.12. Again, circular dots represent actual price changes, and triangular dots represent the simulated outcomes from a normal distribution with the same mean and standard deviation as the actual data. Rather than being scale free, the spectacular characteristic of the power-law whereby all sub-segments are copies of the whole, the annual price change data is more closely aligned with

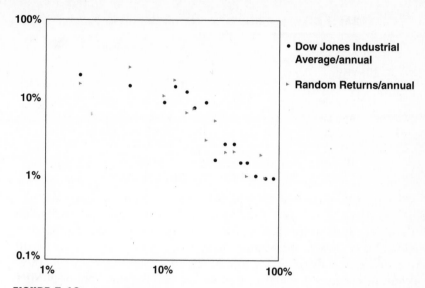

FIGURE 5.12   Annual Returns
Source: Samuel H. Williamson, "Daily Closing Values of the DJA in the United States, 1885 to Present," MeasuringWorth, 2008. URL: http://www.measuring worth.org/DJA/.

what would be expected from an equilibrium system. In other words, the response of the system (i.e., price changes) is slightly more predictable from the information that is introduced to the system. The history is becoming less opaque.

While the sophisticated eyeball test suggests more but not perfect normality, returns can be statistically tested to determine whether they adhere to a normal distribution. Jarque-Bera statistics test if the hypothesis of a normal distribution can be rejected for a given empirical distribution. The p-value of the test is the probability of obtaining a result at least as extreme as the observed distribution, assuming the returns are actually normally distributed. Thus, a low p-value means that the distribution is unlikely to be normal, and a high p-value indicates a high probability that the distribution is normal. Table 5.1 summarizes the Jarque-Bera p-values for various price change frequencies.

For frequencies of 3, 5, and 10 years, it is not possible to statistically reject the hypothesis that the distribution of stock market returns is normally distributed. However, the power of the test is greatly diminished by the decline in data points as the frequency decreases. The progression from short-term stationary criticality to long-term equilibrium can be observed in quintile-to-quintile plots of return magnitudes.

TABLE 5.1 Long-term vs. Short-term "Normality"

Frequency	Jarque-Bera p-value
Daily	<0.1%
Weekly	<0.1%
Monthly	<0.1%
Annual	3.1%
3-Year	17.4%
5-Year	14.8%
10-Year	>50.0%

The quintile-to-quintile (QQ) plots in Figure 5.13 show actual quintiles of returns on the x-axis and simulated returns from a normal distribution on the y-axis. If the price changes followed a normal distribution, the dots would fall very close to the diagonal line. As we can see, as we increase the periodicity from daily to weekly to monthly to annual to three years, there is a convergence to a normal distribution; and thus the assumptions of MPT and fundamental valuation techniques.

Returning to Taleb, the recorded U.S. equity market history is but one history of an infinite number of histories that could have occurred. Perhaps the histories of all equity markets in countries around the world would be more reflective of historical reality. Given that the U.S. equity market is but one history that was uniquely uninterrupted, it is likely that the appropriate

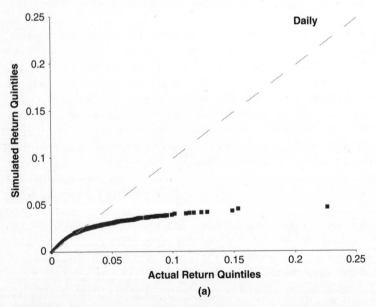

FIGURE 5.13 Return Periodicity and Normalcy

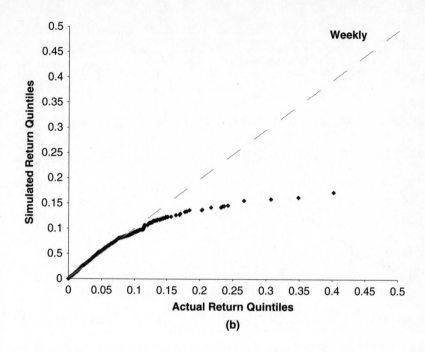

(b)

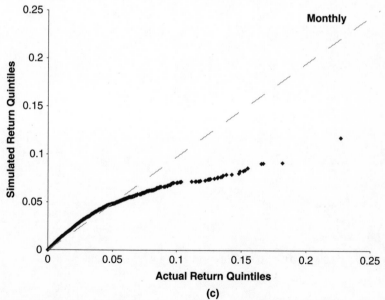

(c)

FIGURE 5.13 (*Continued*)

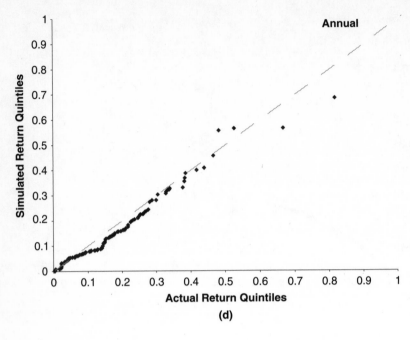

(d)

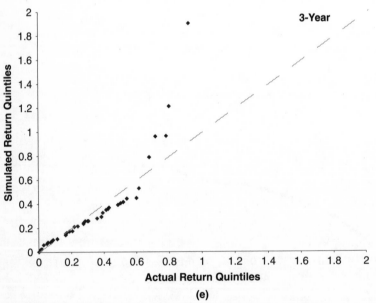

(e)

FIGURE 5.13 (*Continued*)

future investment time horizon for fundamental investors is more on the order of 5, 10, or even 15 years.

Long horizon fundamental investing is likely to be successful for a couple reasons. First, the power-law distribution of returns from a critical state system breaks down as humans begin to think more objectively and reflexively about events and interactions, compelling the system toward fundamental truth and returns toward a more normal distribution.

Drawing from evolution, the magnitude of market response will be dependent upon the current vulnerability that has evolved from the never-ending historical process of interpreting facts, constructing reality, and transacting that results in rewarded investor behaviors persisting in the market-place. As we have discussed, this fosters increasing vulnerability in the system as investors gravitate towards strategies that are rewarded in the short run, increasingly exposing themselves to some major event. Unfortunately, this does not happen overnight; rather, it happens slowly over a period of several years. As this process evolves, the longer-term returns reflect the characteristics of the normal distribution that is at the foundation of equilibrium-based financial theories, the basis for fundamental valuation.

Second, unlike price responses to random information flow that is Taleb's focus, price response to information in financial markets is unrelentingly influenced by the continuous pull of fundamental value. This continual pull is not so strong that prices reflect fundamental values in short periods of time, but the longer the horizon the more we find the fundamental value signal overwhelms the short-term price change noise. Long-term price changes are normally distributed (more accurately the log deviations are normally distributed) around fundamental values. Consequently, active long horizon, fundamental portfolio managers experience idiosyncratic noise in their performance, but over time skill emerges as the dominant influence on portfolio performance.

Due to the long-term nature of the fundamental valuation, the first step of our investment process, it must be augmented by the second step of the process, market behavior analysis. Market behavior analysis tries to wade through the lack of objectivity of market participants to discern why prices deviate from fundamental values at any point in time and evolving vulnerabilities. Market behavior analysis has the potential to improve the timing and magnitude of portfolio strategies. It is not a panacea; however, understanding price/value discrepancies and market vulnerabilities provides an edge in the investment process.

During the low-volatility and high-liquidity environment that ended in 2007, investors focused on short-run fundamentals, implemented carry and credit spread trades, and invested in complex securities that were viable only in that environment. In late 2007 and 2008, that environment disappeared and investors began to realize that the prices of these assets were inconsistent with their fundamental values. The process of transitioning from a low-volatility and high-liquidity environment to a new environment was by no stretch of the imagination normal. The transition was in fact very abnormal, resulting in severe dislocations in the global financial system. The vulnerability evolved over time, and the transition magnitude was large. We really could not expect to anticipate how the transition would occur or what the full magnitude of the transition would be. The specific scenario was beyond comprehension and, perhaps, imagination. However, the dislocation associated with the increasing vulnerability was plainly visible in capital markets.

The success of long-term horizon fundamental investing should be a surprise to nobody. It is amusing that Warren Buffett often emerges to reveal reason as he steps into the maelstrom when prices deviate from fundamental values and fear and greed overwhelm objectivity. Buffet has the luxury of a long-term investment horizon. He invests in a structure that, while not necessarily tax efficient, enables him to have a long-term perspective. Most investors do not have this luxury. Perversely, clients have a tendency to move money every few years in a fruitless attempt to invest alongside the "next Warren Buffett."

Interestingly, endowments are now viewed as the model structure at the beginning of this millennium. It is almost funny to listen to market participants speak of adopting the "endowment model" without realizing that its greatest benefit is a long-term investment horizon. Additionally, each endowment has one client. It does not worry about flows in and out of the endowment based on past performance. Its beneficiaries are far in the future, and it invests accordingly. There is much that we can all learn from these basic observations.

TEAM BEHAVIOR: LESSONS FOR THE CIO FROM JELLY BEANS AND FREUD

For the CIO, not only is fundamental investing complicated by the nuances of *market* behavior that create the opportunities for active investors, but it is also confounded by behavioral issues of *the investment team*. There are two primary behavioral issues that any CIO must at least be aware of, and at best try to manage. First, the CIO must leverage the diverse skills of the investment team. This would be a seemingly simple leadership challenge, but individuals on investment teams suffer from all the same behavioral issues that complicate the market. In particular, the CIO needs to be concerned with groupthink, the dominance of strong personalties and communicators, and the limited willingness of reserved or contrary investment professionals to voice their thoughts and opinions.

The CIO can leverage ideas proposed in James Surowiecki's *The Wisdom of Crowds* to make the most of the information that the investment team possesses at any point in time. Specifically, the CIO can take advantage of information aggregation tools that, when applied across all individuals in the investment team, extract information superior to that from individual specialists or a broad consensus.

Second, Freudian psychoanalysis suggests that the CIO can play an important role in combating the adoption of "phantastic objects" that cloud the judgment of investment team members and skew their construction of reality. The phrase "phantastic objects" comes from standard psychoanalytic thinking. "Phantastic" refers to an imaginary scene that the creator has an unconscious wish to fulfill. The creator is the investor. The word "object" refers to a mental representation.[26] In particular, while individuals harboring hopes and dreams may buy into phantastic objects over short horizons, market participants tend to become more objective over long horizons, causing long-term returns to follow more closely the equilibrium assumptions of Modern Portfolio Theory. The CIO must decide when a mental model held by the investment team is real and when it is hope. Psychoanalysis would suggest that hope is much more prevalent, and more understandable, than most investment leaders appreciate.

> *Most people are other people. Their thoughts are someone else's opinions, their lives a mimicry, their passions a quotation.*
> —Oscar Wilde

We have all likely played a game that provides a prize to the individual who can guess the number of jelly beans in a jar. What we perhaps did not realize was that the best way to win the game is not to guess at all. Rather, by waiting until the game has nearly concluded and submitting an estimate that is the average of all the previous guesses, we are much more likely to win the prize. The average is likely to be an estimate that is superior to over 90 percent of all guesses. How? What does this tell us about markets? Remarkably, the lessons imbedded in this simple game are profound.

As mentioned, a primary distinction of the CIO and other leadership functions is the need to be simultaneously leader and peer. As leader, the CIO has the ultimate responsibility for all investment performance. That does not mean, however, that the CIO should make all of the investment decisions. We have worked in an organization where the CIO seemed to think that ultimate responsibility necessitated ultimate decision authority. We also have experienced environments where the CIO realized his ultimate responsibility, but delegated authority to positions and individuals on the investment team in order to leverage their diversity and skills. It is unquestionable that the latter experience was superior in all regards, particularly investment performance.

We find that nearly all large organizations pay homage to diversity. Unfortunately, our experience suggests that the motivation is primarily political and legal. That is unfortunate, because diversity is perhaps one of the most powerful tools available to the CIO. In particular, diverse backgrounds provide individuals on the investment team with the ability to construct different realities from their observations. Working with a highly diverse investment team at UBS Global Asset Management was highly illuminating and very beneficial to our investment performance.

Diversity enables each individual to develop a mental model of markets and market behavior that is likely to be different from these of other individuals on the investment team. A valuable function of any investment team is to take these models of market behavior and compare them, challenge them, and potentially change them. In the end, the team has the opportunity to leverage the diverse backgrounds of these individuals for better understanding of market behavior that is different from, and better than, that of any individual on the team, in particular, that of the CIO.

The tools outlined in Chapters 1, 2, and 3 provide the CIO with a valuable edge in extracting and rewarding the diverse skills of each investment professional. Additionally, recent research has discussed another tool that has been known to economists for centuries. That tool is the market. James Surowiecki, in *The Wisdom of Crowds*, uses the term "market" in a very broad manner. The market is a place where the sellers of something interact with buyers for a potential exchange. Both parties must have something they can offer in exchange for there to be a potential transaction. Exchanges can involve money and goods, or they can involve money and information. They can even involve information and information. Exchanges can occur in a physical location, but they can be anonymous. For example, the Commodity Clearing Corporation is the opposite party of all transactions on futures exchanges. The buyers and sellers are unaware and unconcerned about the other's identity.

Surowiecki delineates the characteristics that make the market so successful.[27] First, markets work best when there is a *diversity* of opinions to be aggregated. True diversity of the investment team, like at UBS, is a tremendous asset to be exploited by the CIO. The CIO should seek diversity among the investment professionals. It should be a significant driver of hiring and firing decisions, however the CIO only benefits to the degree that he or she can leverage that diversity; and that is what the market is so successful at accomplishing.

Second, the individuals' views and ideas must be *independent*. Interestingly, anonymous exchanges provide for increased independence as buyers and sellers are less able to influence each other. Within investment teams, it cannot be the case that a single idea or several ideas simply travel through the investment team like a chain letter to be repeated by all members during investment strategy sessions. All individuals on an investment team should communicate continually, exchanging ideas and modifying views. The CIO must make sure that investment discussions draw upon independent views and do not simply ratify a collective view that has traveled through the team. Independence is critical, and the CIO must leverage that independence. The anonymity of blind voting on ideas provides a "market" for information that enables those who exchange information or ideas to benefit with limited mutual influence. The market is a tremendous tool at the CIO's disposal.

Third, *decentralization* increases the value of a market. As mentioned, at UBS there was a highly diverse team, drawing from many different nationalities, educational backgrounds, and ethnicities. Investment discussions included the insight from many different countries. The investment professionals were able to draw upon unique perspectives they had of developments in their regions and developments in other regions. The job of CIO was to draw upon this decentralized specialization.

Finally, the market mechanism provides for the *aggregation* of diverse, independent, and decentralized views of individuals in the investment team. The way we implemented this market mechanism at UBS was to conduct surveys of each individual. We would typically ask some question, for example views on earnings or recommended inputs to our valuation model. The objective was to garner feedback from those individuals using the survey as an aggregation tool before discussion of the topic at hand. By conducting the survey we were able to obtain diverse, independent, and decentralized views before our discussions tainted these perspectives.

Some companies use this type of market function to make better decisions, giving their employees money to take positions on such things as release dates of software or the success of marketing programs. This market survey or voting process can be conducted over time, providing ongoing information to and from individuals in the organization seeing the topic from a multitude of perspectives. As time passes, management has a useful set of information to improve their decisions.[28] It is this application of the market tool that we introduce to improve the investment analysis and decision-making processes.

> *There ain't no rules around here. We're trying to accomplish something.*
>
> —Thomas Edison

According to Surowiecki, "If you can assemble a diverse group of people who possess varying degrees of knowledge and insight, you're better off entrusting it with major decisions rather than leaving them in the hands of one or two people, no matter how smart those people are."[29] Suggesting that the organization with the smartest people may not be the best organization is heretical, particularly in the business world caught up in a ceaseless "war for talent" and governed by the assumption that a few superstars can make the difference. It is as if Surowiecki had investment professionals in mind when he drafted those comments.

Our Market versus The Market

So how can an investment organization be structured to use *a* market to beat *the* market? Presumably, the market, drawing upon the diverse views of global market participants, would be unbeatable. However, when market behavior goes astray, the beneficial characteristics of the market disappear. The market becomes vulnerable, a collective view that does not reflect a diverse, independent, and decentralized set of views. The role of the CIO is to make sure that the investment team remains independent and does not become cohesively attached to the evolving vulnerability of a collective market view.

Surowiecki notes that team homogeneity fosters conformity. It is easier for each individual to change his or her opinion than to challenge the group.[30] The CIO must support dissension and fight consensus, for consensus does not reflect an investment team's diversity. Consensus outcomes often feel good because they are the path of least resistance and avoid confrontation; however, it is our belief that consensus has no place in the investment process. The CIO must reward independence and dissent, and the objective Merit Zone evaluation process delineated in Chapter 3 is a tremendous tool. The Merit Zone process enables incentives to penalize consensus behaviors and reward constructive dissent.

A simple recommendation that we employ to help increase independence and diversity is to hire smart, young, and trainable individuals. In a structure of collaborative freedom fostered by the CIO, these individuals have the opportunity to prove themselves and be promoted. We do not recommend hiring senior investment professionals into an investment team, unless the investment team is dysfunctional and needs to be completely rebuilt. A successful investment team is likely to have mutually acceptable values and defined investment philosophy and process. A senior investment professional is unlikely to seamlessly fit into that structure. This is not meant to suggest hiring people similar to those already in the organization, after all, with that you would lose the aforementioned benefits of diversity. While you want diversity from the standpoint of culture, ethnicity, education, and so on, the CIO wants to avoid diversity of values and investment philosophies and processes. Hiring junior people has other positive externalities. They can be trained to understand the investment philosophy and investment processes, without the hindrance of legacy biases. They are young and full of fresh ideas. These young individuals do not have a plethora of responsibilities that result in guarded behavior. Rather, they can take risk, can be the voice of dissent, and can counter the ongoing propensity for cohesion of thought among the investment team. We would recommend bringing young individuals into the investment team and using the Merit Zone process to coax and coach them into higher performance and greater criticality. Success in this process will create a pool of successors for your senior team as your organization grows and its skills expand.

In addition to the objectivity of the Merit Zone process, the CIO should look for additional ways to leverage the skills of the investment team. In this regard, we can learn from Thomas Edison, who provides a good example of how a leader can succeed in this task. Edison was an incredibly hard worker, but he also had a brilliant management style in overseeing groups of "muckers," or inventors. Edison himself was the "Chief Mucker," and often he hired inventors straight out of college and inspired them to work incredibly long hours for workmen's wages. Their creativity and productivity were astounding. He was able to extract a high level of productivity from his workers in part by creating an enjoyable environment. For example, Edison put a pipe organ in the Menlo Park lab for entertainment during breaks throughout the day and when muckers worked late into the night. The atmosphere created by Edison generated a constant spirit of invention and fun.

> *Genius is one percent inspiration and ninety-nine percent perspiration.*
>
> —Thomas Edison

In learning from Edison, the CIO can also foster creativity and inspire hard work by creating an enjoyable environment. The confines of philosophy and process afford the opportunity for the CIO to encourage fun and liberate creativity. Micromanaging within the confines of the philosophy and process reduces the breadth of information and ideas, effectively reducing the size of the investment team. The CIO should inspire, coax, admonish, and support, but he should not burden the team with rules beyond or micromanagement within the philosophy and process.

The CIO versus Phantastic Objects

Earlier in this chapter, we introduced the concept of phantastic objects. In 2008, David Tuckett and Richard Taffler published an article in the *International Journal of Psychoanalysis* discussing phantastic objects as a means of understanding stock market instability.[31]

Tuckett and Taffler base their analysis on clinical experience applied to instability in financial markets. They find that, "when there is news that real prospects have changed, economic agents buy or sell until prices change in line with their changed expectations of 'reality.' In so far as new information is unambiguous and there are enough investors to calculate accurately and act promptly, setting aside their previous attitudes and views, a new equilibrium will be established in a consistent and efficient way."[32] From a fundamental investor's perspective, this equilibrium is nothing more than fundamental value.

CW Smith interviewed senior Wall Street investment professionals and found that they often were uncertain of their views, yet seldom admitted those uncertainties to the public.[33] Even though these professionals claimed to fully understand their position, when pushed by Smith, they admitted that they did not have full comprehension. Consistent with Heuer's observation that more information is less valuable than using the information already possessed more effectively, Smith argued that their lack of understanding was not due to a lack of information, but rather a lack of explanations.

> *"A lot of these companies should never have gone public,"* says *Thomas McDonald, an associate of billionaire Sam Zell. . . . "I think the overzealous bankers convinced founders their dreams would come true, and at valuations they never imagined."*
> —Antonio Regalado, "Brazil's IPO Rush Hits Rough Patch,"
> *The Wall Street Journal*, June 20, 2008

Emotions and states of mind determine the way information about reality is processed. Excitement over a constructed reality leads to euphoria as investors project a mental fantasy of a future in which they attain a reward that is desired in their unconscious mind, but not attainable in the market. In the minds of market participants, reality moves to a euphoric mental state of desire and hope. The psychoanalytic model argues that in the context of uncertainty, investment professionals, think of brokerage firm investment strategists and TV pundits, do not admit to a clear lack of comprehension.

In these instances, there is a previously developed mental state regarding objective facts and constructed realities. However, in the face of the uncertainty and ambiguity observed by Smith, this reality shifts to an unrealistic "reality" that reflects the latent desires of the individual. The tech bubble provides an excellent and, as Figure 5.14 demonstrates, a remarkably typical example. Internet shares ultimately acquired the qualities of phantastic objects and investors were "unconsciously understanding them rather as concrete opportunities to achieve omnipotent and omniscient phantasies, which are usually restrained from becoming conscious reality or treated as delusions. These exciting phantasies had the power to override more realistic calculation and the judgment of the facts."[34]

At this point, the vulnerability model and the psychoanalytic model fed upon themselves. Investors who bought into the tech hype were rewarded by their clients. Investors had a tremendous incentive to align themselves on the characteristics that were rewarded in the market, namely Internet stocks in the tech bubble. This evolution led to the development of phantastic objects in the minds of market participants. Not only did market participants respond to incentives, they skewed the conscious and unconscious perception of these incentives to further load on rewarded characteristics. Market participants loaded on these characteristics by buying more tech stocks, and in a perpetuating cycle found more reasons to support their fantasy. By 1999, the evolutionary model had fully reinforced the psychoanalytic model, which in

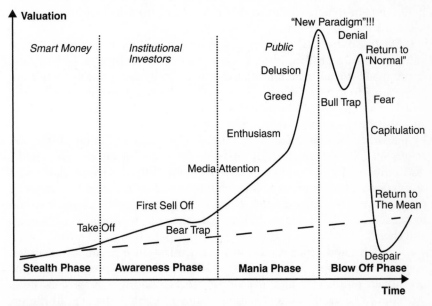

FIGURE 5.14 Main Stages of a Bubble
Source: Dr. Jean-Paul Rodrigue, Dept. of Economics, Hofstra University.

a vicious cycle fed back onto the evolutionary model. The mania was in full force at this juncture.

There were investors who refused to buy in to these phantastic objects; luminaries like Julian Robertson of Tiger Management, Gary Brinson of Brinson Partners, and Jeremy Grantham of GMO stayed out of tech stocks in the later portion of the 1990s and experienced a "short" period of devastating performance. Unfortunately, Julian Robertson closed up shop. Brinson Partners and GMO held to the conviction provided by fundamental value analysis and witnessed a transition to reality that proved to be the most powerful proof of their investment philosophies and processes.

Many concluded that the macro investment skills of fundamental investors such Julian Robertson, Gary Brinson, and Jeremy Grantham were simply untenable in the marketplace. Perhaps an inadequate comprehension of the reinforcing nature of the vulnerability and psychoanalytic models led to the extinction of those who narrowly and uniquely held to fundamental value metrics. Consultants stepped into the void to provide this service to investors, but failure to protect clients during the tremendous downside in 2000, 2001, and 2002, and subsequent failure to capture much of the rebounding upside pretty much ended their tenures as macro investors. Today, a few consultants have stayed true to their discipline and provide fiduciary contributions to their clients. Others abandoned the consulting business and built funds-of-funds investment structures, using the failed style box models and asset-class silo structures of the 1990s.

The role of the CIO in this environment is to make sure that fundamental value remains a beacon in the uncertain storm of chaotic news flow, and that the investment team understands market behavior influences while not responding to unavoidable short-term incentives or a fantasy, what Tuckett and Taffler refer to as "the manifest cover story."[35] The CIO needs to make sure that he does not provide cover for the adoption of phantastic objects by individuals on the investment team. Shiller suggested in his 2005 book *Irrational Exuberance* that authoritative pronouncements can prevent the development of price bubbles.[36] To make these authoritative proclamations at moments of extreme (mandate-altering) greed or fear, the CIO must be confident and highly respected. Only a highly respected individual would have the authority to maintain the confidence of investment professionals and clients.

The CIO and other leaders in the organization have important roles, not only in the unwavering pursuit of superior returns consistent with the investment philosophy and investment process, but also in the consistent, continual, and clear communication of this to every individual in the organization and to every client. This is much easier said than done. The CIO must push back against clients and distribution colleagues. Often this pressure can become insurmountable without the types of governance structures discussed in Chapter 1.

Clearly a CIO must have superior investment capabilities. But there is more to the job than being a good investor. A truly superior CIO must leverage the diversity of the investment team. He must look to hire investment professionals who can challenge consensus and provide fresh ideas. He should look to create an environment that fosters fun, creativity, and hard work. Finally, the superior CIO must use his gravitas to avoid pressures to chase phantastic objects and to prevent investment professionals from responding to short-term incentives that inevitably expose a portfolio to tremendous vulnerability.

PORTFOLIO DESIGN

In addition to a long-term investment horizon, portfolio design is probably the most important aspect in the investment process for generating superior returns. The third and final stage in the investment process, portfolio design, is best built upon the rigorous theoretical foundations of finance, exploiting quantitative methods. We do not, however, advocate quantitative portfolio construction. Rather, we have found that *qualitative* portfolio design, built on a strong, theoretically rigorous, and quantitative foundation, is superior.

In the 1980s, after the extreme volatility of the late 1960s and 1970s, asset allocation and global diversification became the foundation of risk management. Individuals like Sir John Templeton and Gary Brinson pioneered diversification afforded by allocating assets across numerous asset classes, both domestic and international. Unfortunately, in the period from the early 1980s to the end of the tech bubble in 2000, equity and bond markets generally moved almost unwaveringly higher. The market decline of 1987 was one of epic proportions, but it washes out in the quarterly and annual return data, speaking volumes to the focus that fundamental investors should have on long horizons. Unlike the volatility of the 1960s and 1970s, the subsequent two decades experienced declining and low volatility, declining and low inflation, and increasing productivity to varying degrees worldwide. Diversification wasn't necessarily rewarded.

As the 1980s and 1990s progressed, passive investing became vogue. The U.S. equity market, as measured by the S&P 500, came to be increasingly dominated by a small number of overpriced stocks, in the extreme driven by the tech bubble in the final portion of the 1990s. Multiasset class investing seemed to have been discredited in a short period of time. Subsequently, the bursting of the tech bubble detracted from the allure of passive investment portfolios. What emerged was the separation of alpha and beta, alpha being achieved by investing in alternative investments and beta being achieved by investing in index funds. The index funds preserved fees for the more important and expensive pursuit of alpha.

Risk Capital Allocation

Alpha–beta separation reflects an advance in portfolio design, but we believe the way it is normally implemented is a dead end. Rather than achieving beta exposure through index funds and alpha through alternative investments, investors would be better served by realizing that beta is nothing more than a risk that is compensated over time, but not compensated all of the time. In portfolio design, alpha and beta should both be considered on an equal footing by investors seeking compensated risks. Since the separation of alpha and beta inappropriately separated risk exposures that must be considered simultaneously, as practiced, alpha–beta separation was an unsatisfactory method of portfolio design.

Saying that alpha and beta risks should be considered on an equal footing is perhaps a bit generous to alpha and stingy to beta. Why is this? Well, the pursuit of alpha is on average not compensated, and alpha is very difficult and expensive to find. Beta, however, is compensated over time, if not all the time, and is very easy to find via exposure to any asset class. Thus, it is inappropriate to view beta exposure as an afterthought and focus all energy on the pursuit of alpha.

The future of macro investing involves identifying systematic risk exposures (multiple active betas) and evaluating potential compensation. Active betas are not isolated to any individual asset class. The asset class concept is a legacy constraint that offers opportunities for those willing to break down asset-class barriers. The pursuit of compensated systematic risk exposures across all asset classes—active beta management—is a superior way to design portfolios. For example, one could invest in infrastructure as an asset class. Alternatively, one could invest in private equity that has exposure to infrastructure projects, equities of firms involved in basic industries that may support infrastructure, and fixed income assets of those same companies. The exposure is compensated, but not through direct investment in infrastructure. It may be that direct exposure, due to relentless buying driven by some phantastic object, is better achieved outside the asset class through indirect exposure across many different asset classes.

In this new framework, macro investing is "risk capital allocation." The allocation of capital to both systematic (multiple active betas) and idiosyncratic (multiple alphas) risks is superior. Sometimes beta risks are compensated and they should be incurred. Sometimes alpha risks are compensated and should be incurred. Regardless, one should not blindly incur index exposures to obtain beta and then focus all energies on alpha exposure.

To undertake macro investing as a risk capital allocation methodology, the investment organization must first and foremost have a viable, forward-looking risk measurement, analysis, and management tool. It is important to note the use of the phrase "forward-looking." Most risk models are built on short-term historical data. The purpose of this text, however, is not to delve into the construction of consistent forward-looking risk models. Rather, we refer you to the individual and collaborative research of Diermeier, Singer, Staub, and Terhaar for more on this subject.[37]

With this risk system in place, the physical capital can be used to obtain alpha from a number of sources, but sources that are not specifically tied to any asset class. There is no reason for the bottom-up investment process to be constrained by artificial asset classes or style box barriers. The risk analysis system enables the isolation of systematic exposures embedded in the alpha-oriented components. Often these exposures are coming from multiple sources and may compound or offset one another. Sometimes these systematic exposures are compensated and therefore desirable, but some of them may be uncompensated or negatively compensated, in which case they are to be avoided. Derivatives can be prudently used to shift risk capital toward desired compensated risk and away from undesired uncompensated risk. The physical capital is used to obtain alpha exposures, and the risk capital is managed via derivatives to isolate the desired long and short beta exposures.

As it relates to portfolio construction, we are of the belief that there is no reason for a portfolio to be long only. Building a portfolio of desired risk exposures by investing only on the long side is akin to entering a boxing match with one hand tied behind your back. While some people are under the false belief that shorting is a skill that only hedge funds possess, we believe that shorting is a risk management tool that makes any investment process easier. It is likely true that shorting of individual stocks as a means of generating positive returns, requires unique skill, dedication, experience, and a nuanced understanding of market dynamics. However, shorting as a means of hedging risk and isolating exposures is not only the realm of hedge funds, it is the realm of all prudent investors. By utilizing the ability to go both long and short beta in the portfolio design process, an investment firm will be able to more efficiently seek its return objectives while simultaneously avoiding what it deems to be uncompensated risk.

CONCLUSION

At the core of any successful investment management firm are its investment philosophy and process. In order to create a valuable investment edge, these parameters define leadership and behavioral boundaries that must be communicated throughout the organization. Within these boundaries, team members function at the edge of chaos, bringing a wealth of diversity and creativity to the investment process.

We believe our three-part investment process of fundamental valuation, market and team behavior, and portfolio design proves to be a very valuable construct for investment leadership to deliver superior investment performance. The challenges to investment performance presented by market and team behaviors can be overcome by adherence to this process and via leadership that takes advantage of investment team diversity and does not allow investment professionals to get caught up in the short-term emotions that may be driving the market. A strict adherence to this framework is only the first part of achieving investment success. The path to successful stewardship requires investment professionals of the organization to work closely with the distribution professionals to assure that superior investment performance leads to successful client outcomes. Superior client outcomes arise from the symbiosis of equal investment and distribution cooperation. In the next chapter, we discuss how an investment organization can use communication to deliver positive client experiences.

CHAPTER 6

Communication for Superior Client Outcomes

Regardless of how well an asset manager may do in producing top-tier investment performance, a critical and often overlooked component of creating a successful organization is assuring that its clients actually attain the investment results the firm is achieving. What sounds like a relatively simple task (after all, why wouldn't a client achieve the same returns as the portfolio in which they are invested?) is arguably the biggest obstacle to creating successful client outcomes.

The unfortunate reality of the situation is that the long-term returns that an investor achieves are quite often nowhere near as good as the long-term results of the markets, or even the very portfolios in which they are invested. This chapter focuses on the critical role that the business function should play in an investment firm. The end result all too often is a negative client experience, despite what may be superior investment performance produced by the investment firm. So the question this chapter aims to answer is, "What can the firm do to actually *deliver* a positive client outcome?"

Delivering a positive client experience is far more difficult than is commonly believed. There are a multitude of factors that combine to conspire against client outcomes. Simply put, most investors don't stick with the managers they hire long enough to benefit from the skills for which they are paying. Why is this? It is because we operate in an industry consumed with third-party ratings, past performance (often short-term) and manager selection. We have investment firms with severe pressures to grow quickly, who push hardest on that which is easiest to sell, and often neglect to support those capabilities that may simply be out of favor and due for a period of strong performance.

We also have both institutional and private client intermediaries who often focus their efforts and base their primary value proposition on the selection of investment managers. Perhaps this is because it is a task that appears to be very difficult and require great expertise, hence justifying the fees for the services performed. However, the real goal of intermediaries and asset managers alike should be on client behavior modification. That is to say, that there is great value in assisting the process by which investors do not succumb to their natural behavioral biases. Unfortunately this task may appear to be so simple that people are unwilling to pay for this on-going service, despite it being perhaps the greatest source of value creation (or the avoidance of value destruction). These advisors and intermediaries are under constant fear that they themselves will get fired when the managers they select experience periodic underperformance. As a result, they often see themselves as "performance vigilantes" who are paid to hire and fire managers – as it turns out, often to the detriment of their clients.

Most of us in the industry know all too well that past performance is really no guarantee of future results. It is not just a required disclosure, but also an absolute truth. Most of us understand that investor wants are often the opposite of their needs, and that the easy sale is often the wrong sale. Most of us realize that even the very best managers go through multi-year periods of poor performance where the markets are not rewarding their views or approach to investing, and it is during these periods that it is often the best time to be staying the course with, or even hiring, these managers. Unfortunately, the pressures to sell, to grow, and to justify fees often lead to value-destructive actions.

The goal of an investment firm has to be threefold:

1. Attractive risk-adjusted results over time.
2. Explainable performance all of the time.
3. An absolute top-down commitment to exceptional client service.

With respect to client service, we believe three things:

1. Most clients/intermediaries need ongoing education, coaching, and support to extend their time horizons and holding periods with the managers they select. This is job number one. Issues of manager selection, past performance, and fees take a backseat to extending the time horizons and holding periods of investors.
2. Realistic expectations about periodic underperformance of managers, the impact of performance chasing on real client outcomes, and the historic frequency, duration, magnitude, and impact of bull and bear markets are vital to delivering a successful client outcome.
3. An investment firm has to create a culture around client outcomes—not just investment excellence. As discussed in previous chapters, this is about, as Jack Bogle, founder of Vanguard, advocates, "placing stewardship ahead of salesmanship."

An investment firm's best path to sustainable long-term profitability is to do right by its clients. Doing right is multi-faceted. First, it means offering an investment solution that is both sound and repeatable. Second, it means offering this investment solution within acceptable boundaries of risk and volatility. Third, it means a total commitment to keep clients invested long enough so that they can actually benefit from the investment skills for which they are paying. A failure to execute against any one of these objectives will probably perpetuate the hideous gap between manager performance and investor results. Of course we are not saying that investors or advisors are never justified in the termination of a manager, only that a hard look should be taken that places past performance at an appropriate (and lower) priority in the decision-making process.

In this chapter we will discuss some of the key obstacles for most investors to achieving their long-term investment objectives. Further, we will talk about some practical ways for investment firms to help clients stay invested through the course of market cycles and avoid destructive performance-chasing behavior. Finally, we will discuss the ideals and culture that a firm should look to create to assure that a positive client experience is the primary goal at all levels of the organization. It is no accident that you will see a number of quotations from Warren Buffett sprinkled throughout this chapter. Much of the success of Berkshire Hathaway is the result of acute attention paid to avoiding these common mistakes.

THE PROBLEM: HUMAN NATURE

Numerous studies show that both individual and institutional investors tend to underperform the managers with whom they invest. Why is there a gap between invest*ment* and invest*or* performance? Manager selection? Probably not. Expenses? Probably not.

The gap exists because human nature is often in conflict with the tenets of successful investing. Excessive greed in late-stage bull markets and excessive fear in late-stage bear markets causes investors to buy high and sell low. Chasing performance on the way up, and panicking out of an investment on the way down, is too often the order of the day. We routinely witness investors and intermediaries seeking out the hottest managers *after* they've done well, then firing and terminating managers *after* they've done poorly. Holding periods are often too short and expectations are often unrealistic.

As you will see shortly, the average holding period for an equity mutual fund over the past 20 years has been about 37 *months* according to DALBAR, Inc. Investing with a manager for three years may look like an investment because you're placing money with a professional money manager, but in reality it is nothing more than a speculative trade. Whether that particular manager happens to provide attractive returns during any given three-year period is more a random event than a statement of skill. The *lengthening of investor holding periods is essential to achieving better results.*

Equally, while it is realistic to expect superior risk-adjusted performance *over* time, it is unrealistic to expect superior performance all of the time. Most top-quality managers go through multi-year periods when the markets are not rewarding their particular style. In fact, a recent study conducted by Robert W. Baird & Co. finds some astonishing results as it relates to the frequency, magnitude, and duration of underperformance.[1] According to the study (which identified a "high-performing manager" as a domestic or international equity mutual fund with at least a 10-year track record that has outperformed its respective benchmark by a minimum of 1 percent annualized, net of fees):

- One hundred percent of high-performing managers have had a 12-month period of time where they have underperformed their benchmark by at least 3 percentage points, with four out of five of them having experienced a 12-month period where the underperformance was in excess of 10 percentage points.
- Over 80 percent of the high-performing managers analyzed had a three-year period where their portfolios trailed their respective benchmark.
- Sixty-six percent of the high-performing managers spent a minimum of three years in the bottom quartile of their Morningstar peer group.

While there is no doubt that some periods of underperformance may indeed be a cause for concern (e.g. breakdown in process or PM turnover), too many investors fail to see that these periods of underperformance are often a statement of discipline and less a cause for concern or a need to take action. Getting clients to understand the inevitability of periodic underperformance is a critical component to achieving better results.

A CLASSIC TALE

As discussed, investors are constantly shuffling their portfolios around at an alarmingly rapid pace—chasing a fund, asset class, or sector that has experienced a successful run, usually just in time for it to fall out of favor and revert to the mean. So while these individuals may view their actions as investing, in reality what they are doing is little more than merely gambling. While this is a story that has been told time and time again, from tulip bulbs in 1637 Holland to oil in the summer of 2008, perhaps no period of time encapsulates this detrimental behavior more than the technology, media, and telecom (TMT) bubble of the late 1990s, as demonstrated in Figure 6.1.

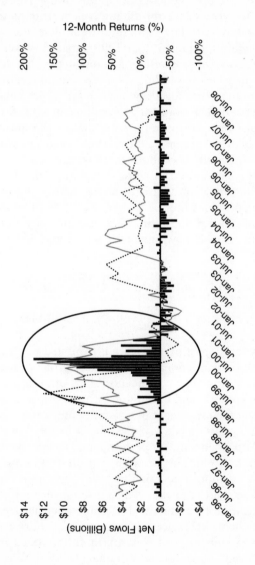

FIGURE 6.1 Technology Funds Saw Largest Inflows, Just before the Bubble Burst

For illustrative purposes only. Past performance is no guarantee of future results. Technology mutual fund sales, redemptions, exchanges, reinvested dividends, and assets under management are based on monthly data calculated by FRC. Performance information based on Specialty Technology sector provided to the FRC by Morningstar. UBS104.2526C.

Source: Financial Research Corporation (FRC); used with permission.

The solid line shows the average rolling one-year returns of technology-focused mutual funds over the past 12 years. As you can see, beginning in the second half of 1998, the performance of these funds experienced a meteoric rise, peaking at a return of over 175 percent in the 12 months ending February of 2000. Unfortunately, the average investor did not benefit from these phenomenal returns. The bars show fund flows into these technology funds, which captured their biggest inflows not in 1998 or 1999 (when they were experiencing their excellent returns), but rather in 2000, just in time for the crash of the TMT bubble. In fact, the dotted line shows the actual returns experienced by investors 12 months after investing in these funds. So while the majority of individuals invested their money at a time when these portfolios had "rear-view mirror" one-year returns in the triple digits, the returns they experienced were in excess of -50 percent in the first year alone! As you can see, these portfolios have essentially been in net outflows ever since.

There is one strategy that is guaranteed to work in investing: Buy low and sell high. If only it were that simple. Interestingly, human nature, behavioral biases, agency issues, liquidity pressures, and a variety of other factors conspire to make this a very difficult proposition. Time and time again individuals do the exact opposite, namely buy high and sell low, and destroy their wealth in the process.

> *It's far better to buy a wonderful company at a fair price than a fair company at a wonderful price.*
>
> —Warren Buffett

The behavior pattern of chasing past performance is exhibited not just by individual investors; we see similar actions with the many professionals involved in the hiring and firing of investment managers. Many of these professionals are judged for compensation and promotion purposes on shorter time frames than the horizon of the investment philosophies they invest in. As a consequence, many professionals do not have the time or inclination to determine whether a period of poor investment performance is a statement of discipline or a real cause for concern. They view any period of poor performance as an opportunity to demonstrate value by taking action—even when the best action to be taken is no action at all. Too many professionals are in the business of what can best be described as combining five-star managers to create a two-star client experience. They are essentially driving forward looking in the rearview mirror, and they are more interested in selling something than in achieving long-term and sustainable client results.

Bill Miller, chairman and chief investment officer of Legg Mason Capital Management, lamented in his Second Quarter 2008 Commentary, "The best time to open an account with us has always been when we've had dismal performance, and the worst time has always been after a long run of excess returns. Yet we (and everyone else) get the most inflows and the most interest AFTER we've done well, and the most client terminations AFTER we've done poorly. It will always be so, because that is the way people behave." The evidence here is more than anecdotal. A number of academic studies and empirical evidence has been collected to demonstrate the futility and destructive power of performance chasing to both individual and institutional investors. A couple of these key pieces of research are summarized below.

CASE 1: INDIVIDUAL INVESTORS, THE IMPACT OF PERFORMANCE CHASING

One of the most well-known studies that attempts to quantify the impact of investor behavior on investment returns is published annually by DALBAR, Inc. Shown in Figure 6.2, Dalbar looks at the 20-year annualized return of the average U.S large-cap equity mutual fund and compares it to the average return realized by the average dollar invested in these funds. For the 20 years through 2007, the results are clear:

So not only is it the case that investors will drastically underperform the market, but they will also drastically underperform the very portfolios in which they are invested! To what can this horrendous gap between the returns the market has provided and the returns the average investor has received be attributed? The answer is chiefly this: human emotion. Investors are constantly shuffling their portfolios around at an alarmingly rapid pace (Dalbar also confirms in its analysis that the average holding period is only three years), chasing a fund, asset class, or sector that has experienced a successful run, usually just in time for it to fall out of favor and revert to the mean. So while these individuals may view their actions as investing, in reality what they are doing is nothing more than misguided speculation.

> *In the business world, the rearview mirror is always clearer than the windshield.*
>
> —Warren Buffett

CASE 2: ARE INSTITUTIONAL INVESTORS THE "SMART MONEY?"

Our own experience, as well as a number of academic studies, has shown that performance-chasing behavior is not confined to the individual investor.

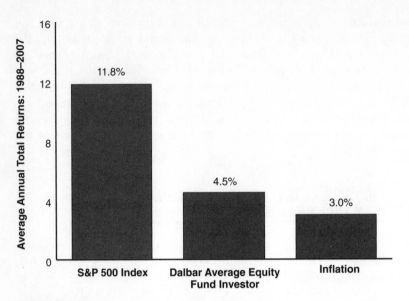

FIGURE 6.2 The Average Investor Underperforms the Average Fund by a Wide Margin

For illustrative purposes only. Past performance does not guarantee future results. Performance calculated assuming reinvestment of all dividends and capital gains. The S&P 500 Index is an unmanaged, weighted index comprising 500 widely held common stocks varying in composition and is unavailable for direct investment. The Dalbar Average Equity Fund Investor is the rate of return investors earned, based on the length of time shareholders actually remain invested in equity mutual funds. Over the time period 1988–2007, the equity mutual fund shareholders held their mutual funds for an average of 3.1 years. Mutual fund sales, redemptions, exchanges, reinvested dividends, and assets under management are based on monthly data provided by the Investment Company Institute. The average annual return of the Dalbar Average Equity Investor is based on all equity funds, represented by the Dalbar Equity Index which was comprised of the S&P 500 Index and the Ibbotson Small Company stock index.

Source: Lipper, Inc. and Dalbar, used with permission.

It seems that the three-year "review mirror" performance evaluation criteria used by many institutional investors is quite detrimental to investor outcomes. An empirical study by Goyal and Wahal examined the selection and termination decisions of 3,400 institutional defined benefit pension plan sponsors and provides strong evidence of this same performance-chasing phenomenon. In their study, Goyal and Wahal concluded that institutional plan sponsors hired investment managers after these managers earned large positive excess returns during the three years prior to their hiring. Despite attractive three-year past investment performance, the hiring of these managers does not deliver positive excess returns thereafter. After hiring these managers, excess returns were in fact indistinguishable from zero.

Similarly, plan sponsors terminated investment managers after observed periods of underperformance. Again, the empirical evidence suggests that the excess returns of these managers after being fired were frequently positive. Finally, and perhaps most interesting, the study found that if plan sponsors had stayed with the original investment managers that they fired for underperformance, their excess returns would be larger than those actually delivered by the replacement managers.

What can be done to help individual and institutional investors alike become better at avoiding the pitfalls of performance-chasing behavior? Communicate, communicate, communicate. Framing, contextualizing and setting appropriate expectations are the key. Making sure that clients are fully aware of the perils of performance chasing is critical, but there are some other key concepts that we look to in an effort to help clients achieve long-term investment success. Two of the more prominent ones are discussed below. Clients must understand the reality of investing in equities and be schooled on the mathematics of recovery. And don't worry; we can get through this without a degree in the evolutionary econometrics of avalanches, Gaussian distributions, thermodynamics, and black swans.

THE REALITY OF INVESTING IN EQUITIES

Stock investing became wildly popular in the bull market of the 1980s and 1990s, and the poster child of the financial industry for getting clients to invest in equities was the return stream shown in Figure 6.3.

The primary point of the chart is fairly self-explanatory: Over time stocks have significantly outperformed bonds, cash, and inflation. While factually correct, that common explanation is incomplete, misleading, and arguably one of the causes for the unrealistic expectations many investors have. For starters, the Ibbotson Chart assumes that clients have an 80-plus year time horizon. As Dalbar and other studies have taught us, the average investor's holding period is much closer to 80 weeks than it is 80 years.

Secondly, the chart makes it seem as if equities go up in a somewhat smooth, linear fashion and grossly minimizes the impact of downturns and bear markets (the 2000–2002 bear market is a proverbial blip on a radar screen and the market crash of 1987 is barely perceivable). Even the current equity bear market (2008–through Q1 2009) does not appear to be a long-term cause for concern. The volatility associated with equity investing gets so lost in this chart that it is easy to understand why many individual

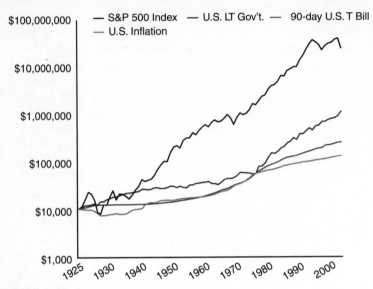

FIGURE 6.3   Compelling Returns on Stock Investments Drew in Clients
Stocks represented by Standard & Poor's (S&P) 500 Index, long-term government bonds by 20-year U.S. Treasury bonds, 90-day U.S. Treasury bills and inflation by the Consumer Price Index (CIP through November, 2008). The S&P 500 Index is an unmanaged, weighted index comprising 500 widely held common stocks varying in composition. Returns consist of income, capital appreciation (or depreciation), and currency gains (or losses). Certain markets have experienced significant year-to-year fluctuations and negative returns from time to time. Stocks are more volatile and subject to greater risks than other asset classes. Indexes are not available for direct investment. Past performance is not a guarantee of future results.
Source: Ned Davis Research, used with permission.

investors fall victim to the myth of the 10 percent return. The myth of the 10 percent return speaks to the incorrect assumptions under which all too many individual investors operate. While it is true that the annualized returns on the S&P 500 going back to the mid-1920s is approximately 10 percent per annum, to anticipate anywhere near this amount in any given year is quite an unrealistic expectation.

In fact, as Figure 6.4 shows, in the past 83 years, there have only been five times that the S&P 500 has even returned between 8 percent and 12 percent in any given calendar year, with a vast majority of calendar year returns nowhere near the 10 percent average.

It is not only the case that individual year-by-year returns can be far away from the historical average of the stock market, but even longer-term

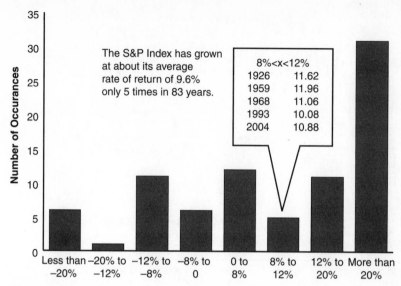

FIGURE 6.4   Rarely Do Stocks Behave As Might Be Expected
Ibbotson data beginning 12/31/26 through 12/31/70. Standard & Poor's data beginning 1/1/71 through 12/31/06. The S&P 500 Index comprised of 500 widely held common stocks varying in composition and is not available for direct investment. Past performance does not guarantee future results. Performance is calculated assuming reinvestment of all dividends and capital gains on a daily basis.
Source: Ibbotson Associates and Standard & Poor's, used with permission.

average returns can stray significantly away from the historical average. For instance, let's examine Figure 6.5, which shows rolling 10-year returns on the S&P 500 for the past 68 years.

While most any investor would probably classify a 10-year holding period as long term, what you can easily see is that even with this time horizon, the average returns on the market are rarely ever near 10 percent, and have been as high as 21 percent per annum and as low as -4 percent per annum over a "long term" 10-year period!

Human emotion is undoubtedly the biggest obstacle to investor success. If not properly informed, an individual investor is set up to fail from the start. The ability to educate (and continuously re-educate) clients on the truths of investing and the reality of market cycles is a critical component in properly managing client expectations. It improves the likelihood that they will stay the course during the inevitable market downturns. It is through this open, honest channel of communication that an investment organization has the best chance to truly deliver positive client outcomes.

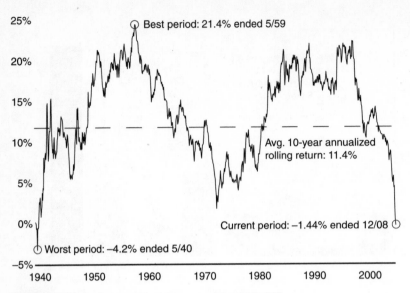

FIGURE 6.5   Rolling 10-Year Return of the S&P 500

The S&P 500 Index is an unmanaged, weighted index comprising 500 widely held common stocks varying in composition and unavailable for direct investment. Past performance does not guarantee future results. Performance is calculated assuming reinvestment of all dividends and capital gains on a daily basis.

Source: Ned Davis Research; used with permission.

THE MATHEMATICS OF RECOVERY

> *Rule #1: Never lose money. Rule #2: Never forget rule #1.*
> —Warren Buffett

There is a reason that most successful investors believe that the best offense is a good defense. The debilitating effects that large losses can have on a portfolio's ability to grow over time are astonishing. The mathematics of recovery are such so that if an investor does not have a plan in place to limit losses during inevitable market declines, they will most likely spend many precious years of their investing lifetime just recouping their losses in an attempt to get back to even. In theory, it is quite simple: If you lose 50 percent on your investment, you need to return 100 percent (not just 50 percent) to get back to even. This rather elementary textbook example does a good job of showing the negative effects that large losses have on a portfolio's ability to compound returns. In reality, however, it is more alarming than it is elementary. As Table 6.1 highlights, there have been

TABLE 6.1 The Last 13 Bears

	Date of Market Trough	Peak to Trough TR Performance	Duration of Bear Market
1	June 13, 1949	−18%	36.5 months
2	October 22, 1957	−15%	14.5 months
3	June 26, 1962	−27%	6.5 months
4	October 7, 1966	−20%	8 months
5	May 26, 1970	−33%	18 months
6	October 3, 1974	−45%	20.5 months
7	March 6, 1978	−14%	17.5 months
8	August 12, 1982	−19%	20.5 months
9	December 4, 1987	−33%	3.5 months
10	October 11, 1990	−19%	3 months
11	August 31, 1998	−19%	1.5 months
12	October 9, 2002	−45%	30.5 months
13	November 20, 2008	−51%	13.5 months
Average Bear Market Performance:		−28%	Average Duration: 14.9 months

There have been 13 bear markets since 1946 (including the bear market started Oct. 2007, or about every 4–5 years on average).
Returns are based on total returns and include the reinvestment of dividends.* 12 months from date of market trough. S&P 500 Index is comprised of 500 widely held common stocks varying in composition.
Source: Ned Davis Research, used with permission.[6]

13 bear markets in the post-World War II era, with an average decline of −28 percent.

What this means is that on average, an investor will have to be prepared for a bear market every 4–5 years, and if they do not have a plan in place to limit losses, they will need to experience an upside recovery of +39 percent just to get themselves out of the hole they've dug! And that is simply using averages. If it happens to be one of the deeper bear markets, such as the post-TMT bear of 2000–2002 or the market crash of 2008, the consequences of not having a plan in place to protect wealth can be life altering.

DILEMMA: INVESTMENT FIRM OR DISTRIBUTION SHOP?

We want to diversify our revenues. We want to always have something to sell. We want to smooth out our earnings. We have to be "commercial."

All are laudable goals, but these are often code words for "distribution shop." Distribution shops sell that which people will buy, regardless of their views on the likelihood of the longer-term merits of the investment. This is a fast path down a slippery slope whose end is all too clear. Distribution shops might be good environments for salesmen (for a while anyway), but they are not good places for true stewards of client assets. Each of the three authors of this book has had the opportunity to observe the resultant damage to clients that occurs when an investment firm shifts its focus from investment superiority to product distribution. As discussed in Chapter 1 and throughout this text, size and complexity are often, though not always, the culprits of this shift. Unfortunately, sometimes the shift happens so gradually that you are unaware it is taking place until it hits you in the face.

As discussed, an ongoing challenge in the asset management business is that client wants are often in conflict with client needs. Clients typically want to invest in the areas of the market that have recently done well, which is normally when they will not be well-compensated for the risks of investing on a go-forward basis. Clients typically have little to no appetite for investments that have recently fared poorly, when in fact their lower prices may provide attractive valuations and significant forward-looking opportunities.

How an investment organization responds to the reality of client behavior often speaks volumes about whether that organization is an investment firm or a distribution shop. Some investment organizations seek to capitalize on client emotion by creating thematic products based on the whims and desires of the market. These firms often produce based on salability rather than sustainability and long-term investment merit. We have witnessed the launching of scores of technology sector mutual funds leading up to the market top in March 2000, the launch of many principal protection funds in the aftermath of the tech bubble, and more recently the launch of scores of emerging market and commodity funds in 2007 and 2008. These offerings are rationalized in the following way: *Clients are going to buy these funds from somebody, so they might as well buy them from us.*

These firms tend to have an asymmetric focus on current sales and revenues, as opposed to quality and sustainability of assets under management, durability of revenue, and protection of the reputation of the franchise. This sort of mentality can lead their client-facing teams to push capabilities with the hottest three-year returns, often just in time for these strategies to cool off. The executives of these firms may be of the cynical—or some may suggest realistic—view that investor behavior is unchangeable, and rather than try to modify it, they seek to capitalize on it by rotating client money from one investment to the next. While few executives would admit that they are more interested in doing business rather than in building a business, the pressure for short-term results is strong, and the evidence would suggest that a positive client experience is not a top priority for many asset managers. History has shown us that reputation is easier lost than restored. Once an investment firm loses its reputation and is instead viewed as a distribution shop, it is hard to impossible to win back clients. Thus, what may provide positive short-term results today can have the unintended consequence of sowing the seeds for disaster tomorrow.

An investment firm that defines success through the actual returns experienced by their clients, as opposed to the advertised returns posted in their marketing literature, must be committed to placing stewardship ahead of salesmanship, and focus on helping clients achieve their goals. This is much easier said than done, and it all starts with culture. What's most important to the leadership of the firm? How are employees recognized, promoted, and compensated? How does management respond when their style is not being rewarded by prevailing market conditions?

THE IMPORTANCE OF CULTURE

Here we go again. As we have repeatedly discussed, the foundation of long-term success begins with the firm's culture, which is a direct reflection of its leadership team. The entire team must live the firm's values and evaluate themselves, and their colleagues, on how well they do so. This all starts with hiring the right kind of people into an organization and reinforcing the positive aspects of the culture that the management team is trying to foster. We have talked about this from a variety of perspectives, but here we focus on the most important aspect as it relates to communication.

The ideal culture for effective communication is one of ownership. By ownership, we mean acting as if your name is on the door (whether it is or not). In this type of an environment, everyone in the organization would make decisions as if they owned the company. It is through this mindset that people truly understand that the business is about gathering and retaining assets, and doing so within a sensible cost and revenue structure. It is also understood that the best way to maximize revenue and long-term profitability is to deliver an excellent client experience. Unfortunately, too many people in the asset management industry mistakenly think of it as a sales business. While gathering assets is vitally important to a successful investment firm, without an equal focus on retaining assets the firm will never achieve excellence.

As it relates to managing and evaluating the sales professionals, there's an old adage: That which gets measured gets done. We talked about the importance of measurable KPIs in Chapter 3. As it relates to the business function, appropriately aligned KPIs are also critical. The more you measure people on the ingredients of client success, rather than strictly on sales goals, the more successful your firm will be. That is not to suggest that the sales of wholesalers/client advisors are not of importance. After all, you need sales professionals who are capable of getting people to invest with you! However, sales data should only be one data point.

Other extremely important metrics are the number of total clients, the length of client tenure, the holding period of particular capabilities, the number of distinct capabilities (for multi-product firms), and number of client meetings—not only with prospects, but with existing clients as well. If you agree with the core philosophy that extending the client holding period is job number one, then the compensation structure should be set up in a way that not only rewards those who bring in the most assets, but also those who have the ability to keep clients invested for the longest period of time. Many compensation schemes pay only for upfront sales, and if they do pay on assets or revenues, it is usually limited to just a few years. Sales professionals should be just as motivated to keep clients invested as they are to get clients to invest in the first place.

Once a successful ownership culture has been created, it is critically important to continuously reinforce it. The best way to reinforce the culture within the business function is also to consistently apply the firm's values in the way you hire, fire, compensate, and recognize employees at the firm. The best-paid client-facing employees should be the ones who are most adept at retaining assets through difficult periods and growing assets with long-term investors. These are those professionals who can win new clients while keeping existing clients invested through the tough times. Many firms make the mistake of rewarding the exceptional sales person who does a fantastic job of bringing in new assets, yet who has little or no regard for what the client does once they invest the money. While this model may bring short-term success, it is inherently flawed and eventually leads to long-term client dissatisfaction. The sales folks who are recognized should be those who truly believe that the key to a successful investment firm is a positive client experience—and that the keys to a positive client experience are realistic expectations and a long time horizon.

SALES AND MARKETING IN AN INVESTMENT FIRM

As has been reiterated throughout this chapter, gathering and retaining assets are the critical components to long-term profitability. While sales are obviously a crucial element towards achieving this success, client retention is every bit as, if not more, important—and all too often not properly recognized. How valuable is a manager's skill if the clients don't stay the course and actually experience the record? Because most successful investment managers experience multi-year periods of poor performance in their path to superior long-term returns, a strong client service commitment is vital. Thus, an excellent investment organization needs strong client advisors and excellent marketing people who can develop high-impact client communication.

Good wholesalers (those who cultivate deep, diversified, and durable relationships with high-quality financial advisors) and good client advisors (who do the same with institutional clients) are those who are committed to client success. They recognize that their efforts have as much (or more) of an impact on the client experience as does the efforts of the portfolio manager. They work hard to make sure that clients understand what they are buying, and they speak to the downside potential of an investment with as much clarity as they do the upside. They make sure that clients understand the reality of market cycles and the impact of extreme loss on long-term returns. They make sure that clients understand the very important concept of time-period bias—the idea that any particular one-, three-, five-, or ten-year period may be heavily influenced by a factor that may not last in future time periods. They want to make sure that clients understand that embedded in the long-term results are periods of underperformance, often measured in years. They provide clients with an understanding of what type of market conditions tend to be most conducive to positive results and what type of market conditions are typically most challenging. They make sure that clients understand that the patient investor typically has been rewarded, and that the impatient investor typically has been penalized. They are as committed to keeping the client invested as they were in getting the client invested.

An excellent investment firm is led by a combination of like-minded investment professionals and business professionals. The first order of business is to identify your competitive advantage, for without a competitive advantage you simply cannot compete. The second order of business is to identify a problem that your competitive advantage is particularly adept at solving. For example, at UBS Global Asset Management, we determined that our most compelling competitive advantage was asset allocation and multi-asset portfolio construction. We determined that the best consumers of this capability were the financial advisors who operated in an open architecture environment where too many choices had led to poor decision making and performance chasing. Rather than continue to package combinations of five-star managers to create two-star client experiences, these financial advisors were open to an alternative to the "best of breed" manager approach. They were increasingly finding that they could manage money or manage clients, but it was extremely difficult to do both with distinction. They discovered that if they found a credible way to liberate themselves from the crushing burdens of manager selection and portfolio construction, they could spend more time with existing clients (and modify their self-destructive behaviors of performance chasing).

A chief marketing officer (CMO) needs to identify the highest conviction forward-looking ideas from the investment team, and then lead the sales and marketing organization around these concepts. Unfortunately, what is sometimes done in the industry is the exact opposite. Some firms have the distribution side dictate to the investment teams what type of strategies to produce. This will inevitably lead to performance chasing and poor client results. It is true that the relationship professionals can often identify the specific problem that their clients need to address (e.g. clients taking insufficient risk to achieve their long-term goals or a mismatch in liabilities relative to assets). When this is the case, they should work with the investment teams on ways to best solve the problem in a credible and sustainable way and not according to what has the potential to raise the most assets.

Once the competitive advantage is established, the client problem is recognized, and the best solution is developed, one must further segment the client base. This is where being privately owned, as opposed to a public company, can be very advantageous. With a privately held asset management firm, there is less pressure to grow just for growth's sake, and no pressure to meet analyst expectations or shareholder demands. This freedom allows an asset manager to selectively identify which clients are best suited to benefit from the firm's investment management skills. It is through identifying the optimal client base (not necessarily biggest client base) that the probability of delivering superior client outcomes is maximized.

Once your business proposition is formed, the next step is building the client-facing team. It is imperative to hire client-facing people who are articulate, driven, and possess conviction in the firm's mission and approach. You need people who can develop marketing material for client solicitation and ongoing communication. Once again, reasonable expectations and longer holding periods are vitally important. Therefore, all communication should be straightforward, easy to understand, and geared toward setting realistic expectations.

The best approach to creating the optimal marketing material is to create it in conjunction with the client-facing teams. It is through the feedback of these people that the material can be tailored to best suit client needs. Once created, most material should be walked through with clients and prospects—not just mailed. If left to interpret marketing pieces on their own, clients will often misconstrue the message that is attempting to be conveyed. Due to time constraints on the client-facing people, the number of individual conversations that can take place to walk clients through marketing material is inherently limited. It is here that a firm can leverage their resources and use technology to broaden the distribution of the message, while still assuring that it is delivered in the manner it is intended to be. A compelling website with video clips of top investment and business leaders can be a very effective tool for a firm to utilize. More and more clients want access to the investment leaders, and they want access when it's most convenient for them to review. Thus, making podcasts and video clips available is a very useful tool in meeting client needs.

CONCLUSION

Human emotion will always be the greatest impediment to investor success. If history has taught us anything, it is that the collective wisdom of the masses will invariably cause investors to do the wrong thing at the wrong time. From an asset management firm's perspective, there are two routes that can be taken: A firm can look to exploit the predictable behavior of investors by catering to their appetite for that which has done well in the past, or it can look to lead clients by managing their emotions, educating them on the reality of market cycles, and making the firm's true mission to deliver superior client outcomes. The former of the two is unfortunately the road most traveled in the asset management industry. It is far easier to give clients that which they desire and that which is easy to sell than it is to give them what they need. The easy sale is often the wrong sale, and this approach eventually leads to a lack of trust from clients, and ultimately diminution of firm reputation. The road less traveled, however, is the path to successful stewardship. Through a culture built around the idea that the best long-term business strategy is to do right by the client, an investment firm has the ability to do more than just raise money and generate fees, it has the ability to help clients truly reach their investment goals.

APPENDIX: CLIENT COMMUNICATION IN EXTREME MARKET CONDITIONS

Creating an organization with a culture built around real-life client results is essential to achieving long-term success; however it is arguably never as critical as during periods of extreme market dislocation. It is in periods of time like this that investor emotion is at its highest and the pressure on clients to succumb to human nature is greatest. While there have been many of these instances throughout time, one of the most extreme, and undoubtedly the most relevant today, is the current panic-driven bear market that started in the fourth quarter of 2007 and has continued through the first quarter of 2009. As investor equity wealth has essentially been cut in half, and the negative news on the economy seems to be never ending, many clients are capitulating to their fears and retreating from their long-term investment plans. In this addendum, we will take a look at how one firm has approached these extremely challenging market conditions in its efforts to communicate with and educate clients. We will not only discuss the key concepts that we want to convey, but we will also take a look at some of the core visuals used to help deliver the right messages to clients.

The events of 2008, particularly in the fourth quarter, could be best described not as a traditional bear market, but rather as a panic-driven market crash led by the indiscriminate selling of risky assets. With volatility and market losses at levels not seen since the Great Depression, many investors have abandoned their long-term investment plans and fled from risky assets to the safety of treasuries and cash; this is the exact same pattern that ultimately leads to the results of the previously discussed Dalbar study. Our goal in interacting with clients is to save them from succumbing to the fears of the moment and to get them focused on their long-term plan. Our path to achieving this goal is through heightened client education and constant client communication. We first want to put 2008 in the proper perspective for clients so that they have the necessary understanding of the historical time period they are presently living through. After that, we look to educate clients on the reality of market cycles so that they are able to put 2008 in its proper context when making decisions that can alter their long-term financial plan.

The first step towards putting 2008 in perspective is demonstrating how this truly is a "take no prisoners" bear market. Unlike previous bear markets, where some asset classes held up relatively well and provided a buffer in a diversified portfolio, this market is one in which there truly was no place to hide for an investor seeking inflation-beating returns over time. Table 6A.1 analyzes the past three major U.S. bear markets and the performance of all Morningstar categories in each.

As you can see, in both the 1987 crash and 2000–2002 post-TMT bubble bear market, there were some asset classes that provided relief as the domestic equity markets declined. In this current market, it did not matter whether a client was diversified in large-cap, mid-cap, or small cap, growth or value, domestic or international, developed or developing markets; with the exception of government bonds, all asset classes have declined, particularly the equity asset classes where the losses have been quite severe.

In a period of time like this, investors who relied upon diversification as a means of loss limitation in difficult times may conclude that its merits are no longer valid. There is a strong tendency for investors to subscribe to the "this time is different" theory and extrapolate the events of the past year in perpetuity. This leads to them making long-term investment decisions based on

TABLE 6A.1 The 2008–2009 Bear Market: No Place to Hide

	Current Bear (annualized) 10/89/07–2/28/09	2000–2002 Bear (annualized) 4/1/00–10/31/02	1987 Bear (annualized) 8/1/87–12/31/87
Global Real Estate	−52.72	10.04	
Diversified Emerging Mkts	−47.60	−18.49	
Foreign Small/Mid Value	−47.56	−11.61	
Foreign Small/Mid Growth	−46.33	−26.23	
Foreign Large Growth	−44.30	−25.07	−16.86
Foreign Large Blend	−44.19	−21.24	−18.17
Foreign Large Value	−43.75	−13.88	−19.81
Small Growth	−42.94	−21.52	−25.38
Small Blend	−42.37	−5.07	−24.05
Large Value	−41.67	−7.44	−19.63
Mid-Cap Growth	−41.42	−25.05	−25.34
World Stock	−41.31	−20.03	−22.05
Small Value	−41.28	4.50	−25.06
Mid-Cap Blend	−40.92	−9.88	−21.50
Mid-Cap Value	−40.76	0.04	−19.99
Large Blend	−39.62	−17.72	−20.82
Large Growth	−38.47	−25.60	−23.83
Natural Res	−36.74	−0.50	−25.01
World Allocation	−29.19	−5.07	−9.89
Moderate Allocation	−28.54	−7.65	−13.65
High Yield Bond	−19.92	−4.39	−3.38
Conservative Allocation	−18.63	−1.14	−5.35
Long-Short	−16.57	4.99	−16.42
Emerging Markets Bond	−14.63	8.43	
Long-Term Bond	−6.22	7.34	1.87
Intermediate-Term Bond	−3.35	7.97	2.67
World Bond	−3.08	5.18	10.27
Short-Term Bond	−2.53	6.90	2.02
Short Government	4.77	7.90	3.04
Intermediate Government	5.28	9.13	2.86
Long Government	9.48	10.10	4.39

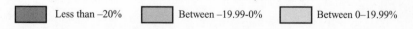 Less than −20%   Between −19.99–0%   Between 0–19.99%

Source: Morningstar category averages. Used with permission.

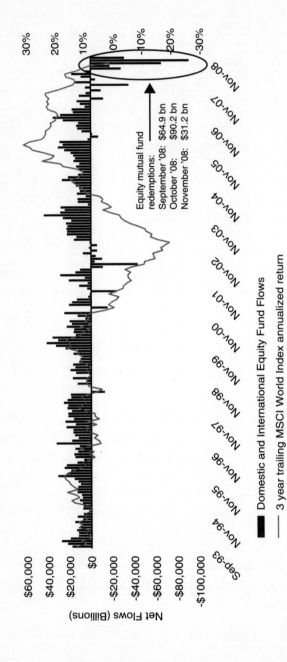

FIGURE 6A.1 Equity Funds' Record Outflows

Includes long-term domestic and international mutual funds. For illustrative purposes only. Mutual fund sales, redemptions, exchanges, reinvested dividends, and assets under management are based on monthly data calculated by FRC.

Source: Financial Research Corporation (FRC); used with permission.

152

the past 12 months, forever altering their wealth accumulation. In trying to put 2008 in its necessary context, we strive to explain to clients that this time is *not* different. Of course, the underlying causes and details of this credit crisis are different than the bursting of the TMT bubble earlier this decade, which in turn is different than the market crash of 1987; however, the one constant throughout each of them is the human response. In periods of market duress, scared investors will inevitably sell their risky assets at panic prices, driving the markets down even further. This concept is more than just anecdotal, for as with previous periods of time, we have the fund flow data to provide factual support.

Very similar to Figure 6.1, which analyzed how investors behaved during the rise and fall of the TMT bubble, Figure 6A.1 shows fund flows into domestic and international equity mutual funds over the past 15 years, and what the trailing three-year annualized return on the MSCI World Index was throughout that time.

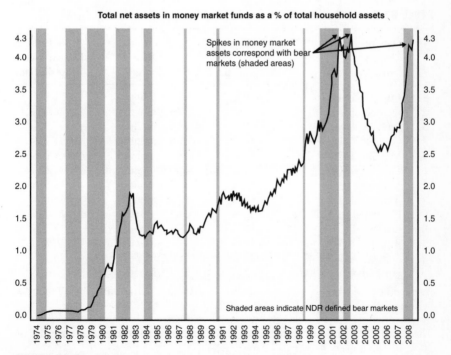

FIGURE 6A.2 The Flight to Quality = A Flight to Cash
Monthly data 1/31/74-8/31/08. A bear market is defined here as a 30 percent drop in the Dow Jones Industrial Average after 50 calendar days or a 13 percent decline after 145 calendar days.
Source: Ned Davis Research. Used with permission.

As you can see in Figure 6A.2 the flight from equity funds into money market funds towards the latter part of 2008 was so incredibly dramatic that investors pulled out over $185 billion in the three months ending in November, with $52.1 billion of that coming in one week alone! (We should add a footnote that this was the weekend ending October 9, 2008.) The net outflows in 2008 will go down amongst the worst on record, and not surprisingly, we are seeing investors flee to the perceived safety of cash and cash-equivalent vehicles. Figure 6A.2 shows the total net assets in money market funds as a percentage of total household assets over the past 35 years.

While flows into money market funds have historically tended to spike in bear markets, what you can see is that during this current bear we are seeing near-historic levels of cash being placed on the sidelines. While this may give investors some short-term piece of mind, it is this behavior that ultimately leads to the hideous real-life investor returns that clients often achieve. That

TABLE 6A.2 The Importance of Staying Invested

	Date of Market Trough	Peak to Trough TR Performance	Duration of Bear Market	% Total Return 1-year post decline
1	June 13, 1949	−18%	36.5 months	51.8%
2	October 22, 1957	−15%	14.5 months	36.4%
3	June 26, 1962	−27%	6.5 months	37.2%
4	October 7, 1966	−20%	8 months	37.7%
5	May 26, 1970	−33%	18 months	49.0%
6	October 3, 1974	−45%	20.5 months	44.4%
7	March 6, 1978	−14%	17.5 months	18.5%
8	August 12, 1982	−19%	20.5 months	66.0%
9	December 4, 1987	−33%	3.5 months	27.1%
10	October 11, 1990	−19%	3 months	33.5%
11	August 31, 1998	−19%	1.5 months	39.8%
12	October 9, 2002	−45%	30.5 months	36.1%
13	November 20, 2008	−51%	13.5 months	?
Average Bear Market Performance:	−28%	Average Duration:	14.9 months

There have been 13 bear markets since 1946 (including the bear market started Oct. 2007, or about every 4–5 years on average).

Returns are based on total returns and include the reinvestment of dividends.* 12 months from date of market trough. S&P 500 Index is comprised of 500 widely held common stocks varying in composition.

Source: Ned Davis Research.

is why after putting 2008 in the proper context, it is important to educate clients on the reality of market cycles.

To begin educating clients on the reality of market cycles, you must first get them comfortable with the fact that bear markets are an unavoidable part of long-term investing. We use Table 6A.2, an enhanced version of Figure 6.6, to demonstrate the inevitability of these difficult periods to clients.

Since 1946, there have been 13 bear markets, meaning that clients should expect to experience one on average of every 4–5 years. Just as important as getting clients to accept bear markets as an inevitable part of investing is getting them to focus on full market cycles, and the truth that bull markets will follow bear markets (and visa-versa) just as surely as night follows day. That is why when discussing this chart with clients we also look at the market recovery from its bottom. The column on the right shows the 12-month post-bear market return for each of the bear markets shown. It is important for clients to see that equity returns coming out of episodes of huge negative returns have historically been quite extraordinary.

The truth, however, is that those exceptional returns were captured only by investors who found the courage to remain rationally exposed to equities before the turnaround. Those who waited in cash for the markets to turn around, as we saw a record number of people doing in the first quarter of 2009, usually missed out dearly on the recovery. It is also important for clients to realize that while the first 12-month returns from the bottom of a market are usually very strong, it is normally the early stages of the first year that experiences the largest increase. Historically, over 40 percent of the first year of recovery comes within the first three months. So even those clients who get back into the market relatively soon after the bottom, which very few do, will have severely hindered their portfolio's ability to compound wealth over time.

While we want clients to realize the importance of having the fortitude to stay invested so that they don't miss out on the early stages of market recovery, it is also important that we refocus their attention to the long term. As previously discussed, we do not think looking at an 85-year average is a responsible way to communicate to clients; that is why we attempt break down the long term in a more realistic manner, using the "Feast or Famine" and "Rolling 10-yr Return Charts." In periods of extreme trepidation, such as the present, we also find it important to show how the market has done over the longer term from different starting points. History has shown that after long periods of poor performance, the market has generally experienced subsequent long-term periods of superior returns. We use Figure 6A.3 and Table 6A.3 to illustrate that point. Figure 6A.3 shows a distribution of rolling 10-year returns of the S&P 500 on a quarterly basis. Rolling 10-year

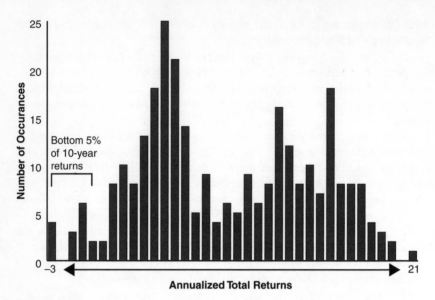

FIGURE 6A.3 Distribution of Quarter-ending 10-Year S&P 500 Returns
Source: Leuthold Group. Used with permission. Past performance does not guarantee future results.

returns below 3.9 percent a year comprise the bottom decile, those north of 17.5 percent per annum make up the top decile.

The current rolling 10-year period on the S&P 500 not only ranks it in the bottom decile, but even in the bottom 5 percent. With the past decade of stock market returns among the worst ever, it is understandable that investors would be hesitant to re-enter the equity markets; that is why, after putting the past decade in its historical perspective, we think it is important to further examine how the markets have generally done following periods of similar disappointing returns. Table 6A.3 builds upon the previous figure by showing the subsequent 10-year return for all data points in the bottom 5 percent.

As you can see, the 10-year returns subsequent to the lowest 5 percent of previous 10-year periods have been very attractive.

While making sure clients understand the nature of the financial markets is imperative, education alone is not enough. The manner and frequency in which clients are communicated with is just as important in managing investor emotions. It is in periods of time like this that there is no such thing as over-communication.

The client-facing professionals need to be proactive and highly visible. They need to emote empathy and conviction. When discussing the cyclicality

TABLE 6A.3 10-Year Returns after Worst Equity Performance Periods

	Prior 10-yr Avg. Ann. Return	Avg. Ann. Return	Cum. Return
Q2 1939 to Q2 1949	−3.65	8.62	129
Q1 1939 to Q1 1949	−2.79	9.12	139
Q3 1939 to Q3 1949	−2.74	7.74	111
Q1 1938 to Q1 1948	−2.54	11.76	204
Q1 1940 to Q1 1950	−1.42	9.65	151
Q2 1940 to Q2 1950	−1.42	12.19	216
Q4 1938 to Q4 1948	−0.65	7.21	101 Worst
Q3 1938 to Q3 1948	−0.10	8.12	118
Q3 1940 to Q3 1950	0.18	12.57	227
Q4 1937 to Q4 1947	0.20	9.61	150
Q4 1939 to Q4 1949	0.23	9.09	139
Q2 1938 to Q2 1948	0.44	9.52	148
Q3 1974 to Q3 1984	0.49	15.58	325 Best
Q1 1941 to Q1 1951	0.71	14.47	286
Q4 1974 to Q4 1984	1.24	14.76	296
		Average 10.76%	183%

Source: Leuthold Group. Used with permission. Past performance does not guarantee future results.

of markets, particularly in periods of time such as the present, it is critical that an investment organization be responsibly confident. It would be very easy for a client-facing individual to misuse any of the aforementioned slides as a market call on why a client should invest now. The fact of the matter is that no one knows when the peak or trough of any market is going to be, and that is why, above anything else, it is paramount that client-facing professionals do not give the impression that they are being predictive about the future. The statement that "past performance is no guarantee of future results" should be more than just a legal disclaimer on an investment organization's marketing literature, it should be the motto by which all client-facing individuals conduct their daily activities. While we do believe that the law of market cycles has not been repealed, and that the market will eventually recover, we do not try to pretend we know when it will happen. Our messaging is that a true long-term investor should not get caught up in the emotions of the moment, but rather should decide on an appropriate long-term investment plan and not stray from their plan when they are feeling overly optimistic or fearful about the current environment.

CHAPTER 7

Where are the Clients' Yachts?

Reasonable Fee Structures

One important issue that has significance for investment performance, business performance, and ultimately investor outcomes, is fees. While fees are always a topic of discussion, the market events of 2008 and 2009 have magnified investors' attention on the issue. In this chapter, we will discuss a number of important considerations related to the topic, with a specific focus on performance fee structures. We have always believed that if the administrative and operational hurdles to performance fees that exist in some product structures could be overcome, performance fees would be one of the best ways to align incentives of investors and managers of active investment strategies.

Base fees, also known as management fees, are typically charged as a percentage of assets under management and range from 10 basis points (.10 percent) to as high as 300 basis points (3.0 percent) or even higher. These fees are collected based on the value of assets under management. Typically these are accrued monthly and paid quarterly. While growth of assets through positive investment performance serves to help align manager incentives with those of investors, this is really true only on the margin.

Performance fees are also wide ranging, and the structures can be complex and cumbersome to administer. In a typical performance fee arrangement, the manager is entitled to some portion of the net gains that she generates for her clients. In a typical hedge fund in recent years, it was not uncommon to see performance fees of 20 percent of net portfolio gains. Further, the performance fee is typically preceded by a base fee. When a manager quotes its fee as "2 & 20," it means that the manger charges a 2 percent base fee plus 20 percent of gains in excess of the base fee. Another, though somewhat less utilized, fee structure includes a base fee, plus participation by the manager in gains beyond a pre-specified hurdle. For example a fee quoted as "1 & 10/5" means that the manager charges a 1 percent base fee plus takes 10 percent of the gains over a hurdle of 5 percent.

In this chapter we explore the ways in which incentive structures like these, while perhaps intended to align investor interests, have some significant pitfalls. We discuss some of the perverse incentives that can ensue, and we put forth ideas for structures that improve the alignment of incentives between asset managers and their clients.

In Chapter 5 we introduced "phantastic objects" to enhance our understanding of market instability, in particular their contribution to market bubbles and panics. Phantastic objects aid our understanding of manager compensation structures as well.

Emotions and states of mind determine our perceptions of reality. Excitement over Soros-like hedge fund returns and prior successes of the Harvard and Yale endowments feed the phantasies of investors world over. Individually and collectively a phantasy of high, market-neutral returns became the mental objects of market participants. So strong were the phantasies of investment success that market prices for hedge funds, private equity, and other alternative investments rose to exceed reasonable expectation for returns. Despite ample research by respected academics like Burton Malkiel[1] about the absence of high excess returns and the commonly posed question, "Are alternative vehicles funds or compensation schemes?" investors bought high-priced funds.

Poor performance of a number of these alternative investment funds during the 2008 financial crisis has likely dealt a crippling blow to their high fee structures. The phantastic objects of investors were revealed to be fantastically unreal. So we ask ourselves, what is a superior manager fee structure? What are its characteristics?

An appropriately designed fee structure must incorporate client needs and align the interests of the manager and the client. But, that is easier said than done. The client can dictate a desired fee structure because he need only compel his unique needs and interest on multiple managers. The manager, on the other hand, must consider the needs and interests of all current and potential clients. The manager incurs the additional burden of comparability with other managers. The objective of this chapter is to propose a compensation structure that can be used by many participants in the market.

With this objective in mind, the attributes of an appropriate compensation structure include:

- Alignment of manager behaviors and client objectives.
- Cover basic operating expenses with a management fee.
- Compensation for investor skill, as opposed to luck.
- Hindrance to inappropriate risk-taking.

- Compensation symmetry.
- Relatively low fee for beta, or market exposure.
- Relatively high fee for alpha, or skill, including active management of multiple betas.
- Limited path dependence to impede gaming.

We seek such a compensation structure as we analyze some of the problems that have reared their heads with existing structures in recent years.

THE "GAMMA TRADE"

Beginning in 1973 with the development of Fischer Black's and Myron Scholes' option pricing model, the investment industry began an exciting financial engineering journey. Derivatives fostered risk divisibility and sharing that economists theorized would enable greater financial efficiency. This efficiency would improve productivity by reducing risk and increasing returns to capital investments.

Shortly after Brian began his career working for ContiCommodity, a Futures Commission Merchant (FCM), he signed on to the financial engineering journey when Black and Scholes modified their option pricing formula for marginable futures contracts. A world of opportunity emerged. Unfortunately, not all of that opportunity was beneficial for clients or, for that matter, ethical.

While undertaking research in financial futures and options, Brian witnessed an incredible practice, the sale of a sure bet, referred to as a "gamma trade." The trade was very simple, involving the sale of out-of-the-money call and put options. There is no need to understand put and call option pricing to understand the insidious nature of the gamma trade. The seller of call and put options collects option premiums at the time of the sale. If the market price of the underlying instrument—a futures contract in this case—remains steady, the premium accrues to the seller. At expiration of the options, often after only a few months, the seller retains the entire premium.

The gamma trade has a payoff pattern that appears solid. The options enable leveraged exposure to the underlying futures instrument, and the client's account is credited with the option premium when the position is initiated. In Figure 7.1, we show this payoff structure. All the client has to do is hope that the price of the underlying futures contract does not move by more than 15 percent in either direction. If it does not, the client keeps the option premiums.

The gamma trade proved to be compelling for many market participants. In fact, I witnessed a U.S. Savings and Loan (S&L) client execute these trades

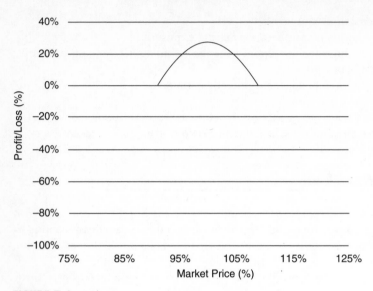

FIGURE 7.1　The Client's View: Gamma Trade Profit and Loss

quite profitably for well over a year. Emboldened by period after period of profitability, the S&L gradually increased its position and the two brokers banked increasingly large commission checks. It seemed both fitting and foreboding that one of the brokers won a Corvette for being that year's most profitable salesman, garnering huge praise from the firm and his clients. The punchbowl was full and the party was raging.

One fateful day, however, that party came to an abrupt end. Prices punched through the lowest levels that either the S&L or the brokers had previously fathomed. The S&L was instantaneously taken to the brink of bankruptcy. The client panicked. One of the brokers simply froze and became unresponsive to the deepening crisis. Luckily, the other broker remained calm. How did this crisis occur?

Hide and Seek

In a gamma trade, more and more options are sold at option strike prices further from the initial market price of the underlying futures contract. Large price moves not only erode option premiums booked on the initial sales, if positions are large enough they can result in colossal losses. Expanding the view of the gamma trade chart shows the losses to which the brokers had exposed the S&L. While a 15 percent rise or fall in the futures price as shown in Figure 7.1 results in a breakeven trade, a move of 20 percent, as can be seen in the expanded view of Figure 7.2, would completely erode not just the margin value, but also the market value of the underlying futures contracts. The broker who remained calm, ignoring his frozen colleague, single-handedly navigated the S&L away from the precipice.

The gamma trade provided stable income in a low-volatility environment, giving it the appearance of a strategy that diversified the portfolio. Variation was mostly due to noise that gave the appearance of a high-return, market-neutral strategy. However, the gamma trade produced losses, which ballooned because of the leverage inherent in derivatives and became crippling as steady returns bolstered confidence and encouraged larger positions. This was especially true when the market moved atypically. In reality, the addition of the gamma trade to increase diversification actually delivered less diversification when it was needed most.

ContiCommodity ultimately collapsed, and REFCO took it over, putting it out of its misery. Brian happened to be on vacation, canoeing through the Canadian wilderness. He returned to Chicago late Sunday night, dragged himself into at the Chicago Board of Trade building early the next morning, and found himself alone in a completely deserted office. An hour or so later, a colleague of Brian's strode in donning jeans and a big smile. He was clearly amused by Brian's suit and tie and quizzical look.

Tom Dittmer, the CEO and owner of REFCO, executed the best takeover Brian has ever been a party to, which is saying something since he

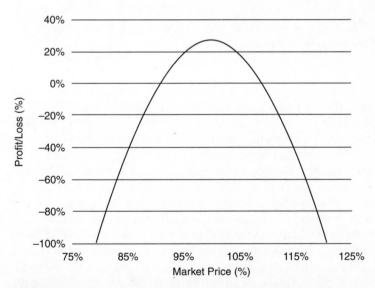

FIGURE 7.2 The Expanded View: Gamma Trade Profit and Loss

has been on the acquiree side of five mergers. Tom interviewed each Conti-Commodity employee and made an immediate hire-or-fire decision. Within a couple weeks, about 90 percent of the ContiCommodity employees were gone and there was no uncertainty for the remaining individuals. Brian stayed with REFCO for a little less than a year, leaving after he became uncomfortable with the reputational risk he assumed through his association. He didn't feel like reliving the past.

Over the course of his short career at REFCO, Tom Dittmer took a liking to Brian, or so his ego led him to believe. When Brian quit, Dittmer dispensed some valuable advice: "If you stay in the business," he said, "make sure that you are always on the receiving end of fees." After watching two brokers take an S&L to the edge of the abyss and walk away highly praised and lavishly compensated, the power of these words was not lost on Brian.

At the time of the S&L disaster, Brian was in awe by how easy it was to make money in finance, as long as you were on the receiving end of fees. The two brokers may have thought that the inevitable would not visit them, or they may have been integrity challenged. Either way, their business model was brilliantly conceived. They made money in a way that made the client feel increasingly comfortable and willing to take on increasingly large positions and incur ever growing fees. When the investment strategy failed, the business model ensured that only the clients lost and those on the receiving end of fees continued to enjoy the comforts of their mansions, sports cars, yachts, and other trophies.

People often have a very hard time distinguishing between good outcomes and good decisions.
—Bob Litterman

Having spent many years in the business and having had numerous lessons in integrity and ethics, we realize things don't change. This simple business model revisited the industry in spades with the proliferation of performance fee structures during the 1990s and 2000s. The investment environment in recent years lured clients to enter the gamma trade game in ever-larger amounts, wanting to increase exposure as much as the new performance fee business wanted clients. Low volatility meant that gamma trades stayed within the profitable range year after year. Everybody wanted in on the party, leading to increased liquidity and market efficiency, but unfortunately less profitability. There was no need for clients to worry; however, as free-flowing liquidity meant that decreasingly profitable positions could be leveraged back to the high returns of previous years. It was the party of the century, and everybody wanted to be there. Boards terminated anyone who could not keep up with the returns of their peers. Investors started niche alpha firms with compensation schemes designed as businesses purveying hopes and dreams. If you were skilled, you jumped on the bandwagon. If not, you remained with the staid traditional dinosaurs of the industry.

Before Brian left UBS, he often had the opportunity to speak with clients about the risks they were taking. By that time gamma trades had become very complex, involving currency carry trades, knock-out options, credit default swaps, leveraged loans, and synthetic credit default structures. Clients had little understanding of the exposure they had incurred. Even if they could understand the strategies, the risks were often hidden behind an opaque veil of mystery and intrigue that shrouded hedge funds and the world's banks alike. Regulators were two steps behind the industry and too busy fighting over who had jurisdiction over derivatives, never fully grasping the systemic magnitude of the issue. Off-balance sheet structured vehicles were capable of concealing the full extent of institutions' exposures.

Some investment firms were either naive or both smart and unethical, establishing businesses that preyed on the low-volatility, high-liquidity environment. As discussed in Chapter 4, it was easy to predict the outcome given the incentives created by the sustained market environment and convex fee structures (make money on positive returns and retain money on negative returns). But it was very difficult to forecast when things would unwind, and nearly impossible to anticipate the magnitude of the financial disaster that would befall the industry.

Of course, much of the blame can and should be placed on the clients who invested with these compensation schemes. Pushed to the cynical extreme, the "Financial Cookery" blog observes that The General Partners' business model is "to raise money at 2+20," not "to deliver alpha." *Theirs is a sales job* at which they have been particularly proficient. Congratulate them for it, at the expense of investors gullible enough not to carry out appropriate due diligence before investing. Whether alpha accrues is of secondary importance, whatever is claimed. If, in applying their business model, General Partners have earned supernormal returns, this speaks more to the limited negotiating capability of hedge fund investors generally. Herein lies the rub. The academics ... want to gnash teeth at those who made easy money with lemon strategies, not question the motivations of the chumps who funded them based on a PowerPoint presentation and confident smile.[2]

As we have pointed out throughout this book, it is inherently difficult to separate luck from skill in this business. The most skillful investors may in fact be entitled to sharing 20 percent (or even more) of the gains they generate for clients. However, it cannot be true that all investment firms or hedge funds are created equal. Nobody held a gun to the client's heads and forced them to invest in a strategy paying 2 & 20. However, the industry at large (investors, managers, advisors, and others) should recognize the complicit role many have played in the process. Industry participants should aggressively pursue an agenda that better aligns incentives and rewards performance in appropriate ways.

Fake Alpha

Dean P. Foster and H. Peyton Young are two academics who understood the incentives behind the gamma trade. In the *Financial Times*, Martin Wolf made their observations widely available to the industry.[3]

Foster and Young proposed a gamma trade that generated what they referred to as "fake alpha." Actually, the gains were quite real within a narrow range of prices, giving the appearance of skill. Since clients do not perceive the magnitude of risk involved, the investment appears to evidence skill as most scenarios result in gains. Foster and Young hypothesize a hedge fund charging a 2 percent base fee on assets under management and a 20 percent performance fee over a hurdle of the one-year Treasury bill return. The hedge fund receives $100 million at the beginning of the year and sells calls on an outcome, such as an equity market rise of a bit less than two standard deviations that will occur with a 10 percent probability at the end of the year. Each call requires the seller to pay $1 million if the event occurs.

Since the calls receive $1 million with a 10 percent probability, each call is worth $100,000 at the beginning of the year. Since the hedge fund can sell each call for $100,000, it will have more than $100 million to invest on day one. The hedge fund can cover exposure to 100 calls with the initial funds plus an additional 11 options with the option sale proceeds. The total that can be invested at the beginning of the year is $111.1 million.

At the end of the year, the hedge fund's investment of $111.1 million in one-year Treasury bills yielding 4 percent results in about $115.5 million. If the event does not occur—a 90% probability—the call options expire worthless and the hedge fund's clients retain $115.5 million gross of fees. If the event does occur, the hedge fund pays $111 million to the call buyers and retains a paltry $4.5 million gross of fees for the clients.[4]

The hedge fund managers receive the base fee of $2 million regardless of outcome. If the event does not occur, they retain an additional 20 percent *(15.5 percent − 4 percent) performance fee, or 2.3 percent. The fund manager makes 4.3 percent and the clients earn 11.2 percent each year that the 10 percent probability event does not occur. Foster and Young observe that there is a 59 percent chance that the hedge fund survives five years and the managers collect $23 million in fees. The clients have a 41 percent chance of losing nearly their entire investment. Add a little leverage to the scheme and the odds of compelling performance for clients and compensation for managers is simply inescapable.

If there is no transparency, even a strategy as simple as this is difficult to detect and can result in tremendous client interest. The incentives are simply too compelling. Clients and consultants chasing three-year performance and fearful of the success of peers are drawn to such funds like bees to honey. Investment firms, seeing the opportunity to garner wealth beyond their abilities and their imaginations, are equally drawn. We are not suggesting that all hedge funds ran out intentionally to put on these types of trades with the goal of enriching only themselves. However, the incentive structure does promote abuses of this nature.

The objective of this example is not to demonstrate a lack of acumen on the part of clients, consultants, or investment firms. Rather, serendipitous investment firm returns combined with asset price volatility create such noise that it is difficult to discern skill from luck, honest investors from con artists, and opportunities from disaster. As Martin Wolf observed in his *Financial Times* article, "what we have then is a huge 'lemons' problem: in this business it is really difficult to distinguish talented managers from untalented ones."[5] The "'lemons' problem" refers to George Akerlof's [p. 1] observation that "returns for good quality accrue mainly to the entire group . . . rather that to the individual seller. As a result there tends to be a reduction in the average quality of goods."[6] Such is the expected outcome behind the incentive structures of the current hedge fund business model specifically and performance fee structures generally.

ANATOMY OF A BLOWUP

We suspect that the investment industry will continue to be visited by this sort of financial crises time and again. The situation is pervasive and the conclusion well-rehearsed. However, denial runs deep. We believe that investors must look to stronger governance as the primary means of protecting investors from these types of situations in the future. As we argued in Chapter 1, clearly articulated mission and client-oriented board composition are the first and second lines of defense protecting investors. Beyond governance, only ethics, integrity, and intelligent independence—not the law or increased regulation—are likely to stand between clients and disaster.

Of course even strong boards, even corporate boards of directors, cannot prevent disaster when the trappings of short-term success seem so readily attainable. Nassim Taleb provided a diagram in *Edge* that portrays the "anatomy of a blowup." See Figure 7.3. The diagram is simple: successive periods of success result in larger risks and growing gains. However, the inevitable crisis brings perceived success to an overwhelming and abrupt end.

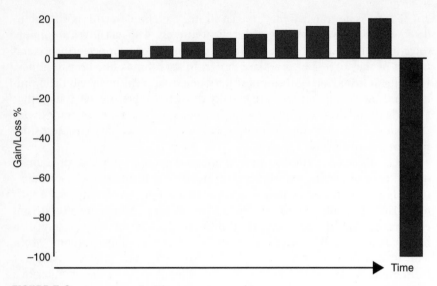

FIGURE 7.3 Anatomy of a Blowup
Source: www.edge.org.

In Figure 7.4 we offer a relatively simple chart of American Insurance Group's (AIG) annual net income for the years prior to its ultimate demise in 2008. The scheme employed by AIG was profitable, but as the number and size of AIG's positions grew, AIG's strategy became increasingly vulnerable. The result was a massive loss in 2008 and federal assistance totaling roughly $170 billion as of March 2009.

CATCH 22

If the gamma trade, incurring exposure to extreme events for high short-term returns, is so devastating, it would seem obvious that the converse of the gamma trade would be successful. Unfortunately, as noted in Chapter 4, the forces of natural behavior prevent success. The investment horizons of most investors would not likely allow for long periods of sequential, if minor, losses that would precede the tremendous return generated by a black swan event. Investment managers are caught in a perpetual Catch 22 that can only be resolved through the integrity of appropriate fee structures and the transparency discussed in Chapter 5.

A major event such as Black Monday in October 1987 would clearly have provided an adequate reward to recoup the continual option premium

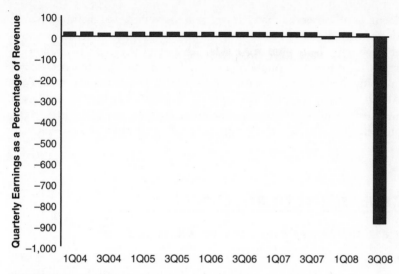

FIGURE 7.4 AIG Quarterly Earnings as Percent of Revenue

losses leading up to the event, but few clients would be willing to stick around long enough to capture the rewards.[7] One investor, the forerunner to Brinson Partners (First Chicago), adhered to its fundamental value philosophy and disciplined investment process in the months leading up to Black Monday. Unfortunately, this discipline led to an outflow of assets as clients felt that the analysis was flawed and they were missing a fundamentally justified rally.

Subsequently, First Chicago became the largest buyer of S&P futures on the day of the crash. Panic created opportunities to buy equities well below fundamental values and resulted in gains that would enable the creation of Brinson Partners. The evolving pre-crash vulnerability was anticipatable. This evolving vulnerability occurred a decade later during the technology, media, and telecommunications (TMT), or dotcom, bubble, and yet again during the credit crisis. Each of these occurrences could have been anticipated and strategies could have been initiated to generate superior investment performance, high returns, and low volatility, which is exactly what our investment team did. The keys were fundamental analysis and understanding incentives. Not all events can be anticipated, and even skilled investors can generate poor investment performance, sometimes spectacularly poor. Such unlucky outcomes from skilled investors make it difficult for clients and agents acting on behalf of clients. Poor performance by skilled investors, although temporary, makes it difficult to design a compensation structure that is beneficial for investment managers, intermediary agents, and clients.

Martin Wolf observed that, "It is, again, hard either to distinguish skill from luck or to align the interests of management, staff, shareholders and the public. It is in the interests of insiders to game the system by exploiting the returns from higher probability events. This means that businesses will suddenly blow up when the low probability disaster occurs," as was the case with AIG.[8] Existing compensation systems fail to reward managers based on cumulative returns over time periods that are truly consequential to the ultimate beneficiaries. As constructed, they fail to distinguish between luck and skill.

FAULTS OF EXISTING FEE STRUCTURES

Alignment of Manager Behaviors and Client Desires

Clients have specific investment objectives subject to numerous constraints. The objectives can usually be summarized as a maximum return subject to an acceptable level of risk. For hedge fund investments these desires tend to include market neutrality. Typically the asset pool is segmented across numerous investment managers. In order to simplify the process, often at the behest of a consultant or a financial advisor, the traditional assets are typically doled out with some benchmark and set of constraints around the benchmark. However, the segmentation of alternative, high-octane alpha and of traditional beta and low-octane alpha is deeply flawed.

First and foremost, almost all added value is systematic. This enhanced return is not alpha at all. For example, any active portfolio achieves enhanced returns by incurring exposures to risk factors. Risk models attempt to measure total portfolio risk by summing risk factor exposures of the portfolio and adding the idiosyncratic risk. Each risk factor exposure is the beta of the portfolio to the risk factor: the portfolio's loading on the risk factor times the factor volatility. Thus the portfolio incurs systematic exposures to common risk factors. Very little of a portfolio's risk is truly idiosyncratic in nature. If all risks were uncorrelated, then risk models would not be necessary.

Second, and perhaps most surprising, is that the majority of alternative investment managers have no benchmark or hurdle rate that they need to beat before taking their performance fee (other than their own base fee). If the manager simply takes the investor's money and invests it in cash, she will be entitled to a performance fee (assuming that the cash rate is higher than the base fee rate). This is an inappropriate and misaligned structure. Of course this cash strategy would not yield long-term results or client satisfaction, however, the existence and persistence of this perverse incentive remains mind bending.

Traditional portfolio risk is also misperceived. Consider the constraints placed on the long-only investment manager. The manager is given a benchmark, such as the S&P 500 equity index. First, the S&P 500, like any index or benchmark that does not encompass the entire market, is active. The S&P 500 index is an active portfolio whose stocks are selected based on a prespecified set of rules such as company market capitalization. Second, managers do not want to underperform the benchmark and will seek to outperform the benchmark with the lowest amount of risk relative to that benchmark. This means that the manager is incentivized to invest in many stocks that are deemed unattractive simply because they have a dominant position in the index. Since the rules for actively constructing an equity index are arbitrary, owning stocks simply because they are in the index forces an arbitrary active investment process onto all managers attempting to generate performance relative to the index. The manager's investment process may even deem some of these securities to be inferior investments.

Moreover, by comparing a manager to an index benchmark, risk management is applied at the micro level of the manager, not the macro level of the client, leading to a multitude of inappropriate holdings that reduce risk relative to the index. Risk management should occur at the client's total portfolio level. Risk incurred by any manager investing only a portion of the funds should be of limited importance because a large portion will likely be diversified away by other managers. Textbooks teach portfolio managers to be concerned with risk-adjusted returns, but often they fail to add that risk-adjusted returns only matter at the aggregate portfolio level.

Another important problem is that the traditional manager has a long-only constraint. This restricts the manager to employing only a portion of his research. Fundamental analysis will result in assets that are deemed to be priced below fundamental values, and therefore attractive candidates for long positions. Conversely, it will identify assets deemed to be priced above values, and thus candidates for short positions. The long only constraint allows positions to be taken only in those assets that are priced below values. Half of the research is wasted because there are a number of assets priced above values that should be sold short, allowing the portfolio to benefit when prices correct to lower values.

Last, the benchmark typically forces the manager to invest within a narrow universe. Suppose an investment manager prefers exposure to attractively priced computer manufacturing stocks, and he thinks that China's Lenovo is much more attractive than Dell. If Dell is the most attractive member of the benchmark, then the manager will place capital in Dell instead of Lenovo. The narrow universe of the benchmark forces the manager to invest in a security in which he would otherwise not invest at all.

By identifying a benchmark and requiring the investment manager to minimize risk relative to that benchmark, the client or agent forces a misalignment of advisor behaviors and client needs. In order to align the two, the constraint and incentives that the client places on the manager must allow and reward behavior consistent with his needs. A benchmark often is more of a confounding construct than one aligning manager behaviors and client needs.

Assuming no unconditional market exposure is desired, rather than constrain a manager by imposing index-based performance benchmarks, we recommend that the investor adopt total return objectives with at least a risk-free rate hurdle. Alternatively, and depending on the liability needs of the investor, a total real return objective may be even more appropriate. Last, while risk management is necessary at all levels of portfolio construction, it should be applied with greatest consequence at the level of the client's aggregate portfolio.

Compensation Symmetry

Perhaps the biggest weakness of most performance fee structures is the failure to equalize compensation across good and bad performance periods. During periods of good performance the investment advisor receives compensation but during periods of poor performance the investment advisor typically fails to receive a performance fee. Note that during the period of poor performance the investment adviser does not lose compensation, he merely fails to receive compensation. This compensation structure creates an incentive to take excessive risk, rewarding random good performance but not penalizing random poor performance.

The single most important thing to focus on in creating a superior compensation structure is performance fee symmetry. The most direct way to create symmetry is to reward good performance and penalize poor performance through a mechanism that claws back previous compensation from the investment advisor. The problem, of course, is that the investment advisor has a free and levered call option on the performance of the portfolio. The advisor's performance fee is based on the entire pool of assets under management, which may be orders of magnitude greater than his individual wealth or in fact the entire wealth of all the advisor's employees.

This leverage can be reduced by simply reducing the percentage that the investment advisor receives for any performance relative to the real return objective. This is an unrealistic recommendation because the market has cleared at a much higher percentage than this would imply. Thus, proposing a low performance fee percentage merely assumes away the problem. Realistically, the structure must take into account the fact that the percentage performance participation is high and be designed accordingly.

We recommend a performance fee structure that retains some compensation asymmetry, but penalizes the investment advisor for poor performance. The structure would need to earn fees during good performance and allow clients to claw back fees previously earned by the manager when performance is poor.[9] Since the manager is exposed to performance on the entire asset base, poor performance could rapidly bankrupt a fund manager. The lower limit on cumulative performance fees over any rolling performance period would need to be zero in order not to eliminate the risk of bankruptcy and, therefore, the incentive for an investment manager to take compensated risk. Despite the risk being compensated, there is always substantial noise around the performance and it would be inappropriate to create a structure that would randomly bankrupt the investment manager.

The high noise-to-signal ratio suggests a lower performance fee decrement percentage during periods of underperformance than during outperformance, further reducing the risk of bankruptcy. If, for example, the performance fee during outperformance is 20 percent, then the decrement during poor performance could be 10 percent.

Path Dependence: A Word about High-Water Marks

High-water marks are features of performance fee structures that limit the ability of investment managers to receive compensation from positive returns that occur below a previous high in the net asset value (NAV) of the fund. For example, if the NAV rises from 100 to 125 and then declines, the high-water mark is 125. If after the NAV subsequently declines to 110, it begins to move higher, the manager does not receive a performance fee until the NAV rises above 125 and establishes a new high-water mark.

A high-water mark further aligns incentives of the investment manager and the client, but it is far from perfect. First, any NAV decline below the high-water mark results in reduced compensation for the employees of the advisor. Some employees may be comfortable with periods of restrained *current* compensation, but others may not. The high-water mark can lead to inappropriate turnover of investment manager employees.

Second, a NAV decline to a level well below the high-water mark leads to expectations of low *future* manager compensation. Compensation remains low until the NAV exceeds the high-water mark. Such circumstances lead not only to employee turnover, but worse to an incentive to shut down the fund. In addition, the manager has more incentive to increase risk as the NAV drops below the high-water mark in order to raise the NAV above the mark and increase compensation. Our operating assumption is that risk will be higher the further the NAV is below the high-water mark.

Generally speaking, an investment manager can only take risk up to a level that does not result in outcomes leading to client terminations. If the investment manager proves to be correct in taking long-term risk, but incurs interim losses that result in client termination, then the client has not received an acceptable outcome from the investment manager. The manager's performance may look good in the end, but that fact is irrelevant to departed clients.

Similarly, clients should be leery of agreeing to performance fee parameters that threaten the persistence of the investment manager. The high-water mark is a performance fee structure that creates such a threat. Thus, high-water marks improve some incentives, but they create other risks that should be closely considered. Modified high-water marks are one way that the industry has proposed dealing with these issues. Essentially, in these structures, the high-water mark that was previously attained disappears after a calendar year. While eliminating some of the malincentives, this structure still does not create proper incentives.

Dissuading Inappropriate Risk

Inappropriate risk taking has two basic dimensions. Incentive structures can encourage outsized risk taking and/or they can encourage managers to inappropriately reduce risk. For example, if a manager has not met their performance objective or is below a high-water mark, they may have the incentive to shoot for the moon to collect a performance fee. On the other hand, a manager can lock-in gains and thus fees after a period of strong performance by reducing portfolio risk. Neither of these approaches is likely to lead to competitive long-term results, however, the incentives to do so often exist.

Over a period of many years our team managed a fundamental currency portfolio that was relatively unconstrained, with the ability to go long and short. A colleague managed a currency hedge fund with a similar fundamental philosophy. For a long period of time both funds performed well and consistently. However, strong performance coincided with exchange rates converging on fundamental values. With exchange rates appropriately priced, there were not any significant opportunities for either of us to take advantage of in our portfolios. Our team chose not to take much risk, and did so for a couple of years. Clients who felt that they were paying fees for active management and want to see active risk-taking behavior were not happy, but they understood our approach and were willing to sustain a relatively long period with little risk embedded in the portfolio.

Our hedge fund colleague was not afforded the same opportunity and had to incur risk. If he did not take risk he would not generate performance fees and would not be able to pay his employees. For the two years that our team did not incur risk, he was forced to take more risk than conditions warranted. Over time exchange rates moved away from fundamentally appropriate levels and created an opportunity to take risk, but since he had been incurring risk anyway, that same movement resulted in poor performance. Having generated fund losses and earning no performance fee, the hedge fund NAV dropped well below its high-water mark. As a result, his employees and clients faded away and the fund closed.

Performance fees, if not appropriately structured, create an incentive to take risk even when there is no investment opportunity and no reason to incur risk. Risk should only be incurred when it is rewarded. Investment advisors need shelter and food, if not mansions, yachts, and wine cellars. They should receive reasonable compensation apart from the base fee that covers operating expenses, but the structure should not reward unwarranted risk taking.

It may be appropriate to reward poor performance relative to the real return objective. Consider a situation in which all prices are at fundamentally appropriate levels. Any risk incurred would have been uncompensated, thus the most appropriate action by the investment advisor would be to hold cash. The portfolio would likely underperform the real return objective as there would be no opportunity for active portfolio management. In this case, a good investment decision results in underperformance. As discussed in Chapter 4, the CIO would want to reward investment professionals for good investment decisions, but the performance fee structure would need to reward poor performance over some periods to enable such compensation.

Relatively Low Fee for Beta

"Beta" is a difficult concept. To market participants, beta is like Supreme Court Justice Potter Stewart's famous observation about pornography: "I'll know it when I see it." Unfortunately, everybody sees it differently. Beta refers to market exposure, yet the market can be defined in many different ways.

In the second quarter of 2006, the UBS Global Asset Management's "Current Perspectives from Brian Singer" stated that:

> *Today's knee-jerk assumption deems beta the weaker cousin of alpha. Alpha derives from skill, and has value. Beta is a commodity, with little or no value. The 'market' has come to mean a rule-based active portfolio, called a passive index. Owning this supposed index via a derivative provides cheap beta at low cost. Beta is cheap and low risk? How did we get it completely reversed? Investors must remember that risk is the currency that pays for returns.*

*The terms "alpha" and "beta" of course relate to risk. But the
frequent use of these terms to describe broad notions of skill and
commodity has unwittingly damaged the investment industry.*

Academics prefer to define the market by indexes for which they have
data. The S&P 500 index has become the index of choice for academics and
quantitatively minded analysts. Over the last couple of decades many indexes
have accumulated acceptably long performance histories. The Russell 2000
index is now a viable index for investment professionals focusing their efforts
on smaller capitalization U.S. stocks.

Still, there is no consensus on how to define the market, so there is no
consensus on defining beta. A good performance compensation structure
should be guided by client needs and conditions. For performance analysis
and fee determination, beta should be defined as a static market exposure and
distinguished from the alpha that is generated by active beta management
and idiosyncratic security risk taking.

Briefly during the 1990s it was fashionable to define beta by "returns-
based style analysis." Portfolio returns were analyzed to determine styles,
which if persistent were considered passive exposures, and therefore not
the result of manager skill. Although elegant, extracting styles is a difficult
statistical process often resulting in bizarre outcomes, adding an unacceptable degree of uncertainty to a process that would determine fees. The
process evolved to identify style exposures (betas) on a rolling basis over
the measurement period, typically three years. Betas would drift up and
down as fundamental managers altered exposures, and the returns-based
style analysis would exclude these evolving betas from the measurement of
manager skill. Although these evolving betas may have added to portfolio
performance, managers were not rewarded for them, and they started to
be viewed as uncompensated risk. The result was a disincentive to undertake active exposure management, even if opportunities seemed large and
acquirable.

We prefer a broad market capitalization-weighted global equity index.
Since a global equity index volatility overwhelms that of a global bond
index, defining the market as a combination of equities and bonds would,
practically speaking, result in a market index with return characteristics
much like a dampened equity index. Simplicity suggests that the global
equity definition of the market would be sufficient, if not perfect. Finally,
we need the ability to recreate the market index with one or more highly
liquid derivatives. The ability to replicate the index enables the manager to
increase or decrease market (beta) exposure as conditions warrant. It would
be inappropriate to define beta as something that cannot be controlled by the

investment manager. By this criterion, the global equity market definition is acceptable, but more difficult to replicate than a single country equity market index. Thus, beta could be defined as exposure to either a global equity or a single country equity index, with a proclivity for a single country index such as the S&P 500.

For our purposes, we assume that beta is defined by exposure to the S&P 500. Since exposure to the S&P 500 can be incurred cheaply through futures, swaps, or ETFs (Exchange Traded Funds), it would seem odd to charge high fees for performance that derives from static S&P 500 beta exposure.

Oddly, investors have been willing to pay high fees for beta that is incurred in alternative investments. We launched a market neutral U.S. equity hedge fund in the mid-1990s. We found that a beta of about 0.30 to the S&P 500 was considered desirable. Despite the fact that clients could buy a truly market neutral fund and add the 0.30 beta at almost no expense, they still preferred to pay hedge funds a 20 percent performance participation fee on market returns that could have been incurred for next to nothing.

Many investment managers exploit this behavior at the expense of their clients. In 2008, at a CFA Institute conference in Chicago, Denis Karnosky and Brian Singer confirmed the persistence of hedge fund market exposure. However, they found beta exposure by the average equity hedge fund, excluding short sellers, had drifted up to nearly 0.70. If adding beta is outside the mandate of the client, the manager should not charge its full performance fee for the collection of beta returns. Market exposure embedded in portfolio performance should incur a fee that is on par with the fee that passive exposure would cost. If the investment philosophy is long term, as Chapter 4 argued most fundamental investment programs should be, then the static betas can only be determined after long periods of time. As a result, performance fees that distinguish static betas from all forms of active management can only be charged after long periods of performance measurement; we recommend five years.

Relatively High Fee for Alpha

The corollary of the beta discussion is that all performance contributors other than static betas result in returns that are characterized as alpha. Alpha requires skill and should garner compensation. The performance fee for alpha should be relatively high; we recommend 15 percent as a general rule. However, we acknowledge that not all managers are created alike and there may be room for differences based on manager quality.

OUR RECOMMENDATION: HIGH INTEGRITY FEE STRUCTURES

Enough has been written about the excessive fees charged by managers using inappropriate performance fee structures. In 2008, overall performance results within the alternative investment industry were well outside of client expectations. As we continue to see the effects of 2008's deleveraging and lower valuations applied to private assets (which happens in a lagged fashion), this will exacerbate client disappointment in 2009—especially in the private equity industry. These factors are finally opening clients' eyes to the reality of these performance-compromising fee structures.

Management fees, or base fees, are appropriate to cover the basic operating expenses of an investment organization. Thus, as assets under management increase, management fees should decline. In fact, investment managers should be transparent regarding operating expenses so that they and their clients can ascertain the appropriateness of management fees.

Beta can be obtained through a number of passive vehicles, from passive collective funds to ETFs and derivatives. The typical price for a highly liquid passive index, such as the S&P 500, is about 25 bps. For broader indexes, such as a global equity index, the price of index exposure is higher, say 50 bps.

Alpha derived from top-down active beta management or bottom-up security selection requires skill and should be paid accordingly. Of course, market forces determine the appropriate price to be paid for skill, but the typical performance fee of 20 percent, including beta, is probably too high. In fact, the disappointing hedge fund returns of 2008 are likely to usher a period of lower fees. A 20 percent fee paid for skill measured as the return above that of Treasury securities, excluding static beta exposure, seems more appropriate.

A hedge fund with a 20 percent participation in a 30 percent decline on $10 billion of assets under management would incur a loss of $600 million. I doubt any hedge fund manager would cough up $600 million to reimburse clients for one year of portfolio losses. The fee for skill should involve a penalty for poor performance, but it cannot be of such magnitude that the manager avoids risk. Of course, it is reasonable to ask why he should have such a leveraged exposure to performance on the upside if he can't sustain the exposure on the downside, but we leave that question to the clients.

Combining all of these considerations is difficult, and clearly departs from the incentive compensation norms of the 1990s and 2000s; however, incentives are the central consideration, regardless of how new or different the performance compensation structure.

Performance Fee Specifics: The Dreaded Equations

A fee structure that has integrity, shaped by the considerations noted above, would include the following features:

- Base fee that declines as AuM increases.
- Relatively low fee on performance derived from static market exposure.
- Relatively high fee on performance derived from alpha over static market exposure.
- Downside participation by investment manager during periods of poor performance.
- Appropriately long horizon to evaluate skill and determine performance fees.

The total portfolio return comprises the static market return plus the alpha return above the static market return.

$$Total\ Portfolio\ Return = Static\ Market\ Return + Alpha\ Return$$

where,

$$Static\ Market\ Return = T\text{-}Bill\ Return + Market\ Beta$$
$$*[(Market\ Return - T\text{-}Bill\ Return)]$$

and,

$$Alpha\ Return = Total\ Portfolio\ Return - Static\ Market\ Return$$

The proposed static market performance fee is based on the *ex post* realized beta of the portfolio with respect to the market.

$$Market\ Beta = Correlation\ of\ Portfolio\ Returns\ with\ Market\ Returns$$
$$*\left(\frac{Portfolio\ Return\ Volatility}{Market\ Return\ Volatility}\right)$$

The alpha return above the static market return is a residual number that is determined by subtracting the static market return from the total portfolio return.

The proposed fee structure comprises a base fee of 1 percent (which should decline as AuM rises) and a performance fee that is divided between static market return and the alpha return. The fee on static market return is

50 basis points, and the fee on alpha return is 15 percent.

Total Fee = Base Fee + Performance Fee

Total Fee = Base Fee + Static Market Return Fee + Alpha Return Fee

Total Fee = 1% + 0.50% ∗ T-Bill Return + Market Beta

         ∗ {[Market Return − T-Bill Return]}

     0.15 ∗ [Total Portfolio Return-Static Market Base Return]

Since the performance fee should penalize the investment manager for poor performance, the proposed fee structure includes a 50 percent fee participation in negative alpha return performance. For example, the alpha performance fee is 15 percent if the alpha return is positive and 7.5 percent if the alpha return is negative.

Since the measurement period required for preliminary observations of skill for a manager that a client *knows* has skill is on the order of five years, we propose the ability to claw back performance fees from the manager from a period of up to five years. If accrued performance fees in any given year are negative, then the client would be able to claw back fees up to the amount accumulated in the most recent rolling five-year period.

If alpha equals the Total Portfolio Returns − the Static Market Return, then

Total Fee = 1% Base Fee + 0.50% + [T-Bill Return + Market Beta

     + (Market Return − T-Bill Return)]

$$+ \begin{cases} 15\% * alpha, & \text{if } alpha \geq 0 \\ 7.5\% * alpha, & \text{if } alpha < 0 \ \& \ |7.5\% * alpha| \\ & < \text{cumulative 5 year } alpha \\ -\text{cumulative 5 year } alpha, & \text{if } |7.5\% * alpha| \\ & > \text{cumulative 5 year } alpha \end{cases}$$

Before addressing the determination of beta, it is instructive to compare the fees associated with a 1 percent base fee and 20 percent performance fee (over the T-Bill return) structure and the proposed fee structure. For this comparison, it is simply necessary to assume an arbitrary investment horizon and commensurate fee determination period. In Table 7.1, assume in each of the four cases provided that the T-Bill

TABLE 7.1   Fee Case Studies – Performance Inputs

	Case 1	Case 2	Case 3	Case 4
	Beta Positive & Alpha Positive	*Beta Positive & Alpha Negative*	*Beta Negative & Alpha Positive*	*Beta Negative & Alpha Negative*
Beta (static market return)	0.75 (7.63%)	0.75 (7.63%)	−0.25 (4.13%)	−0.25 (4.13%)
Alpha Return	6.00%	−2.00%	6.00%	−2.00%
Total Portfolio Return	13.63%	5.63%	10.13%	2.13%
Portfolio Return over T-Bill	8.63%	0.63%	5.13%	−2.87%

return is 5 percent and that the market return is 10 percent per annum. The 1/20 fee structure and the proposed fee structure result in the fees shown in Table 7.2.

The following cases include figures that display the components of the fee structures in a "waterfall chart" demonstrating the accumulation of fees.

Case 1: Beta Positive & Alpha Positive

In Case 1, the market increases and the manager has a positive exposure, benefiting from the market rally. Moreover, the alpha contribution, beyond the gain from market exposure, is positive. The typical 1/20 fee structure, shown in Figure 7.5, earns the 1 percent base fee (blue) and earns the 20 percent performance participation on the static market return (red) and the alpha return (green). The yellow bar measures the total fee of 2.73 percent.

TABLE 7.2   Fee Case Studies – Realized Fees

	Case 1	Case 2	Case 3	Case 4
	Beta Positive & Alpha Positive	*Beta Positive & Alpha Negative*	*Beta Negative & Alpha Positive*	*Beta Negative & Alpha Negative*
1%/20%	2.73%	1.13%	2.03%	1.00%
Proposed	1.91%	0.86%	1.90%	0.85%

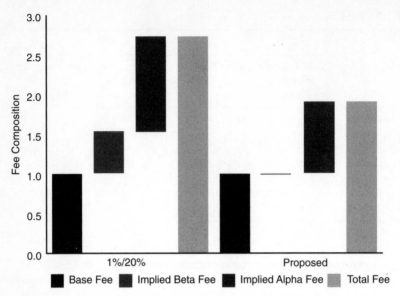

FIGURE 7.5 Fee Comparison (Beta Positive and Alpha Positive)

The inappropriate nature of this fee structure is the accrual of performance fees for market exposure that is obtainable without any skill whatsoever.

The proposed fee structure includes the same 1 percent base fee for ease of comparison. The static market return, acquirable without skill, garners a 50 basis point fee that is similar to what it would cost to replicate a passive global equity portfolio. The 1%/20% structure earns 53 basis points of static market-based performance fees, and the proposed fee structure earns only 1 basis point.

Alpha, the portion of the portfolio's return that is attributable to skill, garners a performance fee of 15 percent rather than 20 percent. The proposed fee structure earns an alpha fee of 90 basis points, below the 120 basis point fee that is excised by the 20 percent participation.

In total the proposed fee structure is 30 percent below the 1%/20% fee structure, and the performance portion of the proposed fee structure is nearly 50 percent lower.

Case 2: Beta Positive & Alpha Negative

A more interesting situation arises when market participation results in a gain that more than offsets a loss due to skill. In Case 2, shown in Figure 7.6,

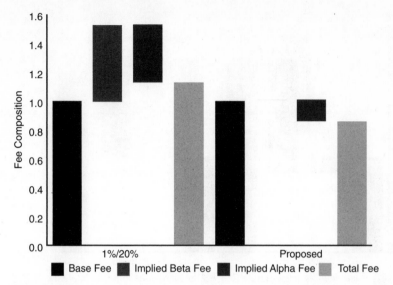

FIGURE 7.6 Fee Comparison (Beta Positive and Alpha Negative)

the market rallies and the manager's beta is positive, resulting in a performance fee of 53 bps. The alpha return is negative, resulting in an offsetting fee loss of 40 bps. Since the combined static market and alpha fee is positive, the full 20 percent performance participation is charged. Despite a loss arising from active portfolio management, the manager accrues a performance fee of 13 bps on top of the 100 bps base fee for a total fee of 1.13 percent.

The proposed fee structure accrues a minor gain of 1 bp due to static market exposure. The alpha return contribution is negative, so the performance participation is 7.5 of the alpha *loss*, or negative 15 bps.

The total fee that accrues to the 1%/20% fee structure is 1.13 percent. The proposed structure earns 86 bps, a fee that is almost 25 percent lower. The 1%/20% structure earns a positive performance fee and the proposed structure incurs a *negative* performance fee.

Case 3: Beta Negative & Alpha Positive

A reduction in portfolio performance that arises from a negative portfolio beta in a rising market or a positive beta in a declining market presents an interesting and perhaps unintuitive outcome. The reduction in portfolio performance due to adverse static market exposure partially offsets the positive alpha return. As a result, shown in Figure 7.7, the performance fee is charged on a smaller portion of the total return. In the 1/20 fee structure

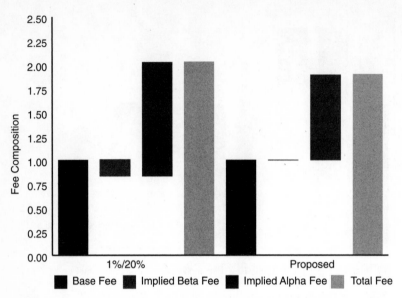

FIGURE 7.7   Fee Comparison (Beta Negative and Alpha Positive)

accrues a negative market performance fee of 18 bps, partially offsetting the positive alpha fee of 120 bps. The total fee is 2.03 percent.

The proposed fee structure has a static market fee contribution that is negative, but rounds to zero. If the beta exposure contribution to the portfolio's performance is negative, then the 1/20 structure, not distinguishing between beta and alpha returns, experiences a performance fee reduction. Of course, a negative beta is an uncommon hedge fund position, except for short-sellers. Thus, the client's fee benefit tends to occur when the market declines, an environment when hedge fund clients tend to be displeased by fund performance to a much greater degree than they are pleased by the performance fee reduction.

The proposed fee structure results in a 90 bps skill-based alpha contribution. The total fee for the proposed structure, at 1.90 percent, is about 5 percent below that of the 1%/20% structure. The performance contribution from the proposed structure is 90 bps, about 10 percent below the 102 bps of the 1%/20% structure.

Case 4: Beta Negative & Alpha Negative

The final case, shown in Figure 7.8, is one in which both the static market and alpha return contributions are negative. The 1/20 is simple, neither the

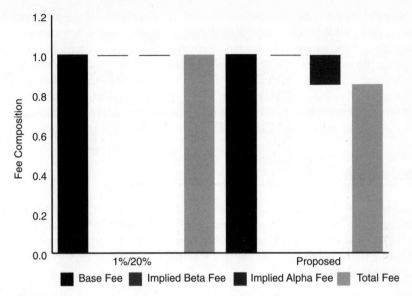

FIGURE 7.8   Fee Comparison (Beta Negative and Alpha Negative)

beta nor alpha activities generate a performance fee. The proposed structure doesn't earn a beta fee, but it earns a *negative* 15 bps from the skill-based alpha activity. In total, the 1/20 structure earns the base fee and the proposed structure earns 0.85 percent, slightly below the base fee.

The glaring problem with this fee structure is the uncertainty of beta. There needs to be a sufficiently long return series to calculate a beta that is representative of reality or statistically significant. Since fundamental investment processes should be long term in nature for full performance benefits to be captured, the performance and the beta determination periods should be consistent with the relatively long investment horizon.

An escrow account for the purpose of paying performance fees can be established to accommodate the longer investment horizon that is needed to reduce beta uncertainty and, therefore, the static market and alpha returns. Each client's investment is separated into a non-escrow (regular) portion equal to 95 percent of the funds invested and an escrow portion equal to the remaining 5 percent. Regular and escrow funds are invested the same. At the end of the performance evaluation period, say five years, the beta is determined so that the static market and alpha fees can be determined. Prior to the conclusion of the first five-year period, the beta is assumed to be consistent with the anticipated market exposure, say 0.50, or a combination of 0.50 and the realized beta up to the time that the relationship concludes.

Some clients may be uncomfortable with the complexity of the proposed fee structure. While such discomfort would be unfortunate given that it is designed for the greatest alignment of interests, two alternative fee structures can be employed with the same expected total fees. First, a simple 1 percent base fee and 10 percent performance fee over T-Bills has roughly the same expected fee. Second, a 1.40 percent fee is equivalent to the performance fee structures over time. Each of the alternative fee structures has a reduced alignment of incentives, with the flat fee reflecting the least alignment.

CONCLUSION

Investing successfully is difficult in the best of times, and even then it takes several years to identify skill that is worthy of compensation. Our objective in this chapter has been to propose ideas for investment manager fee structures that better align the interests of clients and managers. In doing so, we propose a framework that:

- Compensates skill.
- Rewards positive performance and penalizes poor performance.
- Charges low fees for static market-based returns that can be simply obtained.
- Dissuades inappropriate risk taking.

Skill should be rewarded, but fee structures should not be designed to rely on integrity alone for appropriate behaviors. Our recommendation vastly reduces many of the inappropriate incentives of fee structures that arose in the 1990s.

We do not expect this to be the ultimate fee structure. There may be more simple ways of achieving the same ends with rolling period fee structures, and we will endeavor to construct such frameworks. However, we feel our current recommendation is not only a significant advance but also feasible under current regulations. It requires a close relationship and transparent communications beyond investment industry norms, but integrity supports our proposal and transparency. After the financial crisis, the investment industry is ready for change, and we feel that it is ripe for recommendations such as ours.

CHAPTER 8

Final Thoughts

The writing of this book is a project that took more than a year, drawing upon hundreds of conversations with investors on five continents. While the project itself took a year, it is based on the authors' collective experience of more than 65 years in the asset management business. Together, we have worked in private firms and public firms, institutional firms and retail firms, large firms and small firms, investment-driven firms and product-driven firms, well-run firms and poorly run firms, successful firms and dying firms. We have been firm acquirees and acquirors. Between us, we have worked in virtually every facet of the business, including trading, operations, legal, client service, marketing, emerging markets equity, asset allocation, currency management, risk management, product development, research and strategic planning. We have launched firms, built firms, sold firms, and left firms. Over these many years, we have talked to thousands of investors in a multitude of countries from the investment novice to the most sophisticated institutional and private investors. We have continually learned, and we hope that process never stops.

These diverse experiences have taught us a number of valuable lessons and principles, many of which we hope we have been able to effectively pass on in this book. While we have sometimes taken a direct route from point A to point B, there have been times where the route has been more circuitous. Further, with numerous authors making contributions to this text, the reader is certain to notice a few idiosyncrasies as well as instances in which a few dead horses were systematically bludgeoned for good measure. Accordingly, we decided not to leave any observation insufficiently bludgeoned and now take this opportunity to recap some of the main ideas of this book along with some final thoughts.

CHARACTERISTICS OF GREAT ASSET MANAGEMENT FIRMS

It is often noted that the asset management industry is lacking in leadership and management talent. While we are not sure if that is a true statement, we do firmly believe that the number one characteristic that differentiates the premier league of asset management firms from the next tier of competitors is leadership, especially in the formative years. We have all witnessed a number of very good investors promoted to positions of management and leadership. We have also seen individuals with great relationship management skills promoted into positions of management and leadership. In all cases we note investing skill and relationship management skill have very little correlation with leadership skill. While it may or may not be an industry with a void of strong leaders, one thing is clear: Organizations with strong and stable leadership are able to excel where others do not.

Firms that are recognized as best in class share a number of qualities and virtually all of them stem from the vision and execution of strong leaders. Recall in Chapter 1, we assert that the most successful firms share five consistent characteristics.

1. Strong culture
2. Limited size and complexity
3. Clear governance of the business and investment functions
4. First-rate (but non-hierarchical) investment leadership
5. Integrity

Each and every one of these is only possible with strong leadership. Leaders nourish and uphold the culture of an organization. They make choices that inevitably limit the size and scope of activities that the organization undertakes. A good leader will only work in a firm where there is clear and effective governance to protect the culture, philosophy and investment discipline of the firm. The most effective leaders create a non-hierarchical environment in which idea sharing is encouraged, and diligent execution is rewarded. They also establish a solid foundation, a durable framework, and processes for successfully managing an organization that can maintain these qualities. And last, a great investment leader has a zero tolerance policy for breaches of integrity. By integrity, we mean not only honesty and fulfillment of fiduciary obligation, but process integrity.

IT STARTS WITH A SHARED MISSION AND VALUES

Recall the anecdote about "cutting stones" versus "building a cathedral." The best organizations share a sense of purpose. They are not just cutting stones or making widgets. They are aspiring to do more and be better. A firm's shared aspirations begin with its mission statement, a clear articulation of the long-term goals of the team. It is something that every employee knows and is constantly reminded of. The best firms and their leadership teams take care to reinforce the mission with all employees and to continuously view, frame, connect, and recognize the firm's activities and actions in the context of the mission. The connection is enhanced by intertwined employee values and firm mission. A mission statement is not the be-all and end-all of an investment firm. It is simply a starting point. The values that are lived by employees help sustain the mission on an ongoing basis.

The mission statement will only hold water if the management processes within the organization are designed to support it. Setting organizational goals, team goals, and individual goals that tangibly help to drive the organization in the direction of the mission are paramount. As important as a coherent set of goals and objectives is the establishment of a true meritocratic process for evaluating and remunerating employees. In a true meritocracy, employees will seek excellence knowing that appropriate rewards will follow.

TRUE MERITOCRACY

Establishing a meritocracy, however, is no easy task. In a true meritocracy, employees are paid to reflect their contribution to the attainment of the firm's goals and its mission. That means employees must be paid based on both performance (how well they perform their role on the team) and criticality (how important/critical they are to the achievement of the organizational mission). This can only be done with a transparent and communicative management team that is driven to put the firm's collective objective ahead of those of each individual. Further, in a true meritocracy, each member of the team knows and understands her position, and what it takes to improve their own performance and their own criticality. Strong, transparent, and frequent dialogue is required to achieve this. We believe that accomplished leadership measures employees on what they have accomplished and mentors them on what they can accomplish.

Observing that investment industry leadership often originates in the promotion of individuals with strong investment or client relationship skills and little desire to explore leadership theory, in Chapter 3 we furnished a system for meritocratic leadership implementation. The system provides for objective analysis of criticality and performance and prescribes transparent communication that is often avoided by leaders. Importantly, the system provides a means of analysis and communication that is less threatening and more constructive than the ad hoc processes that permeate most investment firms.

AVOIDING THE PITFALLS

When it comes to generating sustainable, attractive risk-adjusted performance over time, "the road to hell is paved with good intentions." By this we mean that all investment firms start out with the goal of delivering consistent value-added investment performance for their clients. They also start with a framework for achieving this general goal. That said, there are literally hundreds of pitfalls and roadblocks that stand between the organization and the generation of attractive long-term results for clients. The most notable potential pitfalls for an investment-driven firm include:

1. Philosophical drift
2. Process drift
3. Behavioral biases
4. Wrong clients

Philosophical Drift

An investment philosophy is a set of core investment beliefs that drive a firm's value-added investment activities. The investment philosophy is the heart of an investment-driven organization. With a damaged heart, the organization can never function quite the same again. While some investment leaders are skilled heart surgeons, it is an infrequent occurrence when an investment organization is able to modify its investment philosophy and maintain its competitive edge. Great care should be taken by any organization in altering its investment philosophy.

Process Improvement and Slippage

A good investment process balances the natural tension between consistency and innovation. It sets reasonable boundaries, but empowers individuals acting within the process. While investment processes can evolve, they should do so in deliberate and methodical fashion. Process shortcuts virtually always end in pain for clients and for the firm. If it quacks, it is probably a duck, or Gilbert Gottfried.

Investment processes should be designed around a framework that understands the potential sources of value creation and seeks to systematically measure and analyze them. An effective long-term process helps the organizations seek compensated risk while avoiding uncompensated risk. With this idea in mind, the investment process is essentially a risk budgeting process designed to allocate the risk capital in the most efficient and compensated manner.

One clear sign of a breakdown in the investment process is inefficiently or misallocated risk. When risk is undetected or outsized relative to the opportunity set present in an area of the risk budget, it should be a warning sign to the manager and to clients. Too often, the manager looks the other way in the face of evidence that suggests the investment process is slipping away. Keep your eyes and ears open. Use risk measurement and analysis to your benefit, but ensure that implementation is not mechanical. We are absolute in our belief that there must be a human interface between risk system and portfolio strategy. If you think you hear a duck, you probably do. Take action.

Behavioral Biases

Biases affect us all and can have particularly ill effects on our investment decision making. A strong process provides some guard against them. However, the inputs to the investment process are often the place that biases can play the most detrimental roles. Being cognizant of and reminded frequently of those biases will provide some guard against them. Further, diversity of skills, cultures, and ideas is another important deterrent of bias.

The most important thing for us to acknowledge is that as human beings we tend to construct and confirm our own realities. As a result, adding information to our analyses does little to improve our decision making. New information in support of our pre-existing ideas is usually welcomed while nonsupportive information is excused. Adopting tools, techniques, or specific processes to avoid these biases will help to improve the consistency and quality of our investment results.

Market Behavior and Fundamental Approaches

Because we construct our own realities, and because the market is a collection of individuals, it too constructs its own reality. And this is the reality that ends up meaning the most. Never under-appreciate the power of the market. The market has the ultimate say in who wins and who loses–in the end, it is never wrong. The market equilibrates current supply and demand, but it does not distinguish when that supply or demand is fundamentally driven or not.

Market behavior plays the role of both friend and enemy to the fundamental investor. Market behavior is what drives prices away from fundamentals, and provides opportunities to buy undervalued assets and to sell overvalued assets. However, market behavior is also the thing that keeps prices divergent from fundamental values, often for longer than the investment strategy and its clients can tolerate.

Wrong Clients

An investment firm is nothing without its clients. Never forget that. However, also don't forget that few things can be as catastrophic to an investment firm as having the wrong clients. By "wrong clients" we mean clients whose timeframe, objectives, or expectations are not aligned with the strategy and approach of the investment manager. A number of once good but now defunct investment firms learned this lesson the hard way during the credit and financial crises of 2008.

Cases in point are those hedge funds that catered to structured product providers and retail investors as a source of capital. Many hedge fund firms offer liquidity terms that are better than the de facto liquidity of their underlying investments. They do this because of the power of pooling of their capital base and clients. As long as a significant number of clients do not act in concert and simultaneously pull their capital, the firm can continue to meet redemptions while effectively managing its portfolio. Unfortunately, the mass deleveraging of 2008 exposed the flawed execution of many managers in this regard. Too high a reliance on certain sources of capital (that as it turns out can act in concert under certain conditions) left a number of firms unable to meet their client commitments. Perhaps these managers did not know they had the wrong clients, but it is the client's responsibility to assure alignment more than it is the responsibility of the manager. A manager with integrity will act in good faith, but the onus is on the client to ascertain good faith.

FOR SUCCESSFUL CLIENT OUTCOMES: COMMUNICATE, COMMUNICATE, COMMUNICATE

As we have said superior client outcomes are equal parts investing and communication. Generating superior investment performance is extremely difficult but is achievable for the highest quality firms. However, actually delivering superior investor outcomes raises additional challenges that most of the investment industry neither acknowledges nor achieves.

Virtually all investors have a tendency to chase past performance as a hopeful indicator of future performance. Unfortunately, it is a certainty that past performance is not an indicator of future results. In fact, past performance over a narrow time frame tends to be a contrary indicator of future results. Despite a number of theoretical and empirical studies that demonstrate the hazards of performance chasing, this is the most dramatic and negative behavioral bias that investors need assistance in overcoming.

Sound, consistent, and transparent communication with clients the highest success strategy for achieving superior outcomes and helping them avoid the pitfalls of performance chasing and other value-destroying behaviors. Firms that communicate consistently, frequently, and realistically are best positioned to retain clients and deliver superior outcomes over time.

IT'S ALL ABOUT INCENTIVES

Incentives are not only financial in nature. They are also emotional and ego-driven. However, financial incentives are very powerful, and misalignment of incentives can and has in fact proven to work to the detriment of investors. We have challenged some of the pervasive and undifferentiated models in the industry today, especially those of the typical 2 & 20 hedge fund fee structure. Proper alignment of incentives requires a minimum set of goal considerations including:

- Relatively low base fees (management fees)
- Hurdle rates for incentive fees (e.g., performance fees are taken on proceeds in excess of an agreed hurdle)
- No or relatively low fees for market (beta-based) return
- Relatively high fees for alpha (true skill)
- Hinder inappropriate risk taking
- Penalize underperformance

While there is no feasible and practical perfect fee structure, we are certain that a better approach exists than that being employed by many investment firms today. Performance fee hurdles and the ability to claw back some portion of outsized incentive fees in the event of future underperformance would go a long way to correcting some of the misalignments of incentives existent in typical structures today.

INTEGRITY

Ethics is knowing the difference between what you have a right to do, and what is the right thing to do.
—Potter Stewart, U.S. Supreme Court Justice

Assessing and encouraging integrity starts with the interview process, employee indoctrination and training, and of course is supported with appropriate internal controls, proceses and procedures. However, integrity is not something that can be simply stated or verbally communicated. It is something that is best demonstrated and done so with the purest consistency from the top of the organization down.

One of the truest tests of integrity is its blunt refusal to be compromised.

—Chinua Achebe

Managing and leading a diverse group of intelligent and sometimes egocentric human beings is never an easy task. And of course, there is no one-size-fits-all means for leading such a group on a meaningful and successful journey. However, there are a few best practices and golden rules that can make the task more manageable. We hope that some of those ideas have been articulately stated and meaningfully conveyed in this text. The most important of these ideas by far is integrity. Without the integrity of its people, an investment firm is ultimately doomed to failure.

Notes

CHAPTER 1   Characteristics of Successful Asset
Management Firms

1. Charles D. Ellis, *Capital: The Story of Long-Term Investment Excellence* (Hoboken, NJ: John Wiley & Sons, 2004), 63.
2. Dov Seidman, *How: Why How We Do Anything Means Everything . . . in Business (and in Life)* (Hoboken, NJ: John Wiley & Sons, 2007), 243.
3. J.C. Collins and J.I. Porras, *Built to Last* (New York: HarperCollins, 1997), 73–74.
4. J.C. Collins and J.I. Porras, *Built to Last* (New York: HarperCollins, 1997), 75.
5. Capital Group website - www.capgroup.com
6. J. Ware and J. Dethmer, *High Performing Investment Teams* (Hoboken, NJ: John Wiley & Sons, 2006), 17.
7. Capital Group, www.capgroup.com/careers/its_different_here/what.html. (Notice that even the URL speaks to the culture).
8. www.capgroup.com.
9. Ellis, page 36.
10. T. M. Hodgson, et al., "The Concept of Investment Efficiency and its Applications to Investment Management Structures," *British Actuarial Journal*, 6, III (2000), 485.
11. T. M. Hodgson, et al., "The Concept of Investment Efficiency and its Applications to Investment Management Structures," *British Actuarial Journal*, 6, III (2000), 456.
12. Gary Hamel, "Moon Shots for Management," *Harvard Business Review*, HBR at Large (February 2009): 3.
13. Ibid.
14. Friedrich A. Hayek, *The Road to Serfdom: Fiftieth Anniversary Edition* (Chicago: University of Chicago Press, 1994).
15. Friedrich A. Hayek, *The Road to Serfdom: Fiftieth Anniversary Edition* (Chicago: University of Chicago Press, 1994), 20.
16. Alfred D. Chandler, *Strategy and Structure – Chapters in the History of the Industrial Enterprise* (Cambridge: MIT Press, 1962).
17. Gary Hamel, *Moon Shots for Management, Harvard Business Review,* HBR at Large (February 2009): 6.
18. Friedrich A. Hayek, *The Road to Serfdom: Fiftieth Anniversary Edition* (Chicago: University of Chicago Press, 1994), 21.

19. Charles D. Ellis, *Capital: The Story of Long-Term Investment Excellence* (Hoboken, NJ: John Wiley & Sons, 2004), 25.
20. Charles D. Ellis, *Capital: The Story of Long-Term Investment Excellence* (Hoboken, NJ: John Wiley & Sons, 2004), 92.

CHAPTER 2   Building a Cathedral

1. https://www.dodgeandcox.com/about.asp.
2. https://www.dodgeandcox.com/about.asp.
3. The terms "accountable," "authority," and "responsibility" are precisely used in this text. "Accountable" and "responsible" are used synonymously and interchangeably to indicate behaviors and actions an individual or a group of individuals are held to explain, justify, and bear remunerative burden. "Authority" refers to the powers an individual or a group of individuals has to influence behaviors and actions. Individuals or groups should be held accountable only for those behaviors and actions over which they have authority.

CHAPTER 3   Building a Meritocracy

1. Extraordinary performance lasting for about three years presages manager hiring and firing decisions." The Selection and Termination of Investment Management Firms by Plan Sponsors," Goyal and Wahal, *The Journal of Finance* Vol. LXIII, No. 4 August 2008.
2. CFA Institute, "Derivatives and Portfolio Management," *CFA Program Curriculum*, Volume 6, Level II (2008), Reading 72, "The Portfolio Management Process and the Investment Policy Statement," by John L. Maginn, Donald L. Tuttle, Dennis W. McLeavey, and Jerald E. Pinto, p. 493. This is a reprint of *Managing Investment Portfolios: A Dynamic Process*, 3rd Edition, John L. Maginn, Donald L. Tuttle, Dennis W. McLeavey, and Jerald E. Pinto, editors 2005, CFA Institute.
3. If returns were serially correlated, this statement would be only approximately true; however, since the returns are assumed to be IID, independent and identically distributed, the statement is accurate. Serially correlated returns of illiquid assets, such as private equity and hedge funds, result in overstated information ratios.
4. Mark Kritzman's *The Portable Financial Analyst* is a very good book on a number of topics and provides a nice summary of hypothesis testing, such as performance analysis on pages 134–136.
5. Denis S. Karnosky and Brian D. Singer, "A General Framework for Global Currency Management," *Securities Analysts Journal*, March 1991.
6. In some organizations, analysts can evidence the same or higher level of criticality as portfolio managers. I use this hierarchy merely for illustrative purposes.

CHAPTER 4 Investment Philosophy and Process

1. William F. Sharpe, "The Arithmetic of Active Management," *The Financial Analysts Journal* 47 (January/February 1991): 7–9.
2. Sanford Grossman and Joseph Stiglitz, "Information and Competitive Price Systems," *American Economic Review* 66 (1976): 246–253.
3. http://www.capgroup.com/about_us/investment_philosophy.html.
4. James C. Collins and Jerry I. Porras. *Built to Last: Successful Habits of Visionary Companies* (New York: Harper Collins, 1994), 73.
5. Herb Kelleher, "A Culture of Commitment", *Leader to Leader*, No. 4, Spring 1997.
6. Dennis McLeavey, et al. *Managing Investment Portfolios*, John Wiley & Sons, (March 2007) Chapter 1.
7. Albert Edwards and James Montier, *Global Strategy Weekly*, Macro Research, Asset Allocation, Global, Dresdner Kleinwort Securities Limited, 7 March 2007, 1.
8. Larry Hathaway, et al., *UBS Weekly Weight Watcher*, UBS Investment Research, Global Strategy Research, UBS Limited, an affiliate of UBS AG, 2 March 2007, 1.
9. Richard Heuer Jr, ed., *Psychology of Intelligence Analysis* (New York: Nova Novinka, 2005), 47.
10. Richard Heuer Jr, ed., *Psychology of Intelligence Analysis* (New York: Nova Novinka, 2005), 21.
11. Nassim Nicholas Taleb, *The Black Swan: The Impact of the Highly Improbable* (New York: Random House, 2007), 144.
12. As the credit crisis has progressed, deleveraging has reduced both the asset and liability side of the household balance sheet. The magnitudes and the impact on household net worth are unknown at this time.
13. Richard Heuer Jr, ed., *Psychology of Intelligence Analysis* (New York: Nova Novinka, 2005), 68.
14. Paul Slovic, *Behavioral Problems of Adhering to a Decision Policy*, unpublished manuscript, 1973.
15. James Surowiecki, *The Wisdom of Crowds* (New York: Anchor, 2005), 254.

CHAPTER 5 Investment Process in an Evolving World

1. Peter L. Bernstein and Aswath Damodaran, eds., Introduction to *Investment Management* (New York: Wiley, 1998).
2. This idea is adapted from Dov Seidman's, *How: Why How We Do Anything Means Everything . . . in Business (and in Life)* (New York: Wiley, 2007).
3. Armen A. Alchian and William R. Allen, *University Economics: Elements of Inquiry* (3rd ed.) (Wadsworth Pub. Co, 1972), 456.
4. Armen A. Alchian and William R. Allen, *University Economics: Elements of Inquiry* (3rd ed.) (Wadsworth Pub. Co, 1972), 674.

5. The CFA Institute program is equivalent to a masters program in investment finance. The program involves three examinations taken over about a three-year period. When completely successfully, the CFA designation provides a mark of excellence in education and ethics for its recipient.
6. Benjamin Graham and David L. Dodd, *Security Analysis: Principles and Technique* (6th ed.) (New York: McGraw Hill, 2009). Aswath Damadoran, *Investment Valuation: Tools and Techniques for Determining Value of Any Asset* (Wiley Frontiers in Finance, University Edition, 1996).
7. Jason Zweig, "For Investors, Dealing with a Loss of Control," *Wall Street Journal*, October 2, 2008.
8. Charles MacKay, *Extraordinary Popular Delusions and the Madness of Crowds*, foreword by Andrew Tobias (New York: Harmony Books, 1980). Or Charles Mackay, *Memoirs of Extraordinary Popular Delusions and the Madness of Crowds Vol. I: The Essential Library Edition* (New York: Xlibris Corporation, 2000).
9. Mark Buchanan, *Ubiquity: Why Catastrophes Happen* (New York: Three Rivers P, 2002).
10. James Surowiecki, *The Wisdom of Crowds* (New York: Anchor, 2005).
11. Philip Ball, *Critical Mass: How One Thing Leads to Another* (New York: Farrar, Straus & Giroux, 2006).
12. The phrase "interactive agents" is used throughout to mean things that act and interact with each other. In markets the interactive agents are investors, advisors, clients, and so on.
13. James Montier, *Behavioural Investing: A Practitioners Guide to Applying Behavioural Finance* (Wiley, 2007); Hersh Shefrin, *Beyond Greed and Fear: Understanding Behavioral Finance and the Psychology of Investing* (USA: Oxford University Press, 2007); Andrei Shleifer, *Inefficient Markets: An Introduction to Behavioral Finance* (USA: Oxford University Press, 2000); Richard H. Thaler, *Advances in Behavioral Finance* (Russell Sage Foundation Publications, 1993); Richard H. Thaler, *Advances in Behavioral Finance, Volume II* (Princeton University Press, 2005).
14. Technically, a normal distribution can have fat tails that result from skewness or kurtosis. We are using the term "normal" loosely as we are trying not to be technical and prefer to move on to other return distribution characteristics.
15. Nassim Nicholas Taleb, *The Black Swan: The Impact of the Highly Improbable* (New York: Random House, 2007).
16. Karl Popper, Benoit Mendelbrot, George Soros, and Nassim Taleb have all contributed in various ways to this debate.
17. These evolutionary observations are drawn from *Ubiquity* by Mark Buchanan. Mark Buchanan, *Ubiquity: Why Catastrophes Happen* (New York: Three Rivers P, 2002), 90–91.
18. Mark Buchanan, *Ubiquity: Why Catastrophes Happen* (New York: Three Rivers P, 2002), 105–106.
19. This can be considered an aspect of what is often referred to as "Social Darwinism." Social Darwinism has a varied history of acceptance and ridicule, however the use in this text is relatively narrow, and there is no desire to make any statement beyond what is explicit.

20. "This Economy Does Not Compute," *The New York Times*, October 1, 2008, Op-Ed section, New York edition.

21. Jeremy Siegel, "The Resilience of American Finance," *Wall Street Journal,* September 16, 2008.

22. James Montier, "Mind Matters: The Quest for the Holy Grail, or, It's Only a Flesh Wound", Societe Generale: Cross Asset Research (December 13, 2007).

23. Philip Ball, *Critical Mass: How One Thing Leads to Another* (New York: Farrar, Straus & Giroux, 2006), 238.

24. Mark Buchanan, *Ubiquity: Why Catastrophes Happen* (New York: Three Rivers P, 2002), 126.

25. Philip Ball, *Critical Mass: How One Thing Leads to Another* (New York: Farrar, Straus & Giroux, 2006), 195.

26. David Tuckett and Richard Taffler, "Phantastic objects and the financial market's sense of reality: A psychoanalytic contribution to the understanding of stock market instability." *The International Journal of Psychoanalysis* 89 (2008): 389–412.

27. James Surowiecki, *The Wisdom of Crowds* (New York: Anchor, 2005), 10.

28. If the reader is more interested in this idea, we recommend going to www.intrade .com to see functioning markets on a number of topics around the world today. We have found these markets to be superior to polls and pundits who claim to have better insight than the rest of us mere mortals.

29. James Surowiecki, *The Wisdom of Crowds* (New York: Anchor, 2005), 31.

30. James Surowiecki, *The Wisdom of Crowds* (New York: Anchor, 2005), 38.

31. David Tuckett and Richard Taffler, "Phantastic objects and the financial market's sense of reality: A psychoanalytic contribution to the understanding of stock market instability," *The International Journal of Psychoanalysis* 89 (2008): 389–412.

32. David Tuckett and Richard Taffler, "Phantastic objects and the financial market's sense of reality: A psychoanalytic contribution to the understanding of stock market instability," *The International Journal of Psychoanalysis* 89 (2008): 392.

33. Ibid.

34. David Tuckett and Richard Taffler, "Phantastic objects and the financial market's sense of reality: A psychoanalytic contribution to the understanding of stock market instability," *The International Journal of Psychoanalysis* 89 (2008): 396.

35. David Tuckett and Richard Taffler, "Phantastic objects and the financial market's sense of reality: A psychoanalytic contribution to the understanding of stock market instability," *The International Journal of Psychoanalysis* 89 (2008): 398.

36. RJ Shiller, *Irrational Exuberance*, second edition (Princeton, New Jersey: Princeton UP, 2005), 207.

37. Renato Staub, "Multilayer Model of Market Covariance Matrix," *Journal of Portfolio Management* (Spring 2006): 33–44.

    Renato Staub, "Global Investment Solutions: Capital Market Assumptions," UBS Global Asset Management White Paper Series (February 2005).

Brian Singer, Renato Staub, and Kevin Terhaar, "An Appropriate Allocation for Alternative Investments," *Journal of Portfolio Management* (Spring 2003).

Renato Staub and Jeffrey Diermeier, "Segmentation, Illiquidity and Returns," *Journal of Investment Management* (First Quarter 2003).

Brian Singer and Kevin Terhaar, "Economic Foundations of Capital Market Returns"(The Research Foundation of AIMR and Blackwell Series in Finance, September 1997).

CHAPTER 6   Communication for Superior Client Outcomes

1. Timothy Byrne and Aaron Reynolds, "Investors' Paradox—All High Performing Managers Underperform," Baird's Advisory Services Research Group, August, 2008.

CHAPTER 7   Where are the Clients' Yachts?

1. Burton G. Malkiel and Atanu Saha, "Hedge Funds: Risk and Return," *Financial Analyst Journal*, 61, 6 (2005).
2. Andrew Clavell, "Poor Academic Grouse at Wealthy Hedge Fund Managers (again)," *Financial Cookery*, April 4, 2008. Available at http://crookery .blogspot.com/2008/04/poor-academics-grouse-at-wealthy-hedge.html.
3. Martin Wolf, "Why today's hedge fund industry may not survive," *Financial Times*, March 18, 2008.
4. This $4.5 million could have been used to sell even more call options at the beginning of the year. The hedge fund could have sold just enough call options to completely extinguish their clients' $100 million investment.
5. Martin Wolf, "Why today's hedge fund industry may not survive," *Financial Times*, March 18, 2008.
6. George A. Akerlof, "The Market for 'Lemons': Quality Uncertainty and the Market Mechanism," *The Quarterly Journal of Economics*, Vol. 84, No. 3, (August 1970): 488–500. This references page 1 of the article, or more appropriately page 488.
7. There is delicious irony in the fact that "portfolio insurance," a put option strategy similar to the one I used capture a black swan event, was exactly the strategy that investors piled into in 1987, leading to the Black Monday crash in October 1987. In trying to reduce risk, the increasing popularity of portfolio insurance was a significant contributor to the black swan crash.
8. Martin Wolf, "Why today's hedge fund industry may not survive," *Financial Times*, March 18, 2008.
9. A simple alternative would vest and crystallize fractionally over a pre-specified number of years.

Bibliography

Alchian, Armen A., and William R. Allen. *University Economics Elements of Inquiry.* Belmont, CA: Wadsworth, 1972.

Ball, Philip. *Critical Mass: How One Thing Leads to Another.* New York: Farrar, Straus & Giroux, 2004.

Bernstein, Peter L. *Managing Investment Portfolios: A Dynamic Process.* Edited by Dennis W. McLeavey. New York: Wiley, 2007.

Bernstein, Peter L., and Aswath Damodaran. *Investment Management.* New York: Wiley, 1998.

Blanchard, Ken, and Spencer Johnson. *The One Minute Manager.* New York: HarperCollins, 1982.

Blanchard, Ken, Donald K. Carew, and Eunice Parisi-Carew. *The One Minute Manager Builds High Performing Teams.* New York: HarperCollins, 1991.

Bronowski, J., and Bruce Mazlish. *The Western Intellectual Tradition From Leonard to Hegel.* New York: Barnes and Noble Books, 1993.

Buchanan, Mark. "This Economy Does Not Compute." *The New York Times* [New York Edition], October 1, 2008: A29.

Buchanan, Mark. *Ubiquity: Why Catastrophes Happen.* New York: Three Rivers Press, 2002.

Canto, Victor A. *Cocktail Economics: Discovering Investment Truths from Everyday Conversations.* Upper Saddle River, NJ: Financial Times/Prentice Hall, 2007.

Canto, Victor A. *Understanding Asset Allocation: An Intuitive Approach to Maximizing Your Portfolio.* Upper Saddle River, NJ: Financial Times/Prentice Hall, 2006.

CFA Institute, *Derivatives and Portfolio Management*, CFA Program Curriculum, Volume 6, Level III, 2008.

Chancellor, Edward. *Devil Take the Hindmost: A History of Financial Speculation.* New York: Tarcher, 1998.

Chandler, Alfred D. *Strategy and Structure—Chapters in the History of the Industrial Enterprise.* Cambridge: MIT Press, 1962.

Collins, James C., and Jerry I. Porras. *Built to Last: Successful Habits of Visionary Companies.* New York: HarperCollins, 1994.

Damodaran, Aswath. *Investment Valuations: Tools and Techniques for Determining the Value of Any Asset.* New York: Wiley, 1995.

Damodaran, Aswath. *Investment Valuation Tools and Techniques for Determining the Value of Any Asset*, 2nd ed. New York: Wiley, 2002.

Dawkins, Richard. *The Selfish Gene.* New York: Oxford University Press, 1989.

De Soto, Hernando. *The Mystery of Capital: Why Capitalism Triumphs in the West and Fails Everywhere Else.* New York: Basic Books, 2003.

El-Erian, Mohamed. *When Markets Collide: Investment Strategies for the Age of Global Economic Change.* New York: McGraw-Hill, 2008.

Ellis, Charles D., and Burton Gordon Malkiel. *Capital: The Story of Long-Term Investment Excellence.* New York: Wiley, 2005.

Friedman, Milton. *The Road to Serfdom.* Edited by F.A. Hayek. Chicago: University of Chicago Press, 1994.

Global Strategy Weekly, "Macro Research, Asset Allocation, Global, Dresdner Kleinwort Securities Limited," March 7, 2007, p 1.

Goleman, Daniel P. *Working with Emotional Intelligence.* New York: Bantam, 1998.

Goleman, Daniel, Richard Boyatzis, and Annie McKee. *New Leaders: Transforming the Art of Leadership.* New York: Warner Books, 2003.

Goleman, Daniel. *Working with Emotional Intelligence.* New York: Bantam, 2000.

Grabo, M. Cynthia. *Anticipating Surprise: Analysis for Strategic Warning.* New York: University Press of America, 2004.

Graham, Benjamin, and David L. Dodd. *Security Analysis: Principles and Technique*, 6th ed. New York: McGraw-Hill, 2009.

Grossman, Sanford J., and Joseph Stiglitz. "Information and Competitive Price Systems." *American Economic Review* 66, 1976: 246–53.

Hamel, Gary. "Moon Shots for Management." *Harvard Business Review*, HBR at Large, February 2009.

Hayek, Friedrich A. *The Road to Serfdom: Fiftieth Anniversary Edition.* Chicago: University of Chicago Press, 1994.

Heuer, Richard J. *Psychology of Intelligence Analysis.* New York: Nova Novinka, 2005.

Hodgson, T. M., S. Breban, C. L. Ford, M. P. Streatfield, and R. C. Urwin. "The Concept of Investment Efficiency and its Applications to Investment Management Structures." *British Actuarial Journal*, 6, III, 2000, p 451–545.

Homer-Dixon, Thomas. *The Upside of Down: Catastrophe, Creativity, and the Renewal of Civilization.* New York: Island Press, 2006.

Jones, Christopher L., and William F. Sharpe. *The Intelligent Portfolio: Practical Wisdom on Personal Investing from Financial Engines.* New York: Wiley, 2008.

Karnosky, Denis S., and Brian D. Singer. "A General Framework for Global Currency Management," *Securities Analysts Journal*, March 1991.

Kelleher, Herb. "A Culture of Commitment," *Leader to Leader*, (4), Spring 1997.

Kindleberger, Charles P. *Manias, Panics, and Crashes: A History of Financial Crises.* New York: Wiley Australia, 2001.

Klein, Gary A. *Sources of Power: How People Make Decisions.* Cambridge: MIT Press, 1998.

Kritzman, Mark P. *The Portable Financial Analyst: What Practitioners Need to Know.* Grand Rapids, MI: Irwin Professional, 1994.

Landsburg, Steven E. *More Sex Is Safer Sex: The Unconventional Wisdom of Economics.* New York: Free Press, 2008.

Lynch, Peter, and John Rothchild. *One Up on Wall Street: How to Use What You Already Know to Make Money in the Market.* New York: Penguin (Non-Classics), 1990.

Mackay, Charles. *Extraordinary Popular Delusions and the Madness of Crowds.* New York: Three Rivers Press, 1996.

Maginn, John L., Donald L. Tuttle, Dennis W. McLeavey, and Jerald E. Pinto. *Managing Investment Portfolios A Dynamic Process (CFA Institute Investment Series).* New York: Wiley, 2007.

Malkiel, Burton G., and Atanu Saha. "Hedge Funds: Risk and Return." *Financial Analyst Journal*, 61(6), 2005.

Mlodinow, Leonard. *The Drunkard's Walk: How Randomness Rules Our Lives.* New York: Pantheon, 2008.

Olson, Mancur. *Power and Prosperity: Outgrowing Communist and Capitalist Dictatorships.* New York: Basic Books, 2000.

Phillips, Donald T. *Lincoln on Leadership: Executive Strategies for Tough Times.* Grand Rapids, MI: Grand Central, 1993.

Ratey, John J., and Eric Hagerman. *Spark: The Revolutionary New Science of Exercise and the Brain.* Boston: Little Brown & Company, 2008.

Regalado, Antonio. "Brazil's IPO Rush Hits Rouch Patch." *The Wall Street Journal*, June 20, 2008.

Seidman, Dov. *How: Why How We Do Anything Means Everything ... in Business (and in Life).* New York: Wiley, 2007.

Sharpe, William F. "The Arithmetic of Active Management." *Financial Analysts' Journal*, 47(1), 1991.

Shiller, Robert J. *Irrational Exuberance*, 2nd ed. Princeton, NJ: Princeton University Press, 2005.

Shiller, Robert J. *Market Volatility.* Cambridge: MIT Press, 1989.

Siegel, Jeremy. "The Resilience of American Finance." *The Wall Street Journal*, September 16, 2008.

Singer, Brian D., Renato Staub, and Kevin Terhaar. "An Appropriate Allocation for Alternative Investments." *Journal of Portfolio Management*, Spring 2003, p 101–110.

Singer, Brian D., and Kevin Terhaar. *Economic Foundations of Capital Market Returns.* Charlottesville, VA: The Research Foundation of the Institute of Chartered Financial Analysts, 1997.

Slovic, Paul. "Behavioral Problems of Adhering to a Decision Policy." Unpublished manuscript, 1973.

Staub, Renato. "Capital Market Assumptions," Global Investment Solutions White Paper Series, *UBS Global Asset Management*, February 2005.

Staub, Renato. "Multilayer Model of Market Covariance Matrix." *The Journal of Portfolio Management* (Spring 2006), p 33–44.

Staub, Renato, and Jeffrey Diermeier. "Segmentation, Illiquidity and Returns." *Journal of Investment Management*, 1(1), 2003, p. 135–151.

Surowiecki, James. *The Wisdom of Crowds.* New York: Anchor, 2005.

Swensen, David F., and Charles D. Ellis. *Pioneering Portfolio Management: An Unconventional Approach to Investment.* New York: Free Press, 2000.

Swensen, David F. *Unconventional Success: A Fundamental Approach to Personal Investment.* New York: Free Press, 2005.

Tainter, Joseph A., Wendy Ashmore, and Clive Gamble. *The Collapse of Complex Societies.* New York: Cambridge University Press, 1990.

Taleb, Nassim Nicholas. *Fooled by Randomness: The Hidden Role of Chance in Life and in the Markets.* New York: Texere, 2004.

Taleb, Nassim Nicholas. *The Black Swan: The Impact of the Highly Improbable.* New York: Random House, 2007.

Tapscott, Don, and Anthony D. Williams. *Wikinomics: How Mass Collaboration Changes Everything.* New York: Portfolio, 2007.

Taylor, William C., and Polly LaBarre. *Mavericks at Work: Why the Most Original Minds in Business Win.* New York: HarperCollins, 2006.

Trone, Donald, Williaim Allbright, and Philip Taylor. *The Management of Investment Decisions.* New York: McGraw-Hill, 1995.

Tuckett, David, and Richard Taffler. "Phantastic Objects and the Financial Market's Sense of Reality: A Psychoanalytic Contribution to the Understanding of Stock Market Instability." *International Journal of Psychoanalysis*, 89, 2008, p 389–412.

Tzu, Sun. *The Art of War: The Denma Translation.* Minneapolis: Shambhala Publications, 2002.

UBS Weekly Weight Watcher, UBS Investment Research, Global Strategy Research, UBS Limited, an affiliate of UBS AG, 2 March 2007, p 1.

Ware, Jim. *The Psychology of Money: An Investment Manager's Guide to Beating the Market.* New York: Wiley Australia, 2001.

Ware, Jim, Beth Michaels, and Dale Primer. *Investment Leadership: Building a Winning Culture for Long-Term Success.* New York: Wiley, 2003.

Ware, Jim, Jim Dethmer, and Michael J. Mauboussin. *High Performing Investment Teams: How to Achieve Best Practices of Top Firms.* New York: Wiley, 2006.

Whyte, Jamie. *Crimes Against Logic.* New York: McGraw-Hill, 2004.

Wolf, Martin. "Why Today's Hedge Fund Industry May Not Survive." *Financial Times*, March 18, 2008.

Zevon, Crystal. *I'll Sleep When I'm Dead: The Dirty Life and Times of Warren Zevon.* New York: HarperCollins, 2008.

Zweig, Jason. *Your Money and Your Brain: How the New Science of Neuroeconomics Can Help Make You Rich.* New York: Simon & Schuster, 2007.

Zweig, Jason. "For Investors, Dealing with a Loss of Control." *The Wall Street Journal*, October 2, 2008: D1.

About the Authors

Brian D. Singer, CFA

Brian Singer is the founder and CIO of Singer Partners. Brian has 27 years of investment experience, much of that dedicated to the management of unconstrained global asset allocation portfolios. He has served on the investment committees of a number of college and university endowments. He is a member of the CFA Board of Governors and an advisory board member of the *Journal of Performance Measurement*. Over the past 20 years, he has written and contributed to a number of academic journals and financial publications. He is a recipient of the Graham and Dodd Scroll and the Dietz award. His published works include Karnosky, Dr. Denis S., and Brian D. Singer. "A General Framework for Global Currency Management," *Securities Analysts Journal* (March 1991), and Singer, Brian D., and Kevin Terhaar. "Economic Foundations of Capital Market Returns," *The Research Foundation of the Institute of Chartered Financial Analysts* (September 1997). He received his bachelor's degree from Northwestern University in 1982 and his MBA from the University of Chicago in 1986. Brian's pastimes include family, fishing (mostly for largemouth bass), and pontificating on the topics of economics, integrity, and liberty to anyone who will listen.

Greg T. Fedorinchik, CFA

Greg Fedorinchik has 16 years of investment industry experience. Greg is head of Investor Solutions at Mesirow Advanced Strategies, Inc., a firm specializing in institutional multimanager hedge fund portfolios. Greg spent most of his investment career with Brinson Partners, Inc. in Chicago, which later became UBS Global Asset Management. He has worked in a variety of investment, client service, and marketing roles and has helped design and manage a number of innovative global investment offerings for public and corporate defined benefit plans, defined contribution plans, and other institutional investors. Greg received a bachelor's degree from the University of Michigan (economics and English) in 1993 and a master's degree in management from the Kellogg Graduate School of Business at Northwestern University (finance and decision sciences) in 2001. Greg grew up in Traverse City, Michigan and returns frequently to that state in pursuit of its trout and walleye.

Index